W9-DHW-663

ARCHERY

About the Authors

Dr. Wayne C. McKinney is an Emeritus Professor of Biomedical Sciences from Southwest Missouri State University in Springfield, Missouri. His professional interests lie in the exercise sciences of anatomic kinesiology, biomechanics, and exercise physiology. He is concerned about the anatomic and physiologic changes that occur in the human organism as a result of physical exertion. His longitudinal research is related to the effect of varying levels of energy expenditure during supplemental aerobic exercise on cardiovascular fitness and the reduction of cardiac risk. Since exercise has been shown to delay or offset hypokinetic diseases in humans, he considers prescribed frequency, intensity, and duration of exercise to be one form of preventive medicine.

Dr. McKinney earned his Ph.D. in 1963 at the University of Southern California. Archery started as a lifetime interest during his undergraduate years at San Bernardino Valley College and California State University at Long Beach. He earned associate of arts, baccalaureate, and masters degrees "with honors" at those institutions. He participated in intercollegiate baseball and football for four years as an undergraduate student. Archery continues as a special avocational and academic interest along with aerobic exercise. The latter includes slow running and walking workouts six days per week. Dr. McKinney has logged over 45,000 training miles plus numerous races and marathons, from Boston to Pike's Peak.

Dr. McKinney has authored or coauthored numerous articles in a variety of publications and scholarly journals as well as several editions of the following books published by Wm. C. Brown and Brown & Benchmark: *Biophysical Values of Muscular Activity* Second Edition, *Kinesiology, Anatomic Kinesiology, Introduction to Biomechanic Analysis of Sport,* and *Analysis of Sport Motion: Anatomic and Biomechanic Perspectives.*

Mike W. McKinney is a professional physical educator and science teacher at Santa Rita High School in Tucson, Arizona. He has had an interest in target archery and bowhunting during most of his life. His baccalaureate degree was earned at Southwest Missouri State University. His master of science degree is from the University of Arizona. He competed in target archery and intercollegiate wrestling as an undergraduate student at SMSU.

Mike McKinney is an enthusiast for gun hunting as well as bowhunting. His archery interests have expanded into the sport of bowfishing over the past few years. The east central portion of the Arizona White Mountains and the desert of southern Arizona rank as his favorite bowhunting territories. The game animals he prefers to bowhunt are white-tailed deer, elk, and javalina.

ARCHERY
Eighth Edition

Wayne C. McKinney

Mike W. McKinney

Brown & Benchmark
PUBLISHERS

Madison, WI Dubuque Guilford, CT Chicago Toronto London
Mexico City Caracas Buenos Aires Madrid Bogotá Sydney

Book Team

Executive Managing Editor *Ed Bartell*
Project Editor *Theresa Grutz*
Production Editor *Patricia A. Schissel*
Proofreading Coordinator *Carrie Barker*
Art Editor *Rita Hingtgen*
Photo Editor *Leslie Dague*
Production Manager *Beth Kundert*
Production/Imaging and Media Development Manager *Linda Meehan Avenarius*
Production/Costing Manager *Sherry Padden*
Visuals/Design Freelance Specialist *Mary L. Christianson*
Senior Marketing Manager *Pamela S. Cooper*
Copywriter *Sandy Hyde*
Proofreader *Mary Svetlik Anderson*

Basal Text *10/12 Times Roman*
Display Type *Helvetica*
Typesetting System *Macintosh™ QuarkXPress™*
Paper Stock *50# Restorecote*

Executive Vice President and General Manager *Bob McLaughlin*
Vice President, Business Manager *Russ Domeyer*
Vice President of Production and New Media Development *Victoria Putman*
National Sales Manager *Phil Rudder*
National Telesales Director *John Finn*

 A Times Mirror Company

PE Series
Consulting Editor *Aileen Lockhart, Texas Women's University*

Cover photograph *courtesy of Precision Shooting Equipment*

Copyedited by *Rose R. Kramer*

Proofread by *Margaret V. Dolan*

Library of Congress Catalog Card Number: 95–83960

ISBN 0–697–27983–9

Printed in the United States of America by Times Mirror Higher Education Group, Inc.,
2460 Kerper Boulevard, Dubuque, IA 52001

10 9 8 7 6 5 4 3 2 1

Contents

Archery in Literature and Art 213

9

The Language of Archery 225

10

Preface

This book was written to provide the reader with a substantive introduction to target archery, related archery sports, and correlated academic subject matter. Archery is an interesting skill to develop as well as a subject worthy of serious scholarly study. The many ways in which archery can be enjoyed as an avocational activity are addressed.

Participation in one or more of the archery sports and/or study of a variety of academic areas related to archery can enhance the individual's leisure time throughout life. *Instruction in target archery is the starting point in this process.* It has been observed that many people who receive target archery instruction eventually participate in one or more of the other archery sports. The National Field Archery Association (NFAA) has reported that seven million Americans own archery tackle. There are now over three million bowhunters and bowfishers in the United States.

The major objective of this book is to introduce the reader to target archery. Target archery is the most demanding of all competitive forms of archery in terms of precision shooting. The minute accuracy requisites of this sport present special mental and physical demands on the archer. *Target archery skill and knowledge serves as the "foundation for success" for virtually all of the other archery sports.*

The authors recommend that a person with a strong interest in archery sports such as bowhunting, field archery, or bowfishing first acquire considerable skill in executing target archery shooting mechanics. As a plus factor, target archery as a competitive sport may be enjoyed at participation levels ranging from community archery clubs to the Olympic Games. Furthermore, the National Archery Association (NAA) now includes target archery divisions for people who shoot recurve (Olympic Bow) *and* compound bows. This rather new evolution in target archery receives attention in this edition.

The book-in-hand includes FOUR UNIQUE FEATURES:

Skill evaluation techniques designed to improve archery shooting performance is ONE UNIQUE FEATURE of this book. Guidelines are provided for utilizing the video camcorder and videotape for analyses of the archer's shooting mechanics. The findings of the videotape analyses may be used to enhance learning efficiency and reduce shooting errors. By using these teaching/learning techniques either with an instructor or through individual analyses of the videotape, the archer is provided with a meaningful instructional basis for establishing his or her "foundation for success" in target archery as well as the other archery sports.

A SECOND UNIQUE FEATURE of this book is an introduction to the archery sports of bowhunting, bowfishing, field archery, crossbow archery, clout shooting, flight shooting, and ski-archery. Ski-archery (Ski-Arc) is the newest of the archery sports, and readers are introduced to this interesting and physically demanding sport in this book. In addition, opportunities for participation in archery by individuals with disabilities are described. Regardless of age, sex, or physical status, a person who desires to participate in archery can find an activity of interest. Archery can be a sport for anyone motivated to accept the challenge. First, however, the individual must know that the archery sport exists. Therein lies the major objective of the second unique feature of the book.

A THIRD UNIQUE FEATURE of this book is a chapter presenting a comprehensive and specific physical conditioning program for serious archers who wish to pursue one or more of the archery sports. One reviewer with expertise in exercise science wrote: "This chapter is one of the best presentations I've ever seen on the specificity of physical conditioning for a given sport." Anatomic detail is presented to explain the joint motions needed to properly execute the shooting fundamentals. This reinforces an earlier discussion of the techniques of shooting. The kinesiological analysis of shooting is followed by scientifically-based fitness guidelines that establish the intensity, frequency, and duration workout criteria for developing flexibility, strength, muscular endurance, and cardiovascular endurance. Energy expenditure values for various conditioning activities and archery practice are included. *The prescribed exercises apply scientifically-based theory to the practice of conditioning specifically to enhance archery performance.*

Specificity of conditioning by the archer leads to realistic attainment of goals such as better scores in target and field archery, more game while bowhunting or bowfishing, greater distances while flight shooting, or better ski-archery times and scores. A *serious archer* with good shooting mechanics plus an excellent performance-related fitness status is more likely to achieve success than an archer with comparable skill who has an average or low health-related fitness level. Archery sports are athletic activities that require specific conditioning for the archer to attain his or her potential.

An introduction to academic areas within archery that can challenge the individual intellectually is the FOURTH UNIQUE FEATURE of this book. Archery has a solid academic foundation in such scholarly disciplines as anatomic kinesiology, archeology, art, biomechanics, exercise physiology, literature, mechanical engineering, mythology, philosophy, physics, and religion. Furthermore, archery has been an integral part of the development and history of the human race. The archer or archery enthusiast who chooses to become intellectually involved with the academic side of the sport will greatly enrich his or her use of leisure time for life.

For readers interested in bowhunting and bowfishing, Appendix A contains the names, addresses, and phone numbers of government wildlife agencies in the United States and Canada. This provides readers with a ready reference for obtaining the latest rules and regulations related to bowhunting and bowfishing anywhere in these two countries.

Appendix B provides the reader with the names, addresses, and phone numbers of archery organizations throughout the world. These are the controlling groups for such things as target archery, field archery, bowhunting, bowfishing, crossbow archery, flight shooting, ski-archery, disabled archers, and senior citizen archers. This gives the reader handy access to learning more about the programs and opportunities offered by the organization(s) that control each of the distinctive areas of archery.

Special acknowledgment is made to Doug Kittredge, an expert bowhunter and toxophilite from Auburn, California. Our informal discussions about archery in the early 1960s at the University of Southern California led indirectly to the writing of the first edition of *Archery*. Dr. Aileene Lockhart is also appreciated and recognized for extending the invitation to write the book.

Many illustrations in this text are from *Anatomic Kinesiology,* third edition, by Gene A. Logan and Wayne C. McKinney, © 1970, 1977, 1982 Wm. C. Brown Company Publishers, Dubuque, Iowa and from *Adapted Physical Education* by Gene A. Logan, © 1972 Wm. C. Brown Company Publishers, Dubuque, Iowa. Reprinted by permission.

Special acknowledgment is made to E. G. Heath of England for granting permission to reproduce several illustrations from *The Gray Goose Wing,* his classic book on the subject of archery, published by Osprey Publishing Limited in Berkshire, England.

The contributions of the following people to the seven earlier editions of this book are appreciated: Doug Allen, Allen Archery; Elizabeth Allen, Allen Archery; H. W. Allen, inventor of the compound bow; William Bartlett, Precision Shooting Equipment; Ken Beck, President, Black Widow Custom Bows, Inc.; Lawrence A. Brady, target archer; Dave Brilhart, expert bowhunter; Patrick S. Brunhoeber, target archer; Diana Carr, Editorial Assistant, *The U.S. Archer;* Wilbur Corley, Corley's Bowfishin' Stuff; J. Robert Davis, expert bowfisher; Jerry Day, Arizona Game and Fish Department; Debbie Finch, Accra 300; Jack Frazier, expert bowhunter; Kathy M. Greene, target archer; G. C. "Butch" Herold, former Executive Secretary, NFAA; Laura Howard, Precision Shooting Equipment; Loyd Howell, Indian artifact hunter; Dr. L. Dennis Humphrey, Emeritus Professor of Biomedical Sciences; Mac Johnson, *Missouri Conservationist;* Gary Koehlke, Precision Shooting Equipment; Justin List, Mr. Teenage Arizona; Diane Logan, artist; Dr. Gene A. Logan, artist, scholar, scientist, and musician; Christine P. McCartney, Executive Director, NAA; Shirley A. Randall, professional secretary; Arlyne Rhode, Editor, *The U.S. Archer;* Bob Rhode, Hoyt/Easton; Larry Rogge, expert bowhunter; Pete Shepley, President, Precision Shooting Equipment; Paul T. Shore, former Publisher, *Bowfishing Magazine;* Ron Skirvin, Shure Shot; and The Wilson Brothers: Jack, Bob, and Norman, the expert bowyers who produced the quality Black Widow Bow for many years.

The contributions of the following people to the eighth edition of *Archery* are appreciated: Robert C. Balink, Executive Director, National Archery Association; William Bartlett, Precision Shooting Equipment; Ken Beck, President, Black Widow Custom Bows, Inc.; Chris Cockrill, Backwater Bowfishing; Wilbur Corley, Corley's Bowfishin' Stuff; J. Robert Davis, archery innovator and expert bowfisher and bowhunter; Kris Facer, Hoyt USA; Cora Coyne Gosson, Oneida Labs, Inc.; Lonnie Hansen, Missouri Department of Conservation; Dayna Nichols, Secretary, Bowfishing Association of America; Michelle Ragsdale, Professional Archer; Arlyne Rhode, Editor, *The U.S. Archer;* Roger E. Slates, Toxonics Manufacturing, Inc.; and Marcia Wyman, New England School of Archery.

Finally, recognition and thanks are bestowed on Iva and Jenni McKinney for their compassion and understanding of the authors during the time-consuming portions of the writing process.

The objectives and content of the book are the sole responsibilities of the authors.

Wayne C. McKinney, Ph.D.
Mike W. McKinney, M.S.

Introduction to Archery

Participation in archery has produced significant challenges for human beings throughout history. The archery skill of primitive people literally contributed to their survival by providing food as well as the skins of animals to clothe and shelter them. Skilled archers in ancient times were able to win battles for their tribes and communal groups. Later, the military use of archery literally changed governments, territorial boundaries, social orders, and the course of world history.

Archery in our contemporary world is viewed as a shooting sport with many fascinating variations. Target archery is an athletic activity for the competitor who appreciates the pursuit of excellence. Archery is valued by the individual who enjoys the test of using meticulously matched and tuned archery tackle with precision on a target range, field archery unit, crossbow range, or during a bowhunt. It is for the person who savors the aesthetics of being in the out-of-doors enduring all types of weather conditions on a bowhunt, during ski-archery competition, throughout a field or target archery tournament, or while bowfishing for sharks on the ocean. A sport like flight shooting appeals to archers who love the ballistics, aerodynamics, and difficulties of projecting arrows over great distances. The diversity of challenges for the archer is virtually endless.

The reader will be shown that archery can be enjoyed within a wide spectrum of physical, intellectual, and academic pursuits. As a result, all archery sports and related activities have the potential to enhance the leisure time of active participants and/or students of archery as long as desired throughout their lives.

The current popularity of archery is well documented. It is used as a sport in its various forms by millions of people throughout the world. Target archery was officially included as a gold medal sport in the Olympic Games in 1972. This added considerable impetus to archery participation in all of the competing nations. For example, a Nielsen Survey taken during the 1970s after archery became an Olympic event indicated that 2,634,000 Americans participate in at least one of the archery sports. That figure has grown in the 1990s to the point that there are now over 3,000,000 licensed bowhunters alone within the United States. When target archery and all of the other archery sports are added to that number, there are over 4,500,000 archers in the United States. American target archers have had considerable success in international competitions (fig. 1.1). Furthermore, new archery sports are being added to the competitive agenda. Ski-archery is an example of a new archery sport.

The major emphasis within this book is placed on introducing the reader to target archery. Target archery is the most demanding of all forms of archery in terms of precision shooting. It is highly recommended, therefore, that a person

Figure 1.1
Mastery of target archery fundamentals serves as "the foundation of success" for target archery and almost any other archery sport you wish to pursue. The shooting line and stadium in Long Beach, California, at the 1984 Olympic Games. (Photo by *The U.S. Archer*)

with a strong interest in archery sports where accuracy is absolutely essential—such as field archery, ski-archery, bowhunting, and bowfishing—first acquire considerable knowledge and skill in executing the fundamentals of target archery. Target archery is a world-class sport, and it can be pursued avocationally at numerous levels of competition by both sexes and all age groups using Olympic (recurve) or compound bows. Furthermore, your target archery skills will serve as a solid "foundation for success" if you wish to pursue one or more of the other archery sports in the future.

As can be seen in figure 1.2, the challenges in archery sports other than target archery can also have exciting dimensions! When bowfishing, for example, how do you accurately shoot through water, hit, and safely land a shark that outweighs you? You will be introduced to several archery sports in chapters 5, 6, and 7. These sports appeal to both sexes. Where appropriate, competition categories are established for men, women, children, and seniors by age groups. Archery is an equal opportunity sport! It provides people of all ages and both sexes with many chances to succeed as well as fail, for success would not be valued as much without the potential of failure!

Bowhunting, especially for deer and elk, is increasing in popularity each year in North America. Many gun hunters are (1) expanding their hunting seasons by using both gun and bow seasons for game, (2) switching to bowhunting due to the fact that the hunter is less likely to be shot by an unskilled gun hunter during the hunting season, and/or (3) changing to bowhunting because it is a purer form of hunting wild game than hunting with a rifle or shotgun.

Bowfishing is also increasing in popularity. One reason for this is that many bowhunters simply like to extend their game seasons by "hunting" fish with the

Figure 1.2
Target archery skill also allows the archer to pursue specialized archery sports such as bowfishing. "Suzie" J. Davis with a 6´ 11½", 165-pound, brown shark she landed while bowfishing. (Courtesy J. Robert Davis, 32191 Spearin Road, Salisbury, MD 21801)

bow and arrow. If a person likes angling, gigging, boating, and bowhunting, bowfishing is a natural combination of those activities. You are introduced to bowhunting in chapter 6 and bowfishing in chapter 7.

Most individuals become involved in archery initially out of an interest either in target archery, bowhunting, field archery, or bowfishing. Once involved in the sport, many people learn that archery is a topic with a rich academic heritage in subjects such as world history, literature, art, religion, archaeology, and philosophy. In this book an attempt is made to introduce the reader to some of these academic areas of interest. The serious student of the humanities, for example, can satisfy intellectual curiosity by studying archery as it is portrayed by authors and artists in literature, philosophy, and art throughout history. To cite one field of study, mythological literature from throughout the world abounds with tales of archers and their diverse use of archery skills. Archery feats have been romanticized over the years in literature, music, and via the modern entertainment media. Art museums throughout the world contain many famous works of art depicting archers in action. The scholarly student may want to pursue the sport beyond the demanding challenge of shooting. *The study of archery from a liberal arts perspective throughout the history of the world should not be overlooked as a fascinating intellectual and academic pursuit.*

There are also numerous scientific dimensions to archery. The physics of the sport has long engaged the interest of professionals and amateurs. (See the Bibliography.) The sophisticated mechanical engineering changes seen in archery tackle over the last half of the twentieth century represent one pragmatic result of these pursuits. *There have been more scientific advances in archery tackle since 1966*

Figure 1.3
"The Toxophilites." A pen and ink sketch by W. Murray, 1840. (From E. G. Heath, *The Grey Goose Wing*)

than throughout the entire history of humankind! Archery tackle manufacturers have improved bow and arrow construction based on better research, engineering, and the utilization of new materials. Arrow velocities and ballistics are improving, and that has led to excellent performances when quality archery tackle is placed in the hands of expert archers.

The biomedical sciences concerned with the archer are fascinating. The study of human anatomic motions and physiologic functions as they relate to the demands of performing archery skill techniques has kept pace with the tackle changes. Archers are improving as a result of scientific study. Physiologically, the archer is an athlete who needs to be physically and mentally conditioned in order to meet the demands of his or her specialty. From a scholarly perspective, the anatomic kinesiology, biomechanics, exercise and metabolic physiology, sport psychology, and sport medicine related to archery are each interesting areas for study. The reader is introduced to some facets of these academic areas in chapter 8.

Archery can be a very rewarding lifetime activity when one combines the intellectual and neuromuscular (skill) perspectives of the sport. A person who pursues archery as a scholarly participant has long been known as a *toxophilite* (fig. 1.3).

Benefits of Archery

Each sport has the potential to provide unique benefits to its participants. The benefits and values of an eclectic sport such as archery are not the same for all participants.

The outcomes are dependent upon such factors as the facet of the sport pursued, intensity and frequency of participation, personal goals and expectations, and many other individual factors related to one's involvement in the sport.

Archery brings fulfillment as one achieves periodic improvement in skill level. Another potential value of archery is that it can humble an individual periodically due to its complexity. Experiences of this type can be of potential personal value to human beings. The pursuit of excellence and the attempt to master archery are worthy goals with many potential benefits to the individual. Value lies in the pursuit even if the sport is never truly "mastered." Skill improvement should be based on realistic expectations. This will serve as a motivator for the participant even when he or she encounters the recurring frustrations of trying to attain perfection in archery.

Shooting the bow and arrow appears to be an easy and uncomplicated procedure to the naive observer: NEVER UNDERESTIMATE THE COMPLEXITY OF A SKILL THAT APPEARS TO BE THE EPITOME OF SIMPLICITY WHEN PERFORMED BY AN EXPERT! The meaning of that statement will become more apparent as you struggle with the demands of developing target archery skill, and as you learn more about the breadth, scope, and intricacy of the various facets of archery.

To gain some insight into and appreciation of the challenge of attaining archery accuracy, try shooting six arrows from 70 meters at a regulation target archery face the next time you are on a target archery range. Sixty would be a perfect score. Can you score 54 or more points with those six arrows? Elite women and men target archers average nine points per arrow at the 76.55 yard distance! How will you do? Therein lies one of the challenges of target archery for motivated people.

Those not aware of its many uses and physical requirements may consider archery an "easy sport." (The anatomic and physiologic demands on archers and specific conditioning for the sport are discussed in detail in chapter 8.) It is true that an hour of target archery practice in one's backyard or on the local archery range is not as physiologically demanding as comparable time spent playing singles tennis or running. As an example, an hour of anaerobic target archery practice would expend 269 kilocalories of energy for a 152-pound archer. Jogging an hour at a 9-minute-per-mile pace for the same individual is an aerobic activity that would produce an energy expenditure of 799 kilocalories, that is, 530 more kilocalories than target archery practice. As you will learn, however, there is more to archery than just the acts of nocking, drawing, and releasing the arrow.

The serious target archer as an athlete must prepare for competition by specifically developing his or her strength, muscle endurance, and flexibility to excellent levels. That has the potential to enhance accuracy when combined with regular target practice and good shooting mechanics. It is also recommended that the target archer's conditioning include work to develop above average cardiovascular endurance for his or her age as measured by maximal oxygen consumption (see chapter 8). This becomes an absolute requirement if the target archer wishes to compete in ski-archery as discussed in chapter 5. If that is accomplished, the archer's daily shooting and conditioning workouts will be just as demanding in terms of energy expenditure as comparable time spent in other sports perceived to be more demanding physiologically than target archery.

The serious, conditioned bowhunter also benefits by having a good level of health-related fitness. A total conditioning program in addition to target practice is also recommended for bowhunters. This enhances one's chances of stalking, shooting, field dressing, and packing a large game animal out of a wilderness area for human consumption. The *unconditioned bowhunter* may find him/herself in the embarrassing position of being the "animal" packed out! That would not endear you to the other hunters in your party. Due to archery's diversity in terms of participation outlets, the archery sports can be as easy or difficult as the individual desires. The choice is yours.

One major benefit of archery is that the participant can find an area within the sport and adjust it to meet his or her own interests, needs, and physical capabilities. In its many forms, archery can be enjoyed by men and women, old and young, wheelchair athletes, the blind, and superbly conditioned athletes of Olympic caliber. These archery areas are described for the reader within the book-in-hand. Its versatility has the potential to provide numerous benefits for archers with assorted abilities and interests. This is one reason why archery has fascinated humans in virtually all cultures and societies throughout history.

Regular archery practice may counteract specific problems exhibited by people who spend a great deal of time seated at desks, such as students and office workers. They tend to protract their shoulders—the shoulder blades or scapulae are pulled away from the spine and held in that position for prolonged periods of time. The head is thrust forward as the neck is flexed. To observe these atypical positions, look at people as they read, write, or work at desks. These shoulder girdle and cervical spine static positions abnormally lengthen muscles in the back and shorten muscles in your chest and shoulders. Holding the protracted position of the shoulders for several hours each day causes physical discomfort. Normal breathing is inhibited, which has a negative impact on respiratory function. Such a posture adds to the tired feeling a desk worker has at the end of the work day, because energy metabolism is adversely affected.

Shooting a bow for a period of time daily helps to directly counteract the atypical, static body positions described above. To draw a bow, the archer must concentrically contract (shorten) back muscles that have been lengthened throughout the day. These muscles are attached to your scapulae or shoulder blades. During the bow drawing process against the resistance of the bow weight, your scapulae are being adducted or moved toward the spinal column. The neck is stabilized in the extended position during shooting. Those muscles lengthened during the day are shortened or contracted in this process. Conversely, the chest and shoulder muscles shortened while sitting are lengthened when the bow is drawn. The greatest benefit of this for the office worker or student who reads several hours per sitting is to offset the potential for chronic, adaptive shortening of chest and shoulder muscles. Breathing mechanics and respiratory processes are improved. Energy metabolism becomes more efficient and the individual simply feels better.

There is a myth that the practice of target archery contributes to the development of good posture at any age. There is no scientific evidence to support that hypothesis. What archery practice does do for the adult is offset potential static or hypokinetic problems such as the one described above. Archery practice could have some positive effects on proper alignment of the spine, shoulder joints, and shoulder girdles of young children who have not yet reached anatomic maturation. Target archery practice with progressively increased workloads (bow weights) for a child with musculoskeletal problems in these body segments could be utilized as an enjoyable rehabilitative exercise. The use of shooting the bow and arrow most certainly has intrinsic motivating qualities not seen in most rehabilitative modalities.

One major criticism of our society made by sociologists and psychologists is the decline of family unity. To paraphrase a familiar theological statement: The family that plays together stays together. With the onset of a wide variety of avocational activities for children as well as *adult-centered activities for children* (examples are Little League Baseball and Pop Warner Football), the family in modern society often finds itself literally and figuratively going in different directions during leisure time. That is not a good trend.

Archery is one sport that can be enjoyed by all members of the family—at home shooting at a hay bale, on a field archery unit, ski-archery course, target archery range, or on bowhunting and bowfishing trips. There are psychological and sociological benefits inherent within an activity such as archery because it has the potential to develop family unity. As one example, participation in the archery sport of bowfishing has been a leisure time activity for the Rob Davis family for several generations (figs. 1.4 and 1.5).

Many athletic activities learned early in life cannot be used throughout a lifetime. Age is not a limiting factor in archery. It can be enjoyed as soon as the individual is old enough to learn how to handle the tackle safely. Target archery competition, as one example, is found for both sexes in local archery clubs, high schools, universities, the Olympic Games, and the U.S. National Senior Sports Classic. The latter usually includes participants from 55 to 90 plus years of age competing in the sport of target archery.

If you played a team sport such as American football as a teenager or young adult, as one example, you will not continue to utilize your skills in that sport over the next sixty years. One does not see many middle-aged people and senior citizens getting together, putting on the pads, blocking, and tackling each other from August through December each year! American football, like most of the other team sports, is not an activity adults choose to participate in during their leisure time.

In contrast to team sports such as football and basketball, archery can be enjoyed on a regular basis, indoors or outdoors, and as an individual or team activity twelve months per year throughout a lifetime. Furthermore, you do not have to assemble a group of people to practice archery on a daily basis. That factor contributes to the continuity and frequency of archery participation by individuals over many years. One will find that scheduling and depending on adult friends for your regular recreational sport practices, games, and workouts can develop into a figurative pain in the gluteus maximus!

Figure 1.4
Archery sports have been an integral part of the Davis family for years: Robie Davis, his wife, "Suzie" Davis, and father, J. Robert Davis. (Courtesy J. Robert Davis, 32191 Spearin Road, Salisbury, MD 21801)

Figure 1.5
Grandfather and bowfisher, J. Robert Davis, shows granddaughter, Erin Lynch, a BIG carp. The 47.2 pound carp was larger than Erin! (Courtesy J. Robert Davis, 32191 Spearin Road, Salisbury, MD 21801)

One major biophysical value of exercise, when used at proper intensity, frequency, and duration levels, is its contribution in helping the individual cope with distress. Uncontrolled *prolonged distress* has been identified as one of the major risk factors contributing to the onset of coronary heart disease. (CORONARY HEART DISEASE IS THE MAJOR ILLNESS PROBLEM IN OUR MODERN, SEDENTARY WORLD!) Emotional stress of this type tends to be cumulative in humans, and this is devastating to the cardiorespiratory anatomy. Using a "short-term stressor," such as some mode of physical exertion on a daily basis, helps counteract the negative biochemical, anatomic, and physiologic effects of long-term stress on the cardiovascular mechanisms. Exercise at the proper intensity, frequency, and duration levels is one positive way to help cope with prolonged stress situations.

Psychiatrists and other physicians recommend "blowing off steam" daily in a socially acceptable way when you find yourself in a prolonged stress situation. Exercise as a short-term stressor helps maintain homeostasis and contribute positively to one's mental health. Exercise in the form of daily target practice on an archery range or field archery unit *plus* associated conditioning as described in chapter 8 is a great way to expend energy and release emotional tension. This is true whether you only had one of those "bad days" or you are entangled in a prolonged stress situation at work or home.

Shooting the bow and arrow for an hour or more after a stressful day has the potential to relax the archer. Indeed, most exercise or physical exertion modes with good intensity and duration performed on a regular basis will serve as a relaxant. *The concept of intense physical exertion or exercise being a relaxant is so abstract that it is not too well understood by most people.* Exercise is a much better relaxant than the drugs used by many individuals ostensibly for that purpose. Vigorous exercise intensity will work to relax the participant while alcohol, nonprescribed tranquilizers, and other indiscriminate use of legal and illegal drugs are medically contraindicated and counterproductive. From the standpoint of health-related fitness, an hour of target archery practice (exercise) works better as a relaxant for the archer than either being a "couch potato" or using drugs such as alcohol and nicotine allegedly to relax.

The difficulty of mastering archery skill is cited by many participants as a part of the sport's mystique and value. The attempt to master archery skill is a major motivating factor because it is one sport where pure excellence is very difficult to achieve. You may work at it for a lifetime and never master archery skill to your satisfaction! As one example, a perfect FITA or Olympic Round score in target archery is 1440, but a score of 1300–1350 would make many expert archers very happy!

Archery does provide you with many opportunities to overcome human error. This facet of the sport, believe it or not, has the greatest appeal to many individuals who place personal value on pursuing excellence in their lives. Shooting tight groups of arrows consistently into the center ring during a FITA Round at distances of 90 meters (98.42 yards) or 70 meters (76.55 yards) is extremely challenging and difficult to accomplish. When an archer makes continued progress toward realistic shooting goals through intensity of effort, he or she places value on the process and enjoys the outcome. The end result may not be perfection, but a feeling of healthy personal satisfaction on the part of the participant will be enjoyed and valued.

Archery can be a good social activity. Most cities of any size have archery clubs that provide opportunities for archers to share interests with fellow archers. These clubs are usually affiliated with a state and/or national archery organization such as those listed in Appendix B. The clubs, however, are locally operated and funded by modest dues. Archery clubs usually have access to outdoor and/or indoor practice ranges, and intraclub and interclub tournaments are held on a regular basis. Members also compete in large professional and amateur tournaments conducted within the state and region, and also nationally. Clubs in communities are usually organized to accommodate specific interests for target archers, bowhunters, bowfishers, and field archers. Also, most community-based archery clubs are family oriented. As a result, competitions and other activities are scheduled for both sexes and all age groups.

Archery clubs are also found in secondary schools, community colleges, colleges, and universities. Intramural athletic competition is held on a yearly basis in many secondary schools and universities. Archery as an intercollegiate sport is usually part of the athletic club programs of community colleges, colleges, and universities throughout the United States. Intercollegiate competition starts at a local league level and concludes in a national championship. These activities receive considerable attention and support from the National Archery Association (NAA). Several secondary school and collegiate target archers have progressed to compete at the international level.

While people join archery clubs and use archery as a social activity, an archer can also practice and compete without contact with other people if he or she so desires. No partner or team is necessary to enjoy archery in any of its forms. It has been said that the greatest form of competition is with one's self. Archery sports allow the archer to compete as an individual even in highly competitive tournaments when the archer is a member of an organized team. Uniqueness is a trait valued by archers, and archery can be individualized as much or as little as the participant desires.

Appendix A contains the names, addresses, and phone numbers of most of the official wildlife agencies in the United States and Canada. These are provided primarily for readers interested in bowhunting and bowfishing. Current rules, regulations, and information regarding seasons and limits can be obtained by contacting the agency of your choice. Archers and students interested in areas such as biology, zoology, ecology, botany, and conservation may also want to contact these agencies to determine whether or not the game laws related to archery are written based on sound natural science principles.

Appendix B lists the names and addresses of archery organizations throughout the world. These are the controlling organizations for target archery, field archery, bowhunting, bowfishing, flight shooting, clout shooting, crossbow competition, archery for senior citizens, and archery for the disabled. The reader is encouraged to contact the organization(s) of interest to see what they offer in terms of programs, services, and competitions for the archer.

Review

1. Identify the factors that determine the benefits and values of a specific sport of your choice. Compare these values with those pertaining to archery.
2. Discuss with a friend the statement: "Success would not be valued so much without the potential for failure."
3. Find out whether there is an organized target archery club in your community. Visit one of the meetings.
4. What are the areas of liberal arts related to archery?
5. What is the basis for the statement that archery practice has the potential to counteract the negative impact of many sedentary hours spent by such groups as students and office workers?
6. What is the technical name for a person who pursues the scholarly aspects of archery?
7. Discuss the apparent paradox that intense exercise is a relaxant for the human organism.
8. Archery has influenced the course of human history. Can this be said of other sports—which and why?
9. Why is it recommended that a person who is interested in fishing or hunting with archery tackle first become skillful at target archery?
10. How many points per arrow do elite archers score on the average at the distance of 76.55 yards (70 meters)?

The Evolution of Archery

2

The history of archery is directly related to the early development of humankind. A few selected events are included in this chapter to help place archery's historical importance in perspective for the reader. The bibliography contains several excellent references which contain considerable detail about the history of archery.

The student interested in world history and archery is also encouraged to search for archery art and artifacts in museums throughout the world. Insights can be gained about people from various societies and cultures by studying the archery art and tackle they used to survive and conquer their enemies. The Charles Grayson Collection of Archery Tackle housed at the Museum of Anthropology at The University of Missouri in Columbia, Missouri, is one example of a museum that provides the serious student with such opportunities.

Archery skill was of vital importance for human survival for thousands of years. It played a prominent role in the growth and development of individuals, societies, and governments within nations. Archery as an invention was as important to early human development as the discovery of the wheel and control of fire. Ancient people learned how to use the bow and arrow effectively out of dire necessity. If today's archer had to depend upon archery skill for protection from enemies, food, and animal skins to make clothing and shelters, the motivation to attain great skill with the bow and arrow would be dramatically accelerated!

Primitive artists drew bowhunters on cave walls in many locations throughout the world. Many caves in Spain and southern France in particular have excellent examples of cave art with archery themes. Ancient sculptors carved archer warriors in Egypt and other parts of the Middle East to honor them for their feats. The bow has been used by primitive tribes on all continents as a musical instrument. Many theologians, as an example, believe that David's biblical harp was also his bow. A bow can be plucked much like the bass fiddle, harp, and other stringed instruments. Bows, arrows, and their functions became an integral part of cultures, religious rituals, and ceremonial rites of various ethnic groups throughout the world.

Archery feats have given rise to many myths throughout history. Mythologic literature includes archery exploits by such famed characters as Apollo, Diana, Hercules, and Eros. The romance surrounding Wilhelm Tell and his crossbow skill is a part of both classic literature and music. The people of the United Kingdom have idolized Robin Hood for years. Ancient cultures in the Far East also had archer heroes in their literature. The tales from China and Japan were written centuries prior to the ballads and yarns about Robin Hood. Modern novelists and script writers continue to rely upon and embellish fables about Robin Hood. A serious or comedic Robin Hood movie is usually produced about every decade either in the United States or the United Kingdom.

Archery has been used as an integral aspect of ceremonies by numerous religions and sects in the past. As one example, the Assyrians concluded a religious ritual by shooting an arrow toward the sun. This same type of liturgy, The Sun Vow, was practiced by various Indian tribes on the southwest plains of America many centuries later. A sculpture depicting The Sun Vow is on display in the Whitney Museum of Western Art in the Buffalo Bill Historical Center at Cody, Wyoming. The assumed mystical connection of the arrow with the sun, moon, stars, and planets figured prominently in many ancient religions and cultures. From the standpoint of ancient astronomy, the "archery connection" is seen in the naming of a few constellations (see chapter 9).

The Zen Buddhists place considerable value on the practice of archery. The Zen sect does not recognize any dichotomy between "mind" and "body." The Zen philosophy includes the concept that various exercises of the body (including such things as archery and some forms of the martial arts) can bring the practitioner into a state of one complete being. There are times when Buddhists hold the bow at full draw for many hours until they feel the union of "mind" and "soul." At that time, *Satori* is reached. When the archer is no longer conscious of himself or the target, the arrow is released. (The modern target archer holds the bow at full draw about two to five seconds prior to release.)

Figure 2.1 shows Eugen Herrigel, the German author of *Zen in the Art of Archery*. He was one of the few non-Orientals prior to World War II who was accepted to study what is known as The Way of Archery with Zen Buddhists. His book is considered a short classic regarding the practice of archery and its relation to Zen. After his oriental studies and writing of the book, however, Herr Herrigel returned to Germany where he became an impassioned member of the Nazi Party. That behavior was in conspicuous contradiction to the philosophy he learned while studying The Way of Archery and Zen Buddhism.

The reader should compare and contrast Herrigel's stance and nonexistent anchor point in figure 2.1 with the archer's technique in figure 4.16. The extended draw without an anchor point is typical of how Zen archers hold the bow for hours prior to releasing the arrow into flight. That is not an easy task!

The ability of individuals and armies to skillfully use the bow and arrow to advantage changed the course of world history on several occasions. Let us look at just a few of these events chronologically.

Upper Paleolithic Period

It is virtually impossible to document exactly that time in prehistory when humans started using bows and arrows. Ancient bows are very difficult to find because the wood and animal products from which they were constructed tend to deteriorate. Modern radiocarbon testing techniques, however, can be used to date artifacts such

Figure 2.1
A rare photograph of the late
Eugen Herrigel, author of *Zen in
the Art of Archery.* (From E. G.
Heath, *The Grey Goose Wing*)

Figure 2.2
Mesolithic hunting scene from a rock
painting at Los Caballos, Valltorta,
Spain. (From E. G. Heath, *The Grey
Goose Wing*)

as arrow points and stone tools believed to have been used in making archery
tackle. It is generally agreed by archaeologists and others, that humans started using
crude archery tackle at a time during the Upper Paleolithic period, or ten thousand
to twenty thousand years ago.

Drawings in caves, believed to have been inhabited by Cro-Magnon people,
depict archers hunting for wild game. Their bows and arrows appear to have been
constructed with considerable engineering sophistication. Due to the time estimated for archery tackle to evolve in isolated cultures, it is logical to assume that
archery tackle must have been in use many centuries prior to the time of Cro-
Magnon people. The results of radiocarbon testing techniques applied to stone artifacts tend to support this assumption. Figure 2.2 shows a Mesolithic hunting
scene from a rock painting at Los Caballos, Valltorta, Spain. Note the various
types of bows carried by the archers, and that the artists depicted the archers as
being very accurate. They had to be excellent bowhunters, stalkers, and shooters
in order to survive!

The oldest extant bows in museums date back to about 6000 B.C. These are
one-piece wooden bows made of yew or elm found by archaeologists in Scandi-
navia. More sophisticated, tillered bows were recovered from the Holmgaard
bog on the island of Zealand in Denmark. These bows are estimated to be from
the Mesolithic period. In contrast, some museums in America have bows made
by Indians of the southwest or arid region of the United States. These American
Indian bows date back no more than a few hundred years.

Holocene Period

5000 B.C.

The Egyptians were able to free themselves from the Persians during this age. They became superior archers through development of archery tackle and diligent practice. The ability to kill from a distance with arrows eventually proved to be the Egyptians' most important combat technique. Spears, slingshot devices, thrown darts, and slings were the primary weapons of war carried by the foot soldiers in this and other areas prior to the refinement of the bow and arrow. Enemies simply could not get close enough with these crude weapons to have a significant impact upon the Egyptian archers. The development of archery tackle made such things as rocks, spears, clubs, and slings obsolete as weapons of war.

1350 B.C.

King Tutankhamen reigned over the Eighteenth Dynasty of Egypt during this period. The Egyptians were known to used an angular composite bow at this time. Howard Clark, an archaeologist, entered the tomb of Tutankhamen in 1922 and recovered 32 angular composite bows, 14 wooden self bows, 430 arrows, and an array of quivers and bow cases. The mechanics of the angular composite bows found were superior to other bows known to exist during this era.

1000 B.C.

The Persians moved to the area north and east of the Black and Caspian Seas to battle the Scythians. The Persians had learned the value of archery skills and combat tactics from their earlier defeats. Each army had the usual trained archers as foot soldiers, but the Persians added mobility by training some of their archers to shoot while mounted on horses. Shorter bows were designed for utilization by archers on horseback. This proved to be too much for the Scythians. Mounted archers added mobility as well as other military strategies, and they were used time and again by military leaders throughout the world for several centuries.

53 B.C.

Parthia was an ancient country southeast of the Caspian Sea at this time. This territory is now a part of Iran. It was considered to be valuable real estate because whoever controlled it had command of the important economic silk road to China. The Parthians used archers on horseback. They had composite bows and carried large numbers of arrows with them. Camel trains carried additional archery tackle into combat as backup support for the archers.

The Parthians used a tactic of shooting arrows from horseback while either fleeing or pretending to flee from their opponents. This act became known in the language as a "Parthian Shot." The term lives on and now also denotes a sarcastic remark one individual gives to another upon departing. The earlier expression has evolved into the term, "parting shot."

Figure 2.3
The Battle of Hastings, showing the positions of the Saxon and Norman armies at 9:00 A.M. on the 14th of October, 1066. (From E. G. Heath, *The Grey Goose Wing*)

The Parthians and Romans battled in 53 B.C. and again in 37 B.C. with huge losses suffered on both sides. The Parthians did not fare well in the earlier conflict, but they returned to their mounted, mobile tactics in 37 B.C. and slaughtered thirty-five thousand Romans in that battle.

A.D. 850–950

There are records indicating that during this century the Vikings, who could be very obstreperous, helped design another military strategy for use with the bow and arrow. It appears that prior to some amphibious assaults, the Viking archers launched great clouts, or volleys, of arrows from ships into their intended target area. This was an early form of naval bombardment. The English would later utilize clout bombardment on land as an effective killing and panic technique in many of their wars. The current archery sport of clout shooting (see chapter 5) grew from this foreboding origin.

A.D. 1066

The Norman archers taught the English a lasting lesson at the Battle of Hastings (fig. 2.3). The Normans planned and executed a false retreat maneuver designed to draw the English archers out of their hiding places to pursue what seemed to them to be fleeing Normans. When the English made their move into the open, they were attacked by the waiting Norman archers and slaughtered. In this particular situation,

Figure 2.4
A portion of the Bayeux Tapestry. (From
E. G. Heath, *The Grey Goose Wing*)

Figure 2.5
Mounted Samurai warriors of Japan wore
plated armor as protection, a horned
helmet, and a guard cover over the back.
(Courtesy *Bow and Arrow Magazine*)

the English were superior in terms of their archery tackle and skill. They probably would have won the Battle of Hastings if the false retreat by the Normans had not been successful. This lesson was not wasted on the English military leaders because they used the same types of tactics on the French some three hundred years later at the Battle of Poitiers.

A famous work of art, the Bayeux Tapestry, was commissioned by Bishop Odo of Bayeaux. The embroidery was done in England, and when it was completed, the tapestry was taken to Bayeaux Cathedral, where it was preserved (fig.2.4). This tapestry is a band of linen 20 inches wide and 231 feet long. Various aspects of the Battle of Hastings are portrayed on the tapestry. One segment shows clearly and accurately that King Harold was hacked to death by a Norman horseman instead of dying as a result of an arrow wound in the eye, as erroneously recorded by some historians.

Figure 2.4 shows Norman archers carrying short bows and drawing them to their rib cages in order to obtain maximum range. The type of bow depicted on the Bayeux Tapestry is very inefficient from a physics standpoint, especially when compared to contemporary bows such as the Olympic or working recurve bow. Actually, the bows shown on the Bayeux Tapestry are believed to be closer to the Saxon pattern than to the longer Norman version. One explanation of this inaccuracy is that the people who embroidered the tapestry were not bow experts and they depicted the shorter bows used commonly in their area.

A.D. 1220

Like the Persians, Genghis Khan and his generals used archers on horseback with sophisticated short bows. They utilized a high wooden saddle and stirrups that allowed archers to shoot in any direction while riding. They used composite bows with draw weights of up to 160 pounds! (The reader is asked to compare and contrast that bow weight with the weight of the bow you are now using. Most of us could not draw a bow weight of 160 pounds to our anchor point!) Due to these draw weights, thumb ring release devices were employed. An arrow shot from bows of this type could kill opponents at great distances. Khan's "Golden Horde" had great mobility as well as contempt for human life and values. These factors enabled Genghis Khan to capture territory, kill, rape, and plunder from the Pacific Ocean to the Volga River, and from the Caspian Sea to Northern Siberia. Genghis Khan died in A.D. 1227 while on an operation against China.

The Japanese also used mounted warriors (samurai) effectively in combat situations (fig. 2.5). Their combat practice techniques and discipline are legend. They held competitions among the samurai to determine who was the best archer on horseback. To understand the accuracy problems encountered by a mounted archer, the reader might try pulling an arrow from a quiver, nocking, drawing, and shooting at a moving target while mounted on a galloping horse. Keep in mind that the mounted archer was also under the stress of being a target of another archer's hostility! The idea that an arrow could be embedded in your body at any time is a stress factor that cannot be underestimated. Archery could really get exciting in the "good old days" under combat conditions! Kyudo is the Japanese form of archery.

A.D. 1252

It was during this period in English history that the longbow became the national weapon of England. This is a surprising historical fact because recurve bow designs were well known to English bowyers and others. Different types of recurve bows had been used for centuries and are portrayed in various works of art in museums and private collections throughout the world. As one example, there is a series of statues dated 490–480 B.C., from the Temple of Aigina. These statues depict archers using highly sophisticated recurve bows.

Since the working recurve design is superior to the longbow from a physics standpoint in terms of arrow velocity and distance, why did the English choose the longbow as their national weapon? One possible explanation lies in the fact that the recurve bow must be made of a composite of laminated materials glued together. England is a damp country, and the crude glue used at that time was not durable like the epoxy resin glues of today. Consequently, a composite bow might fall apart when put to use by archers fighting in rain and moist environments. Such a malfunction would have been fatal for the archer in the midst of battle. In these circumstances, the longbow, although not as efficient as the recurve bow in terms of creating high arrow velocities, was more reliable for the highly skilled English archers.

The English considered the bow essential to the well-being of the country. As a result, men between the ages of 15 and 60 were ordered to have bows and practice with them. The affluent landowners of the day had to equip themselves with swords and daggers in addition to bows and arrows. Those men who owned small sections of land were required to have bows and arrows only. The English were having political and military problems with the French during this period of time and wanted to enhance their preparation for war status.

Figure 2.6
The Battle of Crécy, August 26, 1346. (From E.G. Heath, *The Grey Goose Wing*)

A.D. 1340–1363

This period marked the start of the rise of English archery superiority. The Hundred Years' War with France was getting under way. The first of the large-scale encounters was the Battle of Crécy in A.D. 1346 (fig. 2.6). Edward III, King of England, had thirteen thousand archers at his disposal, plus three thousand knights and men-at-arms who were deployed in three divisions. It is interesting to note that a teenager, the sixteen-year-old Prince of Wales (the Black Prince), was the commander of one of these divisions. The English used their archers in wedge formations. This tactic, together with their superior skill with the bow and arrow, enabled them to slaughter the majority of the French archers. The French force, numbering approximately forty thousand, was soundly beaten. To recognize the efforts of some of his knights in this battle, King Edward III established the renowned Most Noble Order of the Garter.

It was during this period that King Edward III declared mandatory archery practice for English men. He also declared that all other sports would be illegal. This dictate by the king had a direct effect on the quality of archery skill for all males in the population. The practice of archery by men remained a legal obligation for almost three hundred years! This type of national legislative action would be analogous to President Franklin D. Roosevelt and Congress passing legislation during World War II requiring every American male to practice with

Figure 2.7
The Battle of Poitiers, 1356. (From E. G. Heath, *The Grey Goose Wing*)

Figure 2.8
An archer of A.D.1400 from a design, originally produced for a rifle shooting trophy, by Benjamin Wyon the medalist. This is now the emblem for the Grand National Archery Society of England. (From E. G. Heath, *The Grey Goose Wing*)

the military rifle, and we would still be target shooting with a military rifle today! Although the edict of King Edward III had positive ramifications for England at the time, and later, it is most likely that contemporary Americans and the ACLU would debate the constitutionality of that type of politically-based requirement for one gender.

The Battle of Poitiers took place in A.D. 1356 (fig. 2.7). The English warriors were under the command of the Black Prince. They were outnumbered in this battle more than two to one, but were able to conquer the French. They did this by drawing the French into the open where they could be shot easily. This was accomplished by using false retreat tactics similar to that employed against them by the Normans three hundred years earlier. The French were killed by the thousands. The horses ridden by the French archers were special targets in this particular battle. The strategy was to wound the horses. The riders were unable to control the wounded horses and that added to the chaos on the battlefield. It also made the individual French soldiers slower and easier targets for the English archers.

The Grand National Archery Society of England has a rich historical heritage in the United Kingdom due to the specific importance of archery to English history. Its emblem is based on an archer circa A.D. 1400 (fig. 2.8).

A.D. 1414

The Battle of Agincourt was the last great battle won by English archers. The English were outnumbered by the French four to one, but King Henry V was able to conquer the French chiefly because of superior military strategy and utilization of the skill of the English archers. In his *Henry V,* Shakespeare wrote that twenty-nine English were slain as opposed to ten thousand French archers. The critical day of the Battle of Agincourt is shown in figure 2.9.

Figure 2.9
The Battle of Agincourt, October 25, 1415. Note how the space narrows between the two forests of Agincourt and Tramecourt, which hampered any forward action by the French. (From E. G. Heath, *The Grey Goose Wing*)

A.D. 1453

The date 1453 marked the end of the Hundred Years' War. The fact that the English archers were superior to the French is historically significant both to those countries and to America as we know it. What if the French had won the Hundred Years' War? There would have been an entirely different series of events following the fifteenth century. The sixteenth century was marked by religious and social upheavals in England. Those events helped bring about the subsequent exploratory migrations to America by various English populations. It is doubtful whether the same volume of migration from England would have materialized had the French won that war. America would have been settled in due time, but the political, social, ethnic, and religious structures of The United States would have been entirely different. The edict of King Edward III, and others, requiring the practice of archery by English men for over three hundred years helped shape the histories of England and America! (See figure 2.10.)

A.D. 1455–1471

The Wars of the Roses resulted from the rebellious feudal power displayed by some English lords who had acquired power during the preceding years. Professional military archers returning from France were hired by these nobles for the purpose

Figure 2.10
Archery of Edward IV (1442–1483). The archers in military costume are using the yew longbow and carry twenty-four arrows. (From E. G. Heath, *The Grey Goose Wing*)

of solidifying their place in the political structure of the nation. Generally, the soldiers did a poor job. These military mercenaries lacked both the leadership and discipline they had previously known.

The last battle during the Wars of the Roses was at Tewkesbury. The significance of archery as a weapon of war was still evident, but firearms were beginning to be used. Just as slings, rocks, and spears were not effective against arrows projected by archers with bows in combat, bows and arrows were found to be limited weapons when used against soldiers with firearms. The use of archery as a weapon of war started to decline.

A.D. 1545

Roger Ascham published his classic book *The Schole of Shootynge*. This was the first book ever written in the English language about archery tackle and techniques. This ancient archery textbook was also published later under the title of *Toxophilus*.

King Henry VIII's warship, *Mary Rose*, sank on July 19, 1545. Archaeologists recovered the longbows from that ship and they found that the bows were of superior design and better constructed than earlier versions. One possible reason for this lies in the fact that bowyers had started to use metal tools at this time to construct the longbows.

A.D. 1588

The English and Spanish used gun powder and firearms extensively during the invasion of the Spanish Armada. Most historians use this battle to illustrate the decline of archery as a weapon of war. Nevertheless, archers were used on a smaller scale in battles, wars depicted by politicians as "police actions," and other conflicts for the next four hundred years.

A.D. 1917–1990

The compound bow was invented in January, 1966, by H. Wilbur Allen of Billings, Missouri. His main objective for inventing and subsequently manufacturing the compound bow was to make bowhunting easier and more efficient. The compound bow is now very popular for hunting purposes because it is easier to hold for a longer time at full draw, produces greater arrow velocity, and it has better penetration capacity than recurve or longbows. These are important factors for the bowhunter. It is now legal to use the compound bow for hunting in all fifty states. The compound bow is used extensively by field archers in their competitions and the National Archery Association has established Compound Bow Divisions in target archery tournaments. The compound bow is not used currently in the Olympic Games in target archery competition. The recurve, or Olympic Bow, is used in the Olympic Games.

The basic concepts of bow design have undergone more changes since 1966 than in the preceding five thousand years! This technological breakthrough was primarily due to the efforts and ingenuity of H. Wilbur Allen. (His lead has been followed by numerous mechanical engineers who work for the major archery manufacturers throughout the world in bow research and design.) In recognition of his contributions to archery, the original Allen Compound Bow (fig. 2.11) is now in The National Museum of American History at The Smithsonian Institution in Washington, D.C. In addition, his contribution to archery is recognized by the Wilbur Allen Memorial Wildlife Area located in the Missouri Ozark Mountains. As a fitting tribute, bowhunting is the only form of hunting allowed in the Allen Wildlife Area.

During the Civil War, World War I, World War II, Korean War, and Vietnam War, bows and arrows were used for discreet military purposes. Their use seems incongruous in what is now known as the "atomic age," but it is true. Some military missions call for killing people very quietly. There are not too many ways for the military person to do this efficiently and live, especially from a distance. Expert archers have been trained in the military for sniper duties, reconnaissance work, and sabotage. Special arrows are made for demolition chores, and broadheads kill by penetration of vital organs and hemorrhage. Marines have trained men for this type of activity in their reconnaissance companies. The U.S. Army trains special ranger groups, and others, in the relatively few martial arts that teach techniques for killing human beings silently. Archery is only one of these techniques.

Although outdated compared to more sophisticated killing techniques, an arrow with a broadhead is still a very effective killing instrument whether it be for a bear, elk, or human being. A razor sharp broadhead arrow shot from a bow at

Figure 2.11
The original compound bow, invented by H. Wilbur Allen of Billings, Missouri, in 1966, is now in The National Museum of American History at The Smithsonian Institution. (Courtesy Mrs. Elizabeth Allen and the *Missouri Conservationist*)

short range has greater penetrating, killing, and/or trauma potential, for example, than a .44 caliber bullet shot from a .44 magnum pistol. Furthermore, a skilled military archer on a reconnaissance mission has a better chance of returning from that duty than a soldier or marine who kills with a noisy firearm. Its silent killing capacity is one of the main reasons archery has been used on a very selective basis in modern warfare.

The Present Time

One hopes that archery will never again be utilized for killing human beings. During the last quarter of the twentieth century, archery has been used most extensively as a sport—target archery, field archery, bowhunting, bowfishing, flight shooting, clout shooting, ski-archery, and so on. SPORT IS THE SINGLE BEST USE OF ARCHERY!

Archery has evolved to the point that it is a diversified and significant recreational activity for millions of people all over the world. Target archery has been a part of the modern Olympic Games as an official gold medal sport since 1972, and that has not only focused attention on target archery but increased interest in the other archery sports. As we will learn in the next chapters, people keep finding and refining the ways in which archery may be used as an avocational activity to enhance leisure time.

Review

1. No written documents tell us when archery was first developed but it is believed to have been between ten and twenty thousand years ago. What evidence supports this belief?
2. What explanation has been proposed for the English military's adoption of the longbow rather than the more efficient recurve bow?
3. For what military purposes is archery still employed, and why are the bow and arrows so effective for these uses?
4. What information about the history of archery is depicted on the famous Bayeux Tapestry?
5. Why must documentation on bow designs be accomplished primarily through art rather than via archaeological artifacts?
6. Discuss the ramifications of the political mandate by King Edward III that required his subjects to practice archery.
7. What is the potential for damage by a sharp broadhead arrow shot at close range in comparison with a .44 caliber bullet shot from a pistol?
8. How did the equipment and tackle of Genghis Khan's archers contribute to their amazing military success?
9. Clout shooting is now one of the sport forms of archery. How did the Vikings employ clout shooting as a military strategy?
10. What recent changes were made in the basic concepts of bow design that are so revolutionary technologically for archery?

Target Archery Tackle

3

In terms of precision shooting, target archery is the most demanding of all the competitive forms of archery. It serves as your "skill foundation" for most of the other archery sports if you ever wish to pursue one or more of them in the future. It is a serious oversight for an archer interested in bowhunting and/or bowfishing, as examples, not to attain a good level of competency in target archery shooting skills BEFORE learning to bowhunt or bowfish. Target archery is one of the oldest sports and the opportunities for competition range from the local level to international contests. It is an interesting and challenging sport for the true competitor.

You should be aware that the National Archery Association (NAA) no longer restricts archers who compete in indoor and outdoor target archery tournaments to the use of the recurve or Olympic Bow exclusively. There are Compound Bow Divisions in many target archery tournaments, so it is recommended that archers interested in bowhunting and bowfishing as recreational activities use compound bows in these competitions, hone their shooting accuracy, and also enjoy the challenges offered by the great sport of target archery. *This chapter is delimited primarily to a description of target archery tackle related to the recurve or Olympic Bow. Compound bows are described in more detail in chapter 6.*

The first step in learning target archery is to acquire an understanding of the equipment. *"Tackle" is the term used by archers for all of their equipment such as bows, arrows, quivers, arm guards, and related shooting gear.* There is an axiom in sport that a properly prepared athlete will be as good or poor as his or her equipment. Precision accuracy in target archery demands that you have meticulously matched, quality tackle to attain success.

The beginner should be provided with every opportunity to learn the sport efficiently. It is extremely important that the first set of archery tackle be matched properly. *Matched tackle means that arrows, exactly alike in every detail, should be chosen for use with a specific bow. The bow weight must be suitable for the individual archer and the arrows to be shot. Finally, the bowstring must match the bow and arrows.* Each archer differs in muscular strength, length of limbs, and aesthetic preferences. Therefore, care must be taken to acquire archery tackle suitable for the unique anatomic features and other differences of each archer.

The "matched tackle principle" is just as appropriate for the issuing of archery tackle in class situations as it is for individuals who purchase their own tackle. Students, unknowingly, will take mismatched tackle issued to them and try to learn to shoot with it. Efficient learning becomes improbable in that type of situation. Issuing mismatched tackle is a major mistake that archery instructors should try to avoid if at all possible.

A beginner mismatched for archery tackle will experience considerable frustration. It is possible to perform all shooting fundamentals correctly with inferior (mismatched) tackle and have little success in accuracy. The beginning archer learns bad, as well as good, habits with mismatched tackle. The archer tends to make improper compensatory skill adjustments in shooting mechanics due to poor tackle. That type of adjustment during the learning process becomes a bad habit in the future when the tackle problem is removed. *It is extremely difficult to unlearn bad habits.*

In target archery, it is a must that the archer obtain a consistent, tight grouping pattern on the target. With cheap or mismatched tackle each arrow shot will have a different flight pattern, resulting in very erratic arrow grouping. Overcoming the human factors that contribute to accuracy problems is enough to make archery a challenging sport for beginner and expert alike. The beginning archer should not be additionally burdened by learning target archery using inefficient tackle.

If possible, beginning archers should receive instruction from a qualified archery instructor prior to doing any shooting on their own. The reason is that bad habits can also be learned by the individual who teaches himself or herself by trial and error. As noted, poor shooting techniques become very difficult to unlearn, and this unlearning would have to be accomplished *before* the proper fundamentals can be mastered. As a result, the learning process becomes much more difficult. Would you try to teach yourself to play the piano or perform brain surgery? Not likely! Mistakes learned on your own make perfection of techniques under the guidance of a good instructor more time consuming. As in any other area where neuromotor skills are learned, good instruction along with quality equipment must come first if you are interested in becoming an elite or highly skilled target archer.

Ideally, the first set of archery tackle, matched for the individual, should be issued by a knowledgeable archery instructor. Quality archery tackle is expensive to purchase. Because of this expense, most students will wish to learn and try the sport for a period of time with issued, matched tackle to determine whether or not archery appeals to his or her avocational interests.

If you become interested in archery as a lifetime sport after you have received instruction and gained a functional level of skill, that is the time to purchase your own matched archery tackle. *It is highly recommended that your tackle be purchased from a professional archery shop where the salespeople are aware of the complexities of matching the individual components of the tackle to one another and to the requirements of the archer.* Most of these pro shops have indoor and/or outdoor ranges where the tackle can be used before you buy it. It is highly recommended that you shoot with the tackle you intend to purchase. Places such as sporting goods stores and franchise operations are usually poor places to purchase archery tackle. Salespeople in such stores or franchise operations, as a general rule, simply do not have the technical and scientific information required to match arrows to bows and all tackle to the unique features of the archer.

It is recommended that the archer who plans to use target archery as an avocational activity purchase the following minimum amount of matched tackle:

1. Twelve aluminum, aluminum-carbon, or carbon/graphite arrows matched exactly to each other in terms of straightness, weight, diameter, wall thickness, spine, color coding, fletching, nocks, and target points; matched for use with the bow purchased and to the draw length of the archer; one arrow case.
2. One working recurve or take-down recurve bow (Olympic Bow) with center shot design, cushion plunger, arrow rest, clicker, stabilizer(s), and bowsight. The bow weight must be matched to the archer and to the arrows. It is essential that the bowstring be matched to the bow and arrows to be shot; one bow case (fig. 6.12). (Target archers who wish to compete in Compound Bow Divisions in outdoor and indoor archery tournaments should purchase a quality compound bow *under 60 pounds* in draw weight.)
3. One finger tab with index and middle finger separator feature. (One release aid if using a compound bow.)
4. One arm guard.
5. One arrow quiver (hip or ground).
6. One bowstringer.
7. One finger or bow sling.

This amount of matched tackle is enough to enable the beginning archer to learn the sport efficiently and utilize it avocationally for a long period of time.

The overall cost is related to the quality of tackle purchased. The initial expenditure for archery tackle, although costly, is not too expensive when you pro-rate it over the years of use. Quality target bows are expensive, but they are used by some archers for decades. Archery manufacturers will replace and/or straighten bow limbs on one-piece recurves if and when they become cracked or torqued. Bow limbs on take-down recurve bows can be exchanged to increase bow weight or to lengthen or shorten your bow. Graphite and aluminum arrows can be a costly operational expense for the archer. *Cost for archery tackle should never be reduced by purchasing inexpensive arrows.* Keep arrows in good shape by checking them for damage and cleaning after each use. One motivational factor for developing accuracy is that you do reduce damaging and losing arrows with increased skill. Parts of arrows such as points, nocks, and fletching can be replaced if broken, and aluminum arrows can be straightened if bent.

The Arrow

Although there are some good, inexpensive Port Orford Cedar and other wooden arrows on the market, *wooden arrows are not recommended for use in target archery.* They are not reliable, and it is very difficult to match them for use with various bows. Their use should be limited to bows designed for wooden arrows.

The longbow, as an example, may be best suited for wooden arrows from the standpoint of the physics involved. Finally, it should be remembered that when a wooden arrow is broken it is difficult to replace in terms of an exact match for mass weight, straightness, shaft diameter, point, crest paint, and fletching.

A serious mistake made by too many beginning archers is to be issued a bow for use in a class situation and then purchase cheap, wooden arrows in a place like the university book store. No thought is given to matching the arrows to the mechanical properties of the bow. As noted, that diminishes the probability of learning target archery effectively.

Fiberglass arrows are satisfactory for use by learners *if* they are matched to each other and to the bow that will be used. They cost less than aluminum arrows, but they are manufactured with precision. Research has led to the development of a light, durable, and hollow fiberglass shaft. It is possible for arrow manufacturers to maintain quality control to the point that there are only microscopic deviations in regard to shaft thickness, shaft diameter, and actual arrow weight. The fiberglass arrow shaft always remains straight. This is an advantage of the fiberglass arrow over the aluminum arrow shaft. The fiberglass, like the wooden arrow, will break if it strikes a target stand or other hard object at an odd angle. The frequency with which this occurs is minimal. Fiberglass arrows are damaged beyond repair if stepped on because of compression of the hollow shafts. But, like wooden arrows, fiberglass arrows are not being used too often in target archery. The reason lies in the fact that there are better arrows on the market.

Aluminum and graphite arrows are recommended as the most desirable target archery arrows for beginners and experts alike. Aluminum alloys allow manufacturers to construct arrows that are nearly perfect. When shot by a machine during ballistic testing from 50 yards, it is not uncommon to see arrows grouped within a diameter of two inches. Aluminum arrows are among the most expensive on the market. If the beginner desires to purchase aluminum arrows initially, he or she should keep in mind that there will be times when these arrows will completely miss the target and become lost in the grass. Also, aluminum shafts, unlike fiberglass arrows, will bend when they strike the target stand or other hard objects instead of the target mat. (There are, however, procedures and machines for straightening a bent aluminum shaft.) Aluminum arrows are highly recommended over fiberglass arrows.

It must also be kept in mind that arrow velocities are now greater due to improved bow design. Aluminum alloy arrows are better designed to handle the greater force capacity of modern bows than wooden or fiberglass arrows. They are manufactured in a wide range of sizes and arrow weights to match a greater number of bows, draw weights, arrow lengths, and shaft spine or stiffness needs. It is also easier to purchase an exact replacement for one of your lost or damaged aluminum arrows. These factors are additional reasons for considering aluminum arrows.

The reader should be aware of the fact that archery manufacturers are now using new materials and combinations of "old materials" in making arrows. This

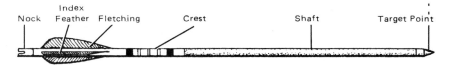

Figure 3.1
Arrow terminology.

practice widens your choice. There are now tapered aerodynamic arrows on the market made of aluminum and carbon materials. These kinds of arrows with superior performance physics will enhance accuracy in years to come. They have lighter mass weight than traditional aluminum arrows even though the diameter of the arrow shaft is larger. The new alloys allow increased strength to reduce mass weight by keeping the wall of the arrow shaft thinner. These factors contribute to better aerodynamics and accuracy.

Carbon/graphite arrows are the latest development on the market. These arrows are being used extensively by expert archers. They do not bend, and they are shatter resistant. These shafts are lighter than aluminum with a higher static spine. Carbon arrows have excellent energy storing and absorption features, and tests have shown that these features enhance their penetrating capacity. Those features translate into higher velocities and flatter trajectories for carbon arrows over some aluminum and the older fiberglass arrows. That can mean better scores in target archery.

It is recommended that the archer go to an archery pro shop and shoot aluminum as well as carbon arrows properly matched for his or her bow. Compare and contrast the arrows for factors such as accuracy, velocity, penetration, and trajectory based on how you shoot them at a specific target over preferred distances. Pragmatically, one should purchase the style of arrow that performs best for you when matched to your bow. The elite and professional target archers are using graphite as well as aluminum arrows in competition. Wooden and fiberglass arrows tend to be a part of the history of the sport.

The term "end" applies to a set number of arrows shot on the range before archers go to the target to score and retrieve. The number of arrows in an end may be designated as three, five, or six in target archery. The most common number of arrows designated as an end in instructional situations is six. That is one reason for recommending that beginning archers purchase a minimum of twelve arrows (two ends) initially. A few extra arrows are always needed in case of loss or damage during classes or tournaments.

Terminology for the various parts of the target archery arrow is shown in figure 3.1. It should also be noted that manufacturers of arrows place informative numbers on the shafts. These numbers indicate the outside diameter of the arrow shaft in closest sixty-fourths of an inch and the wall thickness of the arrow in thousandths of an inch. This information is very important in the matching of ends of arrows when arrows are purchased initially and when an arrow has to be replaced.

Figure 3.2
Arrow designs. From top to bottom: target archery arrow, bowhunting arrow with broadhead, field archery arrow with a field point, and bowfishing arrow with sting-a-ree point.

For comparative purposes, figure 3.2 shows some common types of arrows used in the four most popular archery sports. Each arrow was designed for a unique purpose. The reader should visually compare and contrast these four arrows with that in mind. The arrow designs shown in figure 3.2 are for target archery (target pile or point), bowhunting (broadhead point), field archery (field point), and bowfishing (fishing point).

Spine

The spine of an arrow shaft is the deflection of the shaft, measured in inches, when depressed by a two-pound weight at its center. There are instruments that measure the degree of spine with minute precision. This measurement is important, inasmuch as the degree of spine deflection and uniformity are basic factors to consider when obtaining matched arrows. The spine deflection value must be compatible with the archer's bow weight.

One reason for matching bow weight and spine is a phenomenon known as the *Archer's Paradox.* Contrary to what the archer thinks he or she sees as the arrow leaves the bow, an arrow does not fly directly toward the target immediately upon being released. By means of cinematographic analysis, it has been demonstrated that the arrow shaft actually deflects or bends around the bow immediately after release. The reader can understand that an arrow shaft too stiff or too flexible could cause problems during this phase of its flight pattern. An arrow of sufficient spine, matched for the bow and released properly, tends to stabilize itself rapidly and follows an undeviating flight pattern during its trajectory toward the target. The fact that an arrow first deviates to the left for a right-handed archer when it leaves the bow, but ultimately stabilizes itself in flight to travel straight to the intended target, is known as the Archer's Paradox.

The combination of newer bow designs and materials, the use of cushion plungers and arrow rests, and the changes noted above in the materials used to construct arrow shafts tend to minimize the Archer's Paradox. All of these types of engineering improvements ultimately have led to better accuracy in target archery tournaments throughout the world.

What are some of the consequences of having improperly spined arrows for a bow? (It must be kept in mind that several factors other than spine determine accurate arrow flight. These will be discussed later.) Improper spine can cause the following arrow flight patterns: (1) an arrow naturally starts its flight by deviating a few degrees to the left for a right-handed archer. If the spine is too stiff, the shaft of the arrow or the fletching will actually brush the bow. This causes a reduction in arrow velocity. In addition, a flight pattern change occurs in the opposite direction. The archer's shot will be low and to the right of the intended target. (2) If the spine is too weak and flexible, the arrow may never stabilize and follow its intended trajectory. Instead, it will fly consistently to the left of the target. Improperly spined arrows are a definite causative factor for erratic arrow grouping.

What should be considered when selecting the proper spine for arrows? First, the bow weight, that is, the pounds of pull exerted on the bowstring by the archer for his or her specific arrow length, is very important. Second, the arrow length and weight to the grain must be known accurately. Third, the type and weight of the arrow point are also basic considerations. Target points are made very light. This places the quality target arrow's center of gravity close to its actual center. This makes the arrow aerodynamically sound, as compared to its heavier counterparts in bowhunting and field archery, as seen in figure 3.2.

By knowing these exact arrow measurements, the proper spine can be selected. There are charts for spine and weight specifications as well as shaft selection available from archery tackle manufacturers and in professional archery shops. One should be very careful and follow the guidelines set forth in these charts when matching and purchasing tackle. If you have a question regarding two spine classifications of arrows suitable for a bow, it is best to take the *stiffer* of the two arrows.

Correct arrow selection in terms of spine can mean the difference between tight groups and good scores versus erratic groups and poor scores during a target archery tournament. The stiffer, spined arrow that is light in weight will have a higher velocity. But, the increased spine must be compatible with your bow weight. The increased spine will provide fewer deviations in flight due to human errors at release or to wind conditions on the range. Finally, the technical matching of arrow spine to the proper bow weight that can be handled efficiently by the archer is a major reason archery tackle should be purchased in an archery pro shop. Archers who work there are usually much better informed about the sport than salespeople in your average sporting goods or general merchandise franchise store.

Fletching

The feathers of an arrow are known collectively as fletching. Fletching is as important to an arrow as the tail assembly is to an airplane. The function of the two analogous parts is essentially the same. They both serve to stabilize airborne objects. Fletching stabilizes an arrow by channeling the wind currents encountered by the arrow during flight. Flight equilibrium is also maintained, in part, by high angular velocity (rotation) of the arrow around the longitudinal axis of its shaft.

The type of fletching one uses is largely a matter of personal preference. The trend seems to be away from the old, traditional turkey feather fletching to vinyl and plastic vanes. The latter vanes tend to be more durable than real feathers, and they do

Figure 3.3
Fletching variations. From top to bottom: bowhunting, target archery, flu-flu, spiraled flu-flu, and rubber bowfishing fletching.

not become useless during inclement weather. On the other hand, feather fletching in good condition and shot in dry weather is more likely to exhibit better flight characteristics following a poor release. A poor release usually produces fletching contact with the bow. The relatively rigid plastic vanes striking the bow produce a yaw condition, or lack of stability, during arrow flight. This reduces the arrow's linear velocity and usually results in a low shot. While the same contact may occur between the bow and the feather fletched arrow upon a poor release, the adverse effects on arrow flight are minimized. The flexible feathers are less likely to rebound as much from the bow handle. As a result, the arrow flight is not as adversely affected. The better target archers are using firmer plastic vanes in competition. Plastic weighs more than turkey feathers, so your point weight must be adjusted accordingly for matching purposes when plastic vanes are used.

The length of the fletching is very important because fletching helps stabilize the flight of the arrow after it bends around the bow upon release. Generally, longer and heavier arrows require longer and sturdier fletching. Shorter and lighter target archery arrows require fletching only 3 to 3 1/2 inches in length. Three-vane fletching of either plastic or feathers can be used effectively by target archers. Larger fletching is needed to add flight stability for heavier arrows as used in bowhunting and field archery.

Figure 3.3 shows fletching variations on bowhunting, target, field, and bow-fishing arrows. The fletch on the top arrow, a hunting arrow, is 5 inches in length. The next arrow is a target arrow, and the fletch is 3 inches in length. The larger fletching on the middle arrow is 5 1/2 inches in length. This type of fletch is designed to increase the drag resistance on a field or bowhunting arrow. Obviously, these arrows will not fly as far if a target is missed. Therefore, they are not lost as frequently by field archers or bowhunters. The next arrow shows a spiraled flu-flu fletch. This type of fletching is also designed to increase air resistance (drag) so arrows will not travel as far in flight. The bottom arrow is an example of rubber fletching on a bowfishing arrow. Fletching is not very important on bowfishing arrows because the arrow simply does not have to fly very far to reach its intended target. Some bowfishers remove the fletching completely from their arrows.

Fletching is usually colored in a distinct and traditional manner. On a three-fletched arrow, two vanes will be drab in color and one vane will usually be rather flamboyant. The bright or odd-colored feather is known as the *index feather*, and is placed at a ninety-degree angle to the slit in the nock of the arrow. This can be seen in the upper two arrows in figure 3.3.

As a historical note, the two drab colored vanes were once known as *hen feathers*, and the brightly colored vane was called the *cock feather*. That terminology had an ornithological origin; that is, the feathers of male birds tend to be more colorful than the feathers of the female of the same species. Fletching terminology was changed to indicate arrow placement by using the term *index* for the vane that is usually pointed outward from the bow when it is nocked in the bowstring. It is recommended that experienced archers try shooting periodically on an experimental basis, with the index feather downward or toward the bow. Flight patterns shot both ways should be evaluated. The best technique of fletching placement should be adopted permanently after a satisfactory evaluation period. Most archers prefer that the index feather be placed so it points outward from the bow.

Length

Length of the arrow varies for each individual. The length of your arms and the type of anchor point used are the determining factors. *The anchor point is the placement of the archer's bowstring hand on the chin or face with the bow at full draw.*

The beginner who has not determined his or her anchor point may want to purchase the first six arrows an additional inch longer than the measurement indicates. Anchor point adjustments are made as skill develops. It is much better to have arrows too long for the bow than too short. Accurate arrow lengths can be determined best once all shooting fundamentals are learned properly.

There are several ways to establish an initial arrow length for yourself with and without the use of a bow. If you have a bow and an over-length arrow, mark the arrow in one-inch increments from the bottom of the arrow nock groove to the arrow point. After you have drawn the bow to your anchor point, note the inch mark nearest the back of the bow. That should be your arrow length if the anchor point is established. If not, add an inch as noted to the first arrows purchased.

Another commonly used method of determining arrow length is to have the archer hold both arms out to the sides at shoulder level (abduct both shoulder joints ninety degrees). Obtain the arm spread measurement in inches from the ends of the middle fingers:

Spread Measurement	Arrow Length
57–59 inches	22–23 inches
60–62 inches	23–24 inches
63–65 inches	24–25 inches
66–68 inches	25–26 inches
69–71 inches	26–27 inches
72–74 inches	27–28 inches
75–77 inches	28–29 inches
78+ inches	30 inches

Note: To change from inches to centimeters, multiply by 2.54.

A yardstick may be used to determine arrow length if you do not have a bow and marked arrow. Two techniques may be used. First, stand at right angles to a wall. Place the clenched fist of your bow arm against the wall, simulating a bow hold. The elbow and wrist are extended, and your head is placed in the shooting position looking toward a target (the wall in this case). The distance along the bow arm from the wall to the corner of your mouth is your arrow length. The second technique is to hold, or have a person place, a yardstick on your sternum or breastbone. Hold both arms at shoulder level in front of you and move them to the yardstick. Your correct arrow length will be very close to the measurement at the end of your middle fingertips on the yardstick.

Points

Arrow points are manufactured in a wide variety of types and sizes. Target archery and field archery points are fairly standardized, but you will find a great array of bowhunting and bowfishing points. The beginning archer should start with light points for target archery (fig. 3.4). The various arrow points used in the other areas of archery will be discussed in chapters 6 and 7.

Target archery points are designed to be ultralight to facilitate arrow aerodynamics. Proper point weight for each shaft size is just as essential in target archery as it is for the heavier broadhead points used in bowhunting. The nearly symmetrical equilibrium of the target archery arrow is very important for accuracy. Proper point weight, fletching size, and nocks are the critical components on the arrow.

Most of the more sophisticated target archery points on quality aluminum arrows are designed as nickel-plated steel points fitted to an aluminum sleeve. This unit is then placed solidly into the arrow shaft. Target archery points designed in this manner should not loosen and cause flight problems. They should be checked,

Figure 3.4
The target archery arrow point should be matched in weight to be aerodynamically compatible with the total arrow configuration.

however, after being shot. Arrows should be cleaned with a tassel after each end is shot. The added weight of even very small amounts of dirt causes erratic arrow flight. A *tassel* is a piece of cloth carried by the archer for the specific purpose of keeping arrows clean (see fig. 3.18).

The Bow

The bow has fascinated human beings throughout history. People have used it for hunting land animals and birds on the wing, bowfishing, killing their enemies, making music, drilling holes, and for a variety of other activities.

Bows have been built in all sizes and shapes (see chapters 2 and 9). The following are some examples of different types of bows used throughout history. Some archers in the Far East used seven-foot bows with straight, uneven limbs; some African tribes use a three-foot bow with straight, even limbs; Englishmen of the eleventh century used a self bow made from one piece of wood five feet long with straight limbs; warriors at the Temple of Aigina used composite bows with duo-flexed limbs; the Navajo Indians of the southwestern United States used a short, composite bow for hunting purposes.

Most contemporary bowhunters, bowfishers, and field archers use the compound bow. Target archers now use compound as well as working recurve bows with center shot design and removable limbs. To differentiate between compound and recurve bows—the recurve bow is referred to as the *Olympic Bow* by the National Archery Association. The recurve or Olympic Bow is used exclusively in Olympic competition. Compound bows are used in target archery shooting divisions separate from Olympic Bows.

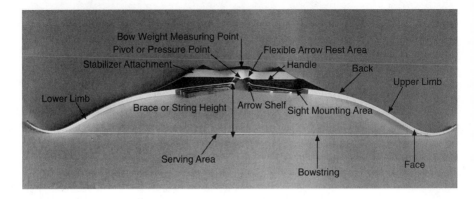

Figure 3.5

Recurve or Olympic Bow terminology. (Courtesy Black Widow Custom Bows, Inc., 1201 Eaglecrest, P.O. Box 2100, Nixa, MO 65714)

*This section is delimited primarily to depicting the **Olympic Bow** for use in target archery. The reader should be aware that FITA and the National Archery Association also include Compound Bow Divisions in outdoor and indoor target archery tournaments. Some relevant information about compound bows will be provided in this chapter, and compound bows are described in more detail in chapter 6.*

The NAA National Championships, for example, have included the following categories for shooting with compound bows in target archery competition: Compound Gentlemen, Compound Ladies, Senior Gentlemen Compound Visitor, Senior Ladies Compound Visitor, Clout Compound Men, and Compound Team Men. Archers who use compound bows do not compete against archers who use the Olympic Bow in outdoor and indoor target archery tournaments. Special rounds and shooting classification definitions for target archery are delineated in chapter 5.

Throughout history the diverse bow designs met their intended objectives in the hands of expert archers. That is an important fact to keep in mind in this age of very efficient archery tackle. *The skill and adaptability of the archer to his or her tackle remains the paramount factor for shooting success.* Bow selection from a variety of quality bows available on the market today is one of those "nice problems" for the contemporary target archer. This type of situation never confronted his or her counterparts prior to the second half of the twentieth century.

The Olympic Bow has unique nomenclature that needs to be learned. This bow terminology is presented in figure 3.5. *The reader should refer to chapter 10 as needed while reading text material for definitions of terms used in archery.* As a historical note, the bow shown in figure 3.5 is an older (circa A.D. 1960) one-piece recurve target archery bow.

Compound bow terminology is included in figure 3.6 for the reader's convenience. The reader may want to compare and contrast it with the Olympic Bow nomenclature in figure 3.5. More information is provided for the compound bow in chapter 6.

Figure 3.6
Compound bow terminology for a two-wheeled bow. (Courtesy Precision Shooting Equipment, 2727 N. Fairview Ave., Tucson, AZ 85705)

Which type of target archery bow should be selected? A well-constructed working recurve bow will be more than adequate. A working recurve bow can be identified by observing the position of the bowstring on the face of the bow. The working recurve bow, as contrasted with longbow designs (see figs. 5.2 and 6.2), will have the string lying on the face of the bow for at least two inches at each end of the limbs. This feature greatly enhances the leverage potential of the bow, adds to better transfer of energy from the bow to the arrow, and increases the velocity of the arrow.

The older model recurve shown in figure 3.5 is an excellent composite bow of solid, one-piece construction. The limbs were made from laminated fiberglass and hard rock maple, with the handle section of Brazilian rosewood. A beginning archer may think about purchasing an older used bow of that type to learn the sport. They are extremely efficient, durable, and functional. In addition, they can be purchased from professional archery shops that trade and sell tackle at prices much below that of a new model take-down recurve bow. From the standpoints of cost and efficient skill development, the purchase of a used working recurve bow

Figure 3.7
A take-down target archery bow showing the lower limb, handle, and upper limb. This quality bow is an efficient, functional work of art. (Courtesy Black Widow Custom Bows, Inc., 1201 Eaglecrest, P.O. Box 2100, Nixa, MO 65714)

is a good way for some people to get started in target archery. You can always "trade up." You must keep in mind, however, that your arrows must match the specifications of any bow purchased.

If the target archer desires an Olympic Bow, the finest tournament archery bows are three-piece, take-down bows. One example of an older model is shown in figures 3.7 and 3.8. Figure 3.7 illustrates a take-down target bow disassembled into the lower limb, riser, and upper limb sections. This bow is made of maple; other take-down models on the market have risers made of a magnesium alloy, aluminum, or carbon graphite. Take-down bows can be assembled quickly and easily. The bow in figure 3.7 is protected by a transparent glass covering over laminated maple curved limbs, thereby making the bow very efficient in terms of leverage, durability, and arrow velocity. The laminated maple also affords the bow an aesthetic quality, which is important to many archers. The bowyers who made this bow have put together an efficient and highly functional work of art.

Draw weights for take-down bows usually range from 22 to 50 pounds. A distinct advantage of a take-down bow over the earlier one-piece recurve models is that the archer can change limb lengths and bow weights as desired. Limbs may be purchased in lengths ranging from 64 to 70 inches.

Figure 3.8
An Olympic Bow equipped with arrow rest, stabilizers, clicker, and bowsight. This is the same bow as shown in figure 3.7. (Courtesy Black Widow Custom Bows, Inc., 1201 Eaglecrest, P.O. Box 2100, Nixa, MO 65714)

Figure 3.8 shows an older version of an equipped "Olympic Bow." This is the same take-down working recurve bow shown in figure 3.7. It is equipped with stabilizers. The bow has three stabilizer inserts in the back of the handle riser plus one on the face of the bow. A clicker is mounted on the sight window. *A clicker is a shooting aid that ensures a consistent draw and helps the target archer concentrate on aiming and release of the arrow.* A bowsight is mounted on the bow. The bow is braced or strung, and the draw is being started in figure 3.8.

Each archer equips his or her bow to meet individual requirements based on such factors as shooting idiosyncracies, target archery rules, and personal preferences. Each competitive target archer is unique.

A quality Olympic Bow has a section cut away at the midline of its upper limb. This is called center shot design. The cutaway area is used as the sight window.

Figure 3.9
Jay Barrs, former Olympic Target Archery Champion, with a state-of-the-art, outfitted Radian Carbon Plus Olympic Bow. (Courtesy Hoyt USA, 475 North Neil Armstrong Road, Salt Lake City, UT 84116–2825)

This feature minimizes the components of the Archer's Paradox by aiding arrow clearance upon release. The arrow is able to move past the bow in a relatively close path to the bowstring alignment with the face of the bow. Another important feature of a bow with center shot design is the practical aspect of allowing the archer to see the intended target.

Figure 3.9 shows a fully outfitted state-of-the-art Olympic Bow—the Hoyt USA Radian Carbon Plus. This is the type of bow now used commonly by elite archers throughout the world in target archery from local to international levels of competition. This take-down recurve bow provides carbon limbs that are impervious to heat, cold, and moisture. Its limb and riser system provides improved arrow velocity as well as better horizontal and vertical limb stability. With a choice of risers and limbs, the individual archer has flexibility in choosing and changing bow lengths and weights as needed. The sight window is unobstructed because the clicker system is eliminated from view within the design of this bow. The clicker system may also be extended easily to meet the needs of the archer. The grip is customized to avoid bow torque and to fit the hand of the archer. The bow in figure 3.9 appears to be the design of target archery bows of the future.

Weight

The bow weight and literal mass weight of the bow are very important for entirely different reasons. *Bow weight is defined as the bow manufacturers' determination of the number of pounds required to draw the bowstring a given distance—usually 28 inches. Mass weight of the bow is the actual weight of the bow in pounds.* Mass weight of a bow should never be confused with bow weight. The mass weight of a good target archery bow with a stabilizer should be in the 3- to 6-pound range. This amount of mass weight helps the archer by adding to the bow's shooting stability. The archer must be strong enough in the shoulder and arm musculature to handle the mass weight of the bow comfortably in competition over a period of several hours.

Due to the efficiency with which good recurve target archery bows can convert potential energy into kinetic energy, considerable force can be transmitted to the arrow. This efficient energy conversion results in excellent arrow velocity. With Olympic Bows, this process is accomplished at relatively low bow weights.

How much bow weight is enough for each archer to attain good scores in target archery? Some guidelines can be supplied to partially answer that question, but the final answer lies in the muscular endurance and strength each individual has in the extensor muscles of the body, the shoulder joints, shoulder girdles, and upper limbs. (A muscle analysis of shooting and conditioning principles for the target archer are provided in anatomic detail in chapter 8.)

Archery instructors generally agree that an archer should select a bow weight that he or she has strength enough to draw and hold without undue strain for multiple repetitions during class, practice sessions, or target archery tournaments. Generally, for most men, this means a bow weight should be found that is comfortable somewhere within a range of 30 to 50 pounds. Although the average adult woman has only 50 percent of the muscle mass seen in men, one should not deduce that a functional bow weight for all women is low. Observations by archery instructors verify that this is not the case. Strength in human beings is a product of genetics, central nervous system efficiency, and muscle mass. Therefore, many small people, male and female, are very strong and can handle higher bow weights. Generally, for most women, a functional target bow weight is found within the range of 25 to 45 pounds. That range does not represent the upper range for all women because some elite, competitive women archers do shoot with higher bow weights. Bow weight is a highly individual matter, and the bow weight must be matched to meet the specific strength of the archer as well as the arrows to be shot from it.

It should be noted that the peak draw weight allowed by the Fédération Internationale de Tir á l'Arc (FITA) for compound bows used in target archery is 60 pounds. This is an important consideration to keep in mind if you are planning to purchase a compound bow for multiple use in target archery and other archery sports. Due to its unique features, the peak draw weight of a compound bow is not attained and held at full draw by the archer. See chapter 6 for more compound bow weight details.

As indicated, bow weights for Olympic Bows are determined according to the number of pounds required to pull the bowstring back to full draw for a given arrow length. Most bows are marked for bow weight at a 28-inch draw. As the draw diminishes in length when using a recurve bow, the bow weight also diminishes in pounds. Conversely, as the draw increases in length, the bow weight increases in pounds. (Greater bow weights are required for bowhunting as compared to target archery. The bowhunter uses an overdraw device, *illegal in target archery,* to increase the bow weight.)

The archer needs to know the actual draw weight for the arrow length being pulled while using an Olympic Bow. The recommended method for doing this was established by the Archery Manufacturer's Organization (AMO). This procedure is accomplished as follows: Divide the draw weight marked on the bow by 20, and determine how many inches, more or less, the actual draw length deviates from 28 inches. Multiply these two answers, and subtract (or add) the answer from the weight marked on the bow. The result of this calculation gives the archer the actual draw weight. As an example, assume that an archer has a 35-pound bow, but he or she is actually drawing 30 inches. Thirty-five divided by 20 equals 1.75. In this example, 1.75 would be multiplied by 2, which is the extra number of inches being drawn above the 28-inch mark. The resultant answer of 3.50 would be added to the 35-pound bow weight. Therefore, an archer drawing a 30-inch arrow on a bow marked 35 pounds for a 28-inch draw would actually be drawing 38.5 pounds. One should use this process to determine the actual bow weight for the length of arrow used.

It is a good idea for some beginners to learn while using a bow weight lighter than they have strength to handle. It is easier to learn shooting fundamentals with a comfortable bow weight because the archer's concentration is not distracted due to fatigue or other physical factors. As skill increases, bow weight can be increased to meet the individual's strength and muscle endurance capabilities. This teaching method is recommended in those learning situations where matched tackle is available and can be issued to the archers.

Some archers like to believe they need a very heavy bow weight. Let us consider what actually happens when the potential kinetic energy of a bow is doubled. What are the differences in terms of arrow velocity between 45- and 90-pound bows? Will arrow velocity be doubled? Tripled? Taking variable arrow weights into consideration, it has been established that an average 90-pound bow increases arrow velocity only 19 to 25 percent over a 45-pound bow. When an archer considers such factors as ease of handling, shooting over prolonged periods of time during tournaments, and accuracy difficulties, is a high bow weight really worth the extra effort needed to draw it? Most archers would answer "No." Contemporary recurve bows have excellent thrust force. This results in superior arrow velocities to handle the standard distances shot in tournaments. *An arrow velocity between 163 and 210 feet per second will be functional for target archery purposes.* Why stress yourself with a bow weight that is too high to handle easily?

The arrow velocity potential for today's bows and arrows is determined by calculating a ballistics coefficient based on the interrelationships of the (1) peak weight of the bow in pounds; (2) total weight of the arrow including point, nock, and fletching in grains; and (3) draw length of the bow. Bows with draw lengths over 30 inches—stable and efficient in terms of longer application of force on the arrow nock after bowstring release—have better ballistic coefficients than bows that do not meet these scientifically based criteria.

A working recurve bow with a ballistics coefficient of 0.140 would produce an arrow velocity of 210 feet per second. In terms of accuracy, flight efficiency, and trajectory, that velocity level could be better than an arrow projection of 240 feet per second. So, the choice of your ultimate bow weight should also be based on these types of technical and scientific factors. The greater bow weight may not be the most efficient. The efficiency of the bow ultimately boils down to three key factors: (1) design, (2) construction materials, and (3) the skill of the archer using it. The last is the most important factor! Knowing the ballistic coefficient of your bow helps to match other tackle to the bow and determine its efficiency for the distances you shoot.

Let us consider some of the basic differences between the designs of the working recurve bow and the longbow (see figure 6.2). This discussion is presented, because, unfortunately, longbows and recurve bows with longbow mechanics are still being issued for learning purposes in some archery classes. First, it should be noted that not all bows sold as recurve bows have recurve actions. In order to work efficiently, the bowstring of the recurve bow must actually touch the face of the bow for two to three inches at the end of both limbs. If the so-called recurve bow is not designed in this manner, it will respond essentially the same as the longbow.

If you have been issued a bow in an instructional situation or for practice, check it out carefully. When the bowstring touches the recurve tips as shown in the bows in figures 3.8 and 3.9, this increases the leverage potential and adds to arrow velocity. There is an increase in the force-time relationship during energy transfer from the bow to the arrow. *The total effect of the force generated by the bow and applied to the arrow via the bowstring-nock arrangement is the product of the magnitude of force over the time during which it operates.*

The principle above is magnified, for example, within the design of compound bows that utilize wheels, pulleys, and cams. These bows with leverage enhancement devices can now be used, as noted, in special divisions in target archery competition if the peak draw weight is under 60 pounds.

The modern design of recurve bows is very efficient. A recurve bow weight of 45 pounds will project an arrow at a rate of speed approximately 20 percent greater than a longbow of comparable weight. A working recurve bow tends to draw more smoothly than a longbow. This is particularly true of the modern take-down bow. These bows have less increase of weight during the last few inches of draw than bows with "longbow mechanics." *The phenomenon of ever-increasing weight as one draws the bowstring hand toward the face is known as "stacking."*

Due to greater arrow velocity, which is derived through increased leverage, the working recurve bow tends to project the arrow on a flatter trajectory than a longbow. This aids accuracy considerably. Finally, the semicircular configuration of a longbow, seen as it is being drawn, tends to cause an uneven distribution of stress in the limbs. This factor also detracts from the overall efficiency and longevity of the longbow. This type of stress within the limbs does not occur within a good working recurve bow.

Can longbows be used in target archery? The answer is yes, but not by serious target archers in highly competitive tournaments against archers using recurve bows. The longbow is making a comeback of sorts as a result of its historical significance. This is due, as one example, to the efforts of organizations such as The British Long Bow Society. This group sponsors tournaments in the United Kingdom and North America. The historic York Round is shot during these tournaments (see chapter 5) and archers must shoot wooden arrows from their longbows. Due to the inefficiency of longbows compared to contemporary recurve bows, the longbow presents a greater challenge to shoot excellent scores on a target archery range. Some target archers and bowhunters enjoy that type of test. Many longbows have been retired to museums, but some are alive and well in the hands of archers who want more sport and a greater degree of difficulty in shooting. More power to them! There are a few archery manufacturers who make quality longbows (fig. 6.2) primarily for use by bowhunters who value the sport of the hunt. A beginning target archer, however, should learn to shoot while using a good, working recurve bow. If, however, you plan to compete in compound bow divisions in target archery, you should learn to shoot with the compound bow. Specificity is a fact of life in sport.

Length

Target archers rarely use short Olympic Bow lengths. They are simply too difficult to use. There is extreme pressure on the bowstring fingers at full draw, which negates a smooth release of the arrow. Most target archers use bows ranging from 64 to 70 inches in length. The added bow length minimizes the pressure the fingers exert on the nock of the arrow during the draw and at release. A smoother release is provided by using a longer bow. In addition, the longer bows generally have greater mass weight. This factor helps the strong archer have better bow arm stability and a steadier bow hand while shooting.

The draw length or arrow length must be considered when selecting a bow for target archery:

	Draw Length	Bow Length
1.	25 inches to 28 inches	64-inch limbs
2.	27 inches to 30 inches	66-inch limbs
3.	29 inches to 32 inches	68-inch limbs
4.	31 inches to 34 inches	70-inch limbs

Personal preference and kinesthetic feeling enter into bow length selection. As an example, a person with a 30-inch draw can use a 66- or 68-inch bow. Whichever length ultimately has the best feeling after shooting numerous ends of arrows is the bow that should be purchased. Most professional archery shops have indoor ranges where bows may be tried prior to purchase. That is highly recommended. Also, keep in mind, that limb lengths can be changed as needed by using take-down bows.

Figure 3.10
Lawrence Brady shoots a bow equipped with one stabilizer. The stabilizer is mounted on the back of the bow.

What can we expect in the future as far as bows are concerned? The mechanical engineers who work for the archery manufacturers are constantly experimenting with new materials. Carbon seems to be a material of choice for designing and building both bows and arrows. Figure 3.9 shows a bow of the future that is now in use. Bows have been manufactured in the past with risers made of carbon, but the bow of the future may just be a bow made completely from carbon material. A prototype bow has been developed with a mass weight of only two pounds!

Stabilizers

One or more stabilizers can be mounted on a target archery bow. The stabilizer can contribute to more efficient arrow flight by minimizing or negating some of the archer's fundamental shooting faults involving the bow arm. A stable bow means less vibration and torque of the bow from aiming through the release. A single stabilizer is shown mounted on a target bow in figure 3.10. The stabilizer is a metal rod screwed into the back of the bow on the bow handle, and it projects forward toward the intended target. The stabilizer can be adjusted for length to fit the personal preference of the archer. (Hydraulic stabilizers for mounting on bows or v-bars are

Figure 3.11
A v-bar stabilizer system mounted on a target archery bow. (Courtesy Black Widow Custom Bows, Inc., 1201 Eaglecrest, P.O. Box 2100, Nixa, MO 65714)

also now on the market.) The number, weight, length, and type of stabilizer is a matter of individual preference. Some archers prefer to use tapered stabilizers mounted on a rotor that pivots 360 degrees. This allows considerable adjustment flexibility for stabilizers. In contrast to figure 3.10, figures 3.8, 3.9, and 3.11 show v-bar stabilizer systems mounted on bows.

A word of advice is in order regarding the use of stabilizers. *The beginner should learn basic fundamentals of shooting before mounting a stabilizer on the bow.* After the fundamentals have been learned to the extent that the archer is grouping arrows consistently, a stabilizer is then recommended for use. However, the archer should try to correct fundamental faults without using the stabilizer. If successfully done, this will mean higher scores when the stabilizer is used later in practice and competitive situations. A stabilizer should not be used as a "crutch" to compensate for fundamental faults of the archer.

Bowstrings

Like arrows, bowstrings must be matched to specific bows as well as the requirements of the archer. This important fact is often overlooked by beginning

Figure 3.12
The bowstring serving is equipped with two nock-locators. A kissing button is on the string above the serving. The bow is also equipped with a clicker, arrow rest, bowsight, and stabilizer. (Courtesy of Patrick Brunhoeber)

archers who tend to settle for any old string that fits the bow being used. Big mistake! Archery manufacturers make recommendations regarding what type of bowstring and exactly how many strands should be used with specific bows. The number of strands in your bowstring can also have an effect on arrow spine. "Matched tackle" means that you are using the correct bowstring for the bow and arrows being shot.

Bowstrings come in varieties of Dacron, Kevlar, and Flemish. Dacron and Flemish tend to stretch too much with use and that can have a negative effect on aerodynamics and accuracy. Kevlar string reduces the elastic component to a minimum and it produces a good shot with an average weight bow when twelve to fifteen strands are used. Dacron strings will vary from eight strands for bows up to 30 pounds to twelve or more strands recommended for bows up to 45 pounds. Bowstrings can be adjusted by twisting, but utilization of this technique should be limited to a maximum of twelve twists to minimize friction and breakage.

The middle portion of the bowstring is called the serving. The arrow is nocked or placed on the string at a specific point on the serving. As can be seen in figure 3.12, two nock-locators have been mounted on the serving. The nock-locators mark the exact nocking point for the arrow. The nock-locators shown in figure 3.12 are found on the serving immediately in back of the arrow rest. The added thread wrapping around the portion of the bowstring known as the *serving* is needed to protect the string from breakage because this area of the bowstring receives the most wear and tear. The total diameter of the serving area is ultimately determined by the number of strands of your bowstring. This serving diameter should not be larger than you can accommodate easily based on your finger size. If it is too large, your release may not be as smooth as it should be.

Bowsights

The excellent bowsight shown in figure 3.13 is the type used by elite amateur and professional target archers who shoot with the Olympic Bow. Use of a bowsight in target archery competition is an absolute essential in obtaining excellent scores. Bowsights should have vertical and horizontal micro adjustment features so the archer can make changes quickly and easily while on the range. These features are seen in figure 3.13. These characteristics are important in a quality target archery bowsight. Factors such as wind velocity and direction can change during a tournament, and bowsight adjustments have to be made fast and accurately in those situations. *The beginning archer should learn target archery by using a bowsight for aiming purposes versus shooting instinctively.* Bowsights are also mounted on the bows shown in figures 3.9, 3.11, and 3.12.

Accessories

The archer must have protection for the bow arm and bowstring fingers. The bow arm must be protected from possible contusions due to being slapped by the bowstring in the general region of your radioulnar and wrist joints (forearm). Bad shooting habits result when adequate forearm protection is not provided or when the arm is moved improperly. Without protection of the shooting hand, the bowstring fingers become severely irritated from the constant pressure and friction exerted by the bowstring. Two common leather accessories designed to protect the forearm and shooting hand—the finger tab and arm guard—are shown in figures 3.14 and 3.15. Both come in several sizes, shapes, and styles. These accessories are relatively inexpensive.

The finger tab should be designed to include a separator or wedge to keep your index and middle fingers apart. This feature will minimize pressure or pinching on the nock during the draw and a tab designed with a separator will help you have a smoother release. The finger tab is rather awkward to use at first, but it is absolutely essential for prolonged shooting during class, practice sessions, or tournaments while using the conventional three-finger release technique. If a finger tab is not used, tender skin may become blistered by the friction created when the bowstring rolls over the fingertips. This, of course, would have an adverse effect on your release and accuracy. If you shoot on a regular basis, the finger tab will become worn, rough, or less pliable. It is necessary to change tabs when that occurs, because a worn tab interferes with a proper release.

Some archers prefer shooting gloves instead of finger tabs. A shooting glove is shown in figure 4.13. The beginner may want to try shooting in practice with gloves and tabs prior to selecting one over the other for regular use. The finger tab with a finger spacer around the arrow nock is recommended over the shooting glove for archers who use the traditional three-finger release technique.

For target archers who use compound bows, the FITA rules stipulate that you may use a release aid in competition. This rule simplifies target archery shooting to some degree for the compound bow shooter. The release aid may not be attached to the compound bow in any way and it may not include any electronic gadgetry in its operation. (Examples of older and newer release aids are shown in figures 6.13, 6.14, and 6.16.) There are many kinds of release aids on the market for use with compound bows.

Figure 3.13
The Toxonics Model 4100 Athenian Recurve
Bowsight used on Olympic Bows by many
elite target archers. (Courtesy Toxonics
Manufacturing, Inc., 1524 Wilmer Road,
Wentzville, MO 63385)

Figure 3.14
Finger tab. (Courtesy Wilson Brothers,
Route 1, Elkland, MO 65644)

Figure 3.15
Arm guard.

Figure 3.16
Finger sling.

The arm guard is placed on the bow arm between the elbow and wrist. The arm guard is shown in figures 3.15 and 3.17. The lower arm in the vicinity of the wrist is an area that can be "slapped" periodically by the bowstring when it is released. Shooting without an arm guard when that occurs can result in painful and serious contusions. Furthermore, following one severe blow by the bowstring on an unprotected arm, an archer has a tendency to flinch—flexion occurs in the elbow and/or wrist—when the arrow is released. These movements at the elbow and wrist are bad habits that the protection afforded by the arm guard tends to eliminate. Archery is fun, but no sport is a pleasure if you are injured frequently and do not experience some success. The arm guard and finger tab lend support to the archer.

A finger sling is another accessory that can help eliminate some problems during release and follow-through. Finger slings are shown in figures 3.16 and 3.17. The finger sling attaches to the index finger or middle finger and the thumb of the bow hand.

Figure 3.17
Arm guard and sling in use. (Courtesy of Lawrence Brady)

Figure 3.18
A hip quiver is designed to carry arrows and other tackle items needed on the shooting line. (Courtesy of Patrick Brunhoeber)

Figure 3.19
Arrow rest without an arrow.

Figure 3.20
Arrow rest holding the arrow at full draw.

It then extends across the back of the bow as shown in figure 3.17. It serves the purpose of keeping the bow from falling to the ground during release of the arrow and the subsequent follow-through. Therefore, the archer can concentrate more on the release and less on losing control of the bow. Target archery is a "mental game," and the more distractions you can eliminate while on the shooting line the better!

An arrow quiver is another accessory that the archer must obtain. *A quiver is a device designed to carry arrows.* There are shoulder, hip, ground, pocket, and bow quivers available. Those come in all sizes, shapes, prices, and materials. Most beginning target archers rely upon inexpensive, ground quivers. The hip quiver, as shown in figure 3.18, is most commonly used by experienced target archers to carry arrows as well as other objects needed during practice or tournaments.

Another important accessory is the arrow rest. This small device is mounted just above the arrow shelf on the bow. The purposes of the arrow rest and cushion plunger are to maintain efficient arrow position, stability, and bow clearance. This device is important from the initial nocking of the arrow onto the bowstring past the time of arrow release and bow clearance. There are one- and two-piece metal and plastic arrow rests on the market. Cushion plungers and arrow rests are produced in a wide variety of choices. Arrow rests are shown in figures 3.19 and 3.20. Some archers simply prefer to shoot from a modified arrow shelf on the bow without an arrow rest, but most serious target archers use cushion plungers and arrow rests.

A clicker is used extensively in target archery. A clicker is shown mounted on the sight window of the bow shown in figure 3.8. *A clicker is a shooting accessory that facilitates a consistent draw and helps the archer concentrate on aiming.* The arrow is ready to be released when the archer hears the "click" or sound as the fully drawn arrow point passes through the clicker.

Care of Archery Tackle

The Bow

The following care and treatment of a target bow will add to its longevity and effectiveness:

1. Always unstring the bow after use with a bowstringer. (It should be noted that some manufacturers prefer that the bow remain braced at all times because improper bracing is a common cause of limb breakage and torque problems.)
2. Place the bow in a bow case for storage purposes. In the case of a take-down bow, remove the bow limbs prior to inserting them in the bow case (see fig. 6.12).
3. Lay the bow in a flat place or hang it vertically if a bow case is not available.
4. To protect the outer surface of the bow, wax it periodically.
5. Use beeswax on the bowstring occasionally to minimize fraying.
6. Do not leave the bow lying on the ground when retrieving arrows from the target.
7. Do not drop the bow.
8. Draw the bow several times to your draw length prior to actually shooting an arrow, but do not release the string at full draw without an arrow in the bow.
9. Always use a bowstringer to brace the bow. Some manufacturers recommend that two feet be placed on the bowstringer for stability as the bow is braced.
10. A take-down bow can be stored while strung if desired. It should be hung horizontally.
11. Maintain proper limb and string alignments.

Arrows

The following care and treatment of arrows will add to their longevity and effectiveness:

1. Store arrows in an arrow case (see fig. 6.12).
2. Wipe arrows clean after shooting.
3. Check fletching after shooting and replace as needed. Fletching can be replaced at a very low cost.
4. Do not carry arrows in a tightly clenched fist. This tends to damage fletching. Place the arrows between the fingers when carrying them back from the target to the shooting line.
5. Check nocks and points after shooting and replace as needed.
6. If an arrow is embedded in a target up to the fletching or nock, remove the arrow by pulling it completely through the target. This protects fletching.

7. If an arrow is embedded or "snaked" into the grass on the target range, remove the arrow from the grass by pulling it in the direction of its flight. This protects fletching.
8. Always check aluminum arrows to determine that they are absolutely straight. Use a precision arrow straightener as needed.

Review

1. Because good quality archery tackle is expensive, it is important to maintain it carefully. Which parts of the tackle can be replaced or repaired if damaged?
2. Compare the efficiency and effectiveness of a working recurve bow with that of a longbow. Can a recurve bow have the mechanical characteristics of a longbow?
3. What do the following terms mean when used in connection with archery: (1) cast, (2) stabilizer, (3) fletching size, (4) tackle, (5) Archer's Paradox, (6) point weight, (7) take-down bow, and (8) thrust force?
4. Why would one spend considerable money on excellent instruction and matched tackle if one is a beginning archer?
5. If you must choose between two spine classifications for arrows to use with your bow, should you select the stiffer or more flexible spine and why?
6. Why is it of great importance to purchase archery tackle from an archery pro shop?
7. If advising a novice on the purchase of archery tackle, which accessory items would you recommend as essential, and which desirable for a beginner?
8. What arrow velocity do you need to compete in target archery?
9. Describe the routine procedures for the care of archery tackle.
10. A stabilizer can contribute to efficient arrow flight by minimizing or negating some fundamental shooting faults. Why, then, is it undesirable for a beginner to learn to shoot with a stabilizer?
11. What is the purpose of a clicker mounted on a bow?
12. The time to seek expert instruction in any sport is after you have practiced on your own and thus have learned a little about the activity. Is this sound advice? Why or why not?
13. Describe the Archer's Paradox and why it is of importance in selecting archery tackle.
14. Describe several methods of determining proper arrow length.

Fundamentals of Target Archery

4

Target archery is a "world class sport." Furthermore, learning target archery shooting skills also serves as your foundation for success in most of the other archery sports. An archer can now compete in target archery tournaments utilizing Olympic or compound bows. There are competitive divisions for target archers using both types of bows, but there is not competition between the divisions. The recurve bow is utilized at the Olympic level of competition exclusively.

Target archery during practice sessions and tournaments necessitates a merger of your physical skills and concentration capacities on every shot. Minute errors in executing the fundamental skills can be frustrating for the target archer because they lead to accuracy problems during the course of an entire round or tournament. A desire to pursue perfection and consistency are attributes the target archer must possess. These qualities are helped considerably if one has an understanding of the shooting fundamentals presented in this chapter.

Target archery is a demanding sport to learn correctly because there are numerous opportunities to err as the archer nocks the arrow, draws the bow, and releases the arrow on its flight toward the target. Those things most difficult to attain in life often are perceived to possess the greatest personal values. Therein lies some of the mystique and benefits of archery, as noted in chapters 1, 2, and 9.

Some basic shooting fundamentals of target archery are modified by champions and other participants in the sport. Such changes in the execution of basic skills occur in all sports due to individual differences of human beings. Elite target archers, like other athletes, have their theories, preferences, idiosyncracies, and variations concerning shooting styles. The beginning archer must remember that skill modifications are developed over a period of years of shooting in practice and competition. Although not all target archers shoot exactly alike, when their fundamental shooting skills are analyzed, their performances display more similarities than differences. As a result, a stereotype of perfect shooting mechanics can be delineated. *Those basic fundamentals of shooting, which are generally agreed upon as the stereotype of perfect skill or mechanics for target archery, are presented in this chapter.*

A few modifications of the stereotype of perfect shooting mechanics are mentioned periodically. The beginner may want to try these variations, but that is recommended only *after* becoming very familiar with your matched tackle and basic shooting techniques.

NOTE: The discussions and illustrations in this chapter pertain to the right-handed target archer shooting the Olympic Bow primarily. Some relevant material about compound bow shooting is presented in this chapter. There are more similarities than differences in terms of shooting fundamentals using Olympic and compound target bows. The main differences between shooting the two bows are found in the drawing and release phases of the shot, and those variations are discussed in this chapter. More information about compound bows may be found in chapters 6 and 7.

Archery and Safety

The archer should always keep the following fact in mind when archery tackle is in hand: *Archery is not a dangerous sport, but an arrow shot from a bow can kill or traumatize another human being on or near the target archery range.*

Safety rules vary from range to range. All rules, however, incorporate the concept of always being aware of the whereabouts of your fellow archers and the trajectory limits of your arrows. When an arrow is placed in a bow it should be pointed *only* in the direction of the intended target. Furthermore, the bow should never be drawn at an angle greater than necessary to hit the target. (Target archery is not clout or flight shooting!) That safety principle always keeps an accidentally released arrow within the safety zone of the archery range. *The archer must know beyond all doubt that no other human being is within arrow distance of the intended target plus the established safety zone.* These limits are usually defined on target archery ranges by instructors or Directors of Shooting.

Practice on a target archery range is performed on a common shooting line for all archers at a specific distance. Whistle signals are usually used to tell the archers when to shoot, stop shooting, and retrieve arrows. An archer should never move in front of the shooting line for any reason until he or she hears the whistle, signal, or voice authorizing retrieval of the arrows. Each archery instructor or Director of Shooting in a tournament will post or announce range safety rules. When these rules are followed in detail, and archers show courtesy and respect for one another on the range, target archery is one of the safest of all sports.

The archer should go to the range in comfortable clothing. Loose-fitting clothing such as golf sweaters, shirts, and blouses, which can become entangled with the bowstring after it has been released, are not recommended for wear on the archery range. It is also good practice to remove such things as watches, pens from pockets, and jewelry prior to shooting. These objects can also become entangled in the bowstring. Footwear should be comfortable enough to enable you to stand for long periods of time and walk to retrieve arrows. Shoes and boots with heels are also not recommended on a target archery range.

From the standpoints of personal safety and proper care of tackle, the bow and arrows to be shot should be given a visual inspection prior to shooting. The bow limbs and the arrows should be checked for stress fractures. Bows with limbs cracked or permanently twisted should be replaced. Arrow nocks and fletching need to be checked to notice if they are damaged in any way. The bowstring should be examined periodically to determine that all strands are intact. The string loops must always be checked to see that they are properly notched on the bow following the bracing process. These simple observations can eliminate potential hazards.

Figure 4.1
Bowstringer. (Courtesy of Bow-Pal)

Bracing

Bracing the bow is the process of attaching the bowstring to the bow in preparation for shooting. Bracing the bow can create problems for some archers. As a matter of fact, bows are damaged more often while being braced than in any other situation. Damage from bracing is one reason why some bowyers recommend that the bow be stored with it braced. *Olympic Bows should always be braced with a bowstringer.* If a bow is broken while using the older push-pull or step-through methods of bracing described below, some bow manufacturers will not replace the broken bows under their guarantees.

A bowstringer is shown in figure 4.1. Figures 4.2 and 4.3 show how to use the bowstringer. The bowstringer shown in figure 4.1 is equipped with two leather pockets, one longer than the other. Place the longer leather pocket on the lower tip of the bow and place the shorter pocket on the upper tip of the bow. Turn the bow face downward, and place the feet shoulder width apart on the bowstringer (fig. 4.2). Grip the bow firmly and pull it straight upward. The palm of the hand should be placed over the back of the bow, with the thumb on one side of the bow and the fingers on the other, to protect the archer in case the stringer should break or the cap should slide off. At the same time, the thumb and fingers slide the loose loop of the bowstring into its notch (fig. 4.3). The archer should be careful not to grip the string with the fingers from the belly side of the bow, or to put the fingers on the belly and slide the string upward. Both of these actions could result in pushing the cap off the end of the bow, causing it to snap upward and injure the archer. Always check both bow notches to see that the bowstring is properly inserted prior to shooting. To unstring the bow the above procedure is reversed. *The use of a bowstringer is simple, safe, and recommended at all times.*

If, however, a bowstringer is not available, there are two methods for bracing a bow manually: (1) the push-pull method and (2) the step-through method. The method used by the archer depends upon the weight of the bow, design of the bow, and strength of the individual.

Figure 4.2
Bracing with a bowstringer—Step One. (Courtesy Patrick Brunhoeber)

Figure 4.3
Bracing with a bowstringer—Step Two. (Courtesy Patrick Brunhoeber)

For most lightweight bows and archers with average strength, the push-pull method of bracing is adequate. (This method works fine for bracing longbows.) The following is the procedure for using the push-pull method of bracing:

1. Place the lower limb of the bow against the instep of the right foot; be certain that the bowstring is placed in the notch on the lower limb of the bow.
2. Grasp the handle with the right hand.
3. Grasp the loop of the bowstring with the thumb and index finger of the left hand and slide it up the upper limb toward the notch of the bow.

Figure 4.4
A Scythian archer in the act of bracing his bow. Since early times this method has proved satisfactory for stringing short and powerful composite bows. From a kylix by the Paraitois painter, after c. 490 B.C. (From E. G. Heath, *The Grey Goose Wing*)

4. PULL with the right hand and PUSH down on the upper limb with the left hand while sliding the bowstring upward and into the bow notch. *For safety, keep your face out of alignment with the upper limb at all times!*
5. Check to see that both bowstring loops are properly inserted (fully) into each bow nock. This is a final safety precaution.

The step-through method of bracing is used more frequently than the push-pull method, especially with heavier Olympic Bows. Again, this bracing technique should be used only when a bowstringer is not available for the archer:

1. Assume an upright stance with the feet apart at shoulder width.
2. Step through or between the bowstring and face of the bow with the right leg.
3. Make certain that the recurve of the lower bow limb encircles your left ankle.
4. Hold the handle of the bow on the upper thigh so both upper and lower bow limbs will bend.
5. Taking advantage of the leverage that this bow position allows, grasp the upper bow limb and bend it forward and downward with the right hand.
6. Move the bowstring upward, placing it in the bow notch with the left hand as the upper limb is being bent downward.
7. Check both bow notches to see that the bowstring loops are properly inserted into each notch. Failure to insert the loops properly exposes the archer to potential injury during the shooting process.

If the bow should slip during this step-through procedure for bracing, clothing such as slacks, pantyhose, and trousers can be ripped. The archer can also receive contusions and abrasions in the process. Steady pressure should be exerted on the bow limb and proper placement of the recurve around the left ankle must be checked to prevent the bow from slipping. Also, if the bow is twisted during this bracing method, it may crack. As can be seen in figure 4.4, variations of this bracing method have been around for a long time. They did not have bowstringers back in 490 B.C. If you have ever tried this bracing method while fully clothed, you might readily understand why the archer in figure 4.4 is bracing in the nude!

The actual distance from the bowstring to the handle or pivot point of the bow is very important. This is known as the brace, or string, height. Bowyers, individuals who make bows, indicate exactly what the brace height should be for each bow.

Brace height is directly related to the length of the bow. As one example, the manufacturer's recommended string height for the bow in figure 3.19 is 9¾ to 10¾ inches for a 69-inch bow and 9½ to 10½ inches for a 67-inch bow. The archer should measure the brace height accurately after bracing the bow. A bowstring too close or too far away from the face of the bow will adversely affect arrow velocity and flight because there is a direct relationship between brace height and spine of the arrows to match the bow.

At times the experienced target archer may adjust his or her brace height to compensate for individual shooting style. A higher brace height of an inch or less, as an example, may reduce bow shock at release and produce more stable arrow flight for some shooting styles. On the other hand, lowering the bowyer's or manufacturer's recommended brace height may compound shooting errors and problems. The amount of energy transferred to the arrow at the time of release will be affected if the brace height is inappropriate for the bow. A part of tuning archery tackle is to make sure that brace height is where it should be for the arrows being shot and for your particular shooting style.

A bowstring can be rotated or twisted in some cases to make minor adjustments for proper brace heights. The twists of the string should be limited to a range of three to ten for any single adjustment. The best situation is to have the proper size bowstring for the recommended brace height and bow weight of your bow. The bowstring must have the proper number of individual strands recommended for your bow weight to be compatible with the spine of your arrows and the bowstring diameter should allow you to use a three finger grip comfortably. Matching and tuning archery tackle are not easy tasks! There are many minute details to consider. Fortunately, archery manufacturers provide good guidelines for use of their equipment.

Stance

The right-handed archer stands with the left side of the body toward the intended target. The archer's stance must be consistent from shot to shot. The exact placement of the feet on the shooting line should be marked at each distance to be shot. Golf tees provide good markers for this purpose on grass ranges. They can be driven into the ground to indicate heel and toe placements for both feet. This procedure enables the archer to return to the exact stance on the shooting line after retrieving arrows. Minute stance deviations can cause sighting and aiming problems, which in turn lead to accuracy problems. *Consistency* is a key word in the sport of target archery. Figures 4.5, 4.6, 4.7, and 4.8 show four different types of stance foot placement used by archers.

Many archers prefer the even or parallel stance shown in figure 4.5. In this stance the shooting line is straddled and weight is evenly distributed over both feet (fig. 8.1). The heels and toes of the feet are aligned, and the middle of the instep of the left foot is positioned with the center of the intended target. The beginning archer may want to try this stance and determine how it feels while shooting several practice rounds. Archers who use the even or parallel stance believe that it minimizes

Figure 4.5
Even stance.

Figure 4.6
Open stance.

Figure 4.7
Oblique stance.

Figure 4.8
Closed stance.

movement to the left by the bow arm before and at release. The open and oblique stances allow the archer to view the target better than while using the even stance. Individual choice and some pragmatism are pleasant facts of life in archery!

The open stance is shown in figure 4.6. The feet should be shoulder-width apart in the open stance. It is recommended that the body weight be distributed evenly on both feet. Initially, the archer should take an even stance with both feet in position so an imaginary line can be drawn through the insteps of your feet to the center of the gold on the target face. To "open the stance," the left foot is moved backwards approximately 6 inches as shown. The open stance allows the archer to see the target better than using the even stance. Many good baseball hitters use an open stance for the same reason; that is, they can see the ball (target) better after it has been released by the pitcher. Archers can use both eyes if desired to see the target face.

Once the placement of the feet has been determined for your open stance and you are comfortable on the line, foot placement should be marked. After shooting an end of arrows, return to the *exact* foot placement each time IF the grouping of the arrows was

Figure 4.9
Body position for addressing the target in target archery—oblique stance. Shooting line is straddled. (Courtesy of Kathy Greene)

good. If not, foot placement may need to be changed. In addition, after gaining shooting experience, you may find that minute body adjustments are in order. The way to make these adjustments is to rotate your trunk (lumbar-thoracic spine). Keep the stance stable while rotating your lower spine as needed until the bow is aligned with the target. This is important both for viewing the target better and for aiming purposes.

Some elite archers prefer the oblique stance shown in figure 4.7. This stance is attained by placing the toe of the left foot nearest the target on a line with the target and pivoting the left foot so it is at a forty-five-degree angle to the target. The heel of the right foot is then placed in line with the toe of the left foot. The oblique stance allows the bow arm to remain in a position where there will be optimum clearance of the bowstring when the arrow is released. Furthermore, with the weight distributed over the balls of the feet, total body equilibrium is enhanced. The target is also seen clearly while using the oblique stance. Body adjustments, as noted above, can also be made as needed.

A closed stance is shown in figure 4.8. The shooting line is straddled and the weight is evenly distributed over both feet. The left foot is simply moved forward a few inches so a heel-toe relationship exists between the left and right feet. This type of stance is not popular among archers, but it is an option.

It is recommended that the beginning archer learn while using either the oblique or parallel stance. After practicing shooting fundamentals to the point where you are comfortable on the range, try various stances during the shooting process. The final stance chosen should be the one allowing the greatest degree of comfort, stability, target visibility, and accuracy for the individual.

The phrase "addressing the target" simply means that the target archer assumes the stance of his or her choice and straddles the shooting line (figs. 4.5, 4.6, 4.7, and 4.8) prepared to shoot. The arrows in those figures show the direction to the target. The overall body position for addressing the target is shown in

Figure 4.10
Nocking the arrow. Note the traditional 90 degree nocking angle. (Courtesy of Kathy Greene)

figure 4.9. The right-handed archer holds the bow in the left hand with the left side of the body nearest the intended target. If a ground quiver is used to hold arrows, it is placed near and in front of the archer so arrows can be reached without changing the stance.

Nocking

Nocking the arrow means proper placement of the arrow in its shooting position on the bowstring. In target archery, this is started only when all archers have assumed their stances on the shooting line. The archer holds the bow next to the hip nearest the target, as shown in figure 4.10. The arrow shaft is laid on the arrow rest. The arrow nock is placed on the bowstring at the serving with the index feather pointing upward. Bowstrings should be equipped with nocking points to define the area for arrow placement on the serving during nocking. Nocking points are placed slightly wider than the width of the arrow nock so adjustments can be made as needed.

The archer should place the arrow nock on the string one-eighth of an inch below the nocking point. A 90-degree angle is formed between the arrow and bowstring. This "traditional nocking angle" can be seen in figure 4.10. The nocking position may be changed one-sixteenth of an inch in the bow tuning process if abnormal flight patterns such as fishtailing, porpoising, or minnowing are noted. (See chapter 10 for definitions of archery terms.) However, for the beginning archer, a problem with flight stability of the arrow is more likely to be the result of poor string gripping and release mechanics than of improper bow tuning. (See the bow tuning section in this chapter.) All skill fundamentals must be executed soundly in order for properly tuned tackle to be effective.

Figure 4.11
Bow hold. The archer must keep the fingers relaxed. Note clicker, arrow rest, stabilizers, and bow sling.

Figure 4.12
Bow hold—hand pressure is exerted high, low, or on the bow's pivot point depending upon the type of bow used and the archer's preference.

Bow Hold

When discussing the bow hand, terms such as "holding" and "gripping" are misnomers. They tend to be misleading as far as archery skill is concerned. The archer does not hold or grip the bow as the draw is made. The bow is literally held only while nocking and after the arrow reaches the target. *During the process of shooting, the bow is actually kept in place by pressure on the bow hand at the pivot point of the bow.* The pivot point pressure felt in your hand against the bow is the resultant counterforce of the force applied to move the bowstring in the opposite direction during the draw to the anchor point. *The bow should never be gripped firmly by the hand during the drawing, aiming, and release phases of shooting.* Why? Avoiding a firmly held bow minimizes torque when the arrow is released. Torque or twisting of the bow prior to and at release causes erratic arrow flight.

As can be seen in figures 4.11 and 4.12, the bow is placed between the thumb and index finger. This bow arm-bow hold alignment technique should position the middle of the bow arm with the center of the bow. That will produce better balance between the pressures exerted on the bow handle and the line-of-pull of the bowstring. Balance between the two forces tends to reduce bow twist or torque as the shot is made and that improves your accuracy. The reason for this lies in the fact that the bowstring travels in a straight line as the release is made. The arrow is not thrown off-line by lateral movement of the bowstring as it starts its flight.

The grip can be high, medium, or low in regard to the position and pressure applied by the hand to the bow at the bow's pivot point. A high grip was the preference of archers who shot with bows made primarily of wood. The high grip was needed to minimize torque. Modern bow designs and materials have reduced (although not totally eliminated) torque problems, so more target archers now utilize medium and low grips effectively. Each archer should experiment with pressure placement of the bow hand high, on, or low in relation to the bow's pivot point. Pragmatically, the pressure placement that works and feels the best with your tackle is the one to use.

There is a tendency for the archer to let the bow pressure position slip slightly to the right or clockwise during the process of shooting. This phenomenon is attributable to a lapse in concentration and/or the fatigue factor, therefore the bow pressure position should be monitored periodically during practice sessions and competitions. This inclination to let the bow pressure slip can be adjusted when noted. The archer accomplishes this by making a very slight counterclockwise rotation of the thumb against the bow handle while concurrently extending the thumb forward toward the target. The "rotation of the thumb" observed in this technique is actually due to a forearm rotary motion known as supination.

There should be a relaxed feeling within the bow hand as much as possible. The palm of the hand should not apply pressure on the bow. The index finger may wrap around the bow, but it should not grip it. Some archers like to have the tip of the thumb and index finger relax and touch gently as a consistency checkpoint for the bow hold, but this is a matter of personal choice. Holding the fingers on the bow hand as relaxed as possible will also heighten accuracy. The opportunity for muscle fatigue in the forearm musculature of the bow arm is lessened considerably by not gripping with the fingers. The bellies of the large muscles that control finger motions (extrinsic hand muscles) are located in your forearm. If they are not contracted to flex the fingers to grip the bow, the fatigue factor is minimized. This reduces the probability of muscle tremors in the bow arm due to tiredness.

An undesired movement even as small as one degree of the bow arm unit at the time of release has a negative effect on accurate arrow flight. Expert athletes in all sports know how to "relax under pressure" to ensure that they reach their potentials. Relaxing musculature consistently during the important bow hold is one of those times for the target archer.

Drawing

Drawing is the act of pulling the bowstring to the chosen anchor point on the archer's face. This is analogous to cocking a pistol prior to firing a bullet. One major difference is that there are opportunities for human error while drawing a bowstring. Cocking a pistol is an error-free mechanical action. The draw may start as soon as the arrow is nocked and the target archer is properly positioned on the shooting line.

Controlled breathing is very important during the drawing and subsequent aiming processes. A breathing system should be found that is comfortable for the archer during the total drawing, aiming, and release time period. One procedure used commonly is to take a deep breath and exhale just prior to starting the draw. Another deep inhalation is made promptly thereafter and the breath is held until the archer sees the arrow strike the target. The total elapsed time for breath-holding for most archers should be no more than ten seconds, which is the approximate time frame for drawing, aiming, releasing, and follow-through.

Some archers use a variation on this breath-holding technique. When the sight pin is in place on the target during aiming, a small amount of the breath from the initial deep inhalation is released or exhaled. The remaining breath is held as aiming is finalized. The release is made, and normal breathing resumes when the arrow hits the target. This procedure relieves some of the internal pressure in the thoracic (chest) region. It also helps reduce muscle tension in the trunk. Beginning archers should try different breathing mechanics until they find one that feels comfortable.

It should also be noted that breathing mechanics and subsequent respiratory functions are more efficient when the archer has a better than average cardiovascular fitness status. The best noninvasive measurement of cardiorespiratory endurance is the maximal oxygen consumption test. Maintaining an above average level of health-related fitness can prolong a competitive target archer's career. (See chapter 8 for fitness guidelines.)

The archer's head position remains fixed from the time the archer addresses the target (fig. 4.9) through the release and follow-through phases of shooting (fig. 4.22). Surprisingly, this simple, stable position of the neck and head tends to be a dilemma for some beginning archers. It is not a problem if the following principle is observed: *The bowstring is drawn to your head (anchor point) instead of moving the head toward the bowstring during the draw.*

Figure 4.13 shows the commonly used three-finger bowstring grip. A shooting glove, such as that shown in figure 4.13, protects the fingers, but a finger tab (fig. 4.14) is recommended for use over a shooting glove in target archery. Most elite archers use a spacer equipped tab. That type of finger tab features a separator which keeps your index and middle fingers apart during the drawing process. Proper placement of the fingers on the bowstring prior to drawing is very important to minimize release problems. The little finger and thumb do not touch the bowstring. The remaining three fingers are placed or "hooked" on the bowstring at or slightly past the first or distal interphalangeal joints of your fingers. Although the middle finger is longer than the remaining two "drawing fingers," it is important that all three fingers be kept even during the draw. This facilitates a smooth and explosive release.

The large knuckle joints of the hand are not flexed at any time during the draw. These joints remain extended and stable at all times. The wrist is also kept extended and stable throughout the draw and release phases. The wrist should never move in any direction (flexed, hyperextended, etc.) during the draw and subsequent release of the arrow.

Figure 4.14 shows the relationship between the index and middle fingers and the nock of the arrow while using a finger tab. The proper position of the fingers on the bowstring next to the arrow nock is difficult to maintain as the pressure increases during the draw. The essence of the problem lies in the nature of the musculature within the hand. As fingers are flexed, it is natural for them to be drawn tightly together into a fist. This type of mechanism within hand musculature helps us grip objects. It is

Figure 4.13
Traditional three-finger grip with shooting glove. (Courtesy of Logan)

Figure 4.14
The three-finger grip while using a finger tab. Care must be taken not to exert undue or unequal pressure on the arrow nock. (Courtesy Wilson Brothers, Route 1, Elkland, MO 65644)

also highly functional, as examples, to hit in the sport of boxing and to grip a baseball bat to hit in baseball. But it can create arrow flight problems for the archer! One should not grip or hold the arrow nock too tightly.

Because the first or distal joints of the index and middle fingers are flexed and the pressure increases during the draw, those two fingers have a tendency to apply pressure on the arrow nock. Beginning archers often find that the points of their arrows will wave around and fall completely off the arrow rest as the draw is made. This common embarrassment is caused by excessive finger pressure on the arrow nock. The archer must compensate for the gripping effect of the hand musculature prior to the draw by placing the index finger one-eighth of an inch above the arrow nock. The middle finger can be placed the same distance below the arrow nock. It may seem that the arrow will become disengaged from the bowstring before the draw can be made, but this feeling will be eliminated by the use of properly placed nocking points and practice. The principle to bear in mind is: *Pressure exerted by fingers on the arrow nock should be kept at an absolute minimum prior to and during the draw and release.* Good finger tabs and nock locators properly positioned on the bowstring help the archer considerably.

As the bowstring is being drawn, it will move from its position across the flexed distal joints of your three fingers involved in the grip to a position *diagonal* to that joint line. If you are gripping correctly, the amount of pressure on each of the three fingers differs. The middle finger should have the greatest feeling of pressure, and the third finger will have control over a good percentage of the remaining force on the hand. The index or top finger has minimal pressure on it because its role is one of control at the time of release.

The problem of pressure against the arrow nock exerted by fingers during the draw process is completely eliminated when using a release aid. As a result, release aids tend to take a considerable amount of "sport" out of archery. *That is one reason that target archery rules forbid the use of release aids with Olympic Bows.* One of the true tests of target archery is the ability of the archer to control finger pressure on the nock during the draw and through release. Release aids that are legal for use with compound bows and in other archery sports are discussed in chapter 6. Some target archery tournaments for compound bows have subdivisions where competitions are separate for release aid shooters and "finger shooters."

As the draw is started, the bow is moved to a vertical position as shown in figure 4.15. The archer in figure 4.15 is midway through the drawing procedure. The bowstring hand is being pulled toward the anchor point on the face. The head and neck remain stable. During this pull or drawing action, it may be necessary for the archer to make a compensatory motion within the forearm (radioulnar joint) to maintain proper string alignment and pressure on the fingers as noted above.

There is a natural tendency to elevate the elbow slightly during the draw. This is an undesired motion. The equal and opposite motion seen in the hand results in a slight diagonal change of the finger-string alignment noted above because the string hand moves downward as the elbow moves upward. If that string position were not corrected, it would cause some unnecessary string torque and pressure downward on the arrow nock at the time of release. Poor arrow flight would be the result. How do you rectify the problem? Correct this by rotating the forearm a few degrees clockwise (supinate the radioulnar joint) during the draw or upon reaching your anchor point. The result of that motion will move your little finger closer to your neck. The little finger should be close to the neck at full draw as seen in figure 4.20. You do not want the little finger in a position analogous to daintily holding a tea cup at a social event!

It is essential for the archer to understand that the force for drawing the bow is provided primarily by powerful muscles on the posterior aspect of the shoulder and within the shoulder girdle. It is recommended that the reader gain an understanding of the specific muscular detail for drawing. That is presented for you in chapter 8. This knowledge will help the archer with his or her focal concentration point for muscular control during the draw.

Since musculature within the drawing arm does not provide the primary draw force, what is the role of this musculature during the draw? It is necessary that the archer keep the arm musculature as relaxed as possible during the draw. These muscles are handling external tension due to the bow weight; therefore, they are stabilizing the joints within the arm. There is no need to contract them further and create more internal tension. That would be counterproductive to good accuracy. The finger grip provides a "hook" on the bowstring. The shoulder and shoulder girdle muscles exert the internal, contractile force to move the string, while the bowstring arm is simply the lever through which the force is exerted. That is accomplished, as much as possible, without adding tension within the drawing arm. This is another time when the skilled archer knows when and how to "relax under pressure." The potential for shot accuracy is enhanced through concentration to each skill detail, and that is the "name of the game" in target archery!

The completed draw by an archer using the traditional grip and an Olympic Bow is shown in figure 4.16. All of the bow weight is held at the anchor point by the archer until the arrow is released. The bow arm and drawing arm should be

Figure 4.15
Start of the draw. (Courtesy of Kathy Greene)

Figure 4.16
Completed draw and anchor point. The bowstring is drawn to the anchor point. The head does not move toward the string. (Courtesy of Kathy Greene)

studied carefully in this figure. The bow arm has been abducted or raised to shoulder height. The wrist and elbow are kept extended at all times, and they remain stable throughout the drawing, aiming, and release phases. A straight line can be drawn from the archer's drawing arm elbow to the arrow point when the draw is completed. At release, the bow arm will react by moving downward.

For comparative purposes, the completed draw by an archer using a release aid and a *compound target archery bow* is shown in figure 4.17. In contrast to drawing the Olympic Bow, it should be noted that the compound bow, when drawn to the anchor point, presents a different bow weight reaction due to the mechanics of its pulley system. There is no stacking effect of weight throughout the draw when using a compound bow. As a result, the archer does not hold all of the draw weight of the bow at the anchor point. The peak poundage of a compound bow is felt by the archer at the mid-draw position. There is a "let-off" of bow weight at mid-draw from 30 to 65 percent depending upon the mechanical efficiency of the compound target bow being used. This means, for example, that if you are shooting a maximum weight 60-pound compound bow in a target archery tournament and the bow has 65 percent let-off capacity, the actual weight held at the anchor point would only be 21 pounds. Upon release, the poundage increases back to peak bow weight. This provides a major augmentation in foot-pounds of energy that transfers to the arrow and adds to its velocity.

The bowstring should not slap the bow arm after it has been released if the bow arm position is correct. The arm guard may be brushed periodically. This can be caused by extraneous shoulder, elbow, or wrist movements. "String slaps" will diminish in

Figure 4.17
Champion professional archer, Michelle Ragsdale, at full draw using a state-of-the-art compound target bow. A release aid is being used. (Courtesy of Precision Shooting Equipment, 2727 N. Fairview Ave., Tucson, AZ 85705)

frequency as the archer increases his or her skill level. Some archers, due to unusual bone anatomy of the elbow, require adjustments of their body segment positions to eliminate painful contusions caused by continued "string slaps" on the bow arm.

If the bowstring hits the bow arm above the arm guard, the archer's stance probably should be changed to the oblique stance described previously. For most individuals this should eliminate the problem. If such a stance adjustment does not work, a bow arm adjustment should be made. The arm should always remain abducted at the shoulder joint and extended at the elbow joint as shown in figure 4.16. To make the bow arm adjustment, the bow should be held in position horizontal to the ground initially. Slowly rotate the bow to the vertical position by laterally rotating the bow shoulder—move the bow counterclockwise—with the elbow extended. This may move the bow arm out of the path of the bowstring. This alignment should be checked visually by an instructor and the archer prior to releasing an arrow.

If the above alignment adjustment does not appear to be satisfactory, the bow arm should be rotated clockwise by medially rotating the shoulder joint until the bowstring can be seen to clear the arm. This is called *canting* the bow. *The elbow should never be flexed to allow the string to clear the bow arm.* Canting should be used only as a last resort to avoid injury.

Each of the above bow adjustment procedures are recommended only for those people who have arm and elbow configurations that elicit continued "string slaps." The sport cannot be enjoyed if the bow arm is contused frequently. That trauma can be avoided.

The alignment of the drawing arm with the arrow and bow as shown in figure 4.16 is important. If the drawing form is perfect, there will be a straight line running from the tip of the elbow through the forearm, wrist, hand, arrow nock, and shaft to the arrow point. Due to anatomic differences, it is not possible for all archers to align the drawing limb perfectly with the arrow. However, all archers should attempt to come as close to this alignment as physically possible. If this is accomplished, there will be a smoother and more efficient transfer of the potential energy within the drawn bow to kinetic energy into the arrow at release.

A straight drawing arm and arrow alignment facilitates a smooth release. If, as noted, the elbow is too high, it is inevitable that the index finger will exert pressure downward on the arrow nock at release. This produces porpoising and erratic arrow flight. The ACTION of releasing the bowstring should produce the desired REACTION of perfect forward or linear motion of the bowstring and arrow as it subsequently clears the bow.

After you have read this chapter and shot a few ends on the range, it is highly recommended, as noted, that you read the first section of chapter 8, "Muscle Analysis of Shooting," to gain some understanding of the muscle control and forces needed as you establish a stance, nock, draw to your anchor point, and release. Finite control and accuracy in archery are reasons for keeping your tackle fine-tuned. Just as important, the archer must be cognizant of "tuning" the muscles most involved in performing the sport of target archery. That knowledge will intensify your concentration during the draw and into the release.

Anchor Point

The term "anchor point" is defined as the place on an archer's face where the hand is placed consistently with the bowstring at full draw. Anchor points are usually described as being low or high on the face (figs. 4.18, 4.19, and 4.20). An anchor point on or under the mandible or jaw bone is termed *low.* A slight adjustment of the low anchor point upward results in a *side of face* anchor point. An anchor point just beneath the zygomatic arch or the large bone inferior and lateral to the eye is considered to be *high.* Preference for a particular anchor point usually involves such factors as facial contour and type of shooting. Many field archers, bowhunters, bowfishers, and instinctive shooters use

Figure 4.18
The recommended low anchor point for beginning target archers.

Figure 4.19
The side of face anchor point. (Courtesy of Kathy Greene)

Figure 4.20
A high anchor point used most commonly by bowhunters. (Courtesy of Kathy Greene)

the high anchor point (fig. 4.20). These archers like to think they sight down the shaft of the arrow. In reality, most archers who use a high anchor point tend to look over the arrow point.

Variations on the low anchor point are used most often by target archers who rely on bowsights for aiming. Low and high anchor points can be used effectively for any kind of shooting. The archer ultimately should use the anchor point that feels most comfortable and is most consistent with good aiming for the type of archery sport of greatest interest.

It is recommended that the beginner utilize a low anchor point while learning target archery fundamentals. Figure 4.18 shows the traditional low anchor point. To learn and perform any athletic activity effectively, one must utilize as many senses as possible. The low anchor point involves the touch, pressure, sight, and kinesthetic senses. The index finger is placed under the chin, and moderate pressure is applied to the mandible or jawbone by the index finger. This low anchor position on the chin allows the bowstring to bisect and *gently touch* the chin, lips, and nose. The archer must not compress or apply heavy pressure on the tissue of these parts of the anatomy. For consistency, the upper and lower teeth must touch gently; that is, the mouth should be shut. The teeth should never be clenched. That type of tension is contraindicated in target archery. As noted, the more one can be "relaxed" during the process of shooting the better. Static contraction of the jaw muscles to clench your teeth has negative reactions in the degree of tension within the muscles of the neck and rib cage, and that interferes with breathing, respiration, and shooting accuracy.

Some target archers use what is known as a "side of face" anchor point if the low anchor point described above seems awkward (figs. 4.17 and 4.19). The head is rotated toward the target as described previously. The bowstring is drawn to a point where it actually touches the side of the mouth, that is, the right side of the mouth for a right-handed archer. The chin is not moved to accommodate the string placement. The hand is anchored *under* the jaw, with the index finger in contact with the side of the mandible (jawbone), similar to the low anchor position. Some archers believe that one advantage of the "side of face" anchor is that a good alignment of the drawing arm and arrow is easier to attain.

Some beginning archers believe that they must change the anchor point and length of draw when shooting from varying distances. This is a disastrous mistake. The anchor point and draw remain constant for all distances. Adjustments for shooting varying distances are accomplished by changing the angles of the bow arm at the shoulder joint. The extent of each adjustment is determined by the capacity of the bow to propel the arrow at velocities needed to cover each precise range distance adequately.

Aiming

Bowsight and instinctive are the two aiming techniques used extensively by archers. *Use of a bowsight for aiming is absolutely essential in target archery and ski-archery.* Furthermore, bowsights are also utilized by serious field archers and bowhunters who know how to gauge distances on field archery units and in hunting environments. (Exact distances are always known in target archery and ski-archery.) The most "sporting technique" for aiming in archery is called instinctive shooting. No aiming device is mounted on the bow, so this is often called "bare bow shooting." Learning how to shoot instinctively is interesting because most archers describe this aiming technique with slight variations and fascinating embellishments.

The beginner should not be too concerned about any aiming procedure until he or she feels comfortable handling appropriate archery tackle and performing the basic fundamentals involving the stance, nocking, drawing, anchor point, release, and follow-through. To gain familiarity and confidence with the tackle and skill fundamentals, shooting should be performed initially over relatively short distances on the range. Shooting point blank eliminates the pressure to aim during the first few shooting sessions. Once a general understanding of shooting fundamentals is acquired, the archer should turn attention toward bowsight aiming and grouping ends of arrows in small patterns on the target from various distances.

Bowsight Aiming

The use of the bowsight will greatly enhance one's ability to hit the intended target; consequently, the use of a bowsight is recommended in preference to any other target archery aiming technique. The archer must establish a bowsight setting on the bow for each shooting distance. This requires the archer to shoot a number of ends at each distance to experiment with bowsight settings. To use a bowsight, the archer places the sighting device in the middle of the intended target—gold on a regulation target archery face—and releases the arrow properly. This procedure is repeated until several ends have been shot. The archer must continually check the grouping patterns on the target face and note the direction of the hits from the gold. For example, if six ends of arrows are shot at a target without changing the bowsight setting and all arrows consistently group low and left on a regulation target face, *the archer must move the bowsight setting device down and left for the next series of shots in order to move the grouping into the center of the target.* If the adjustment of the bowsight is correct and shooting fundamentals are good, the next end should hit the gold. The principle to keep in mind for bowsight adjustments is as follows: THE BOWSIGHT SHOULD ALWAYS BE MOVED IN THE DIRECTION(S) OF THE ARROW GROUPING ERROR.

The bowsight shown in figure 3.13 can be adjusted to compensate for any directional error. It can be moved left, right, up, and down to assist the archer. As noted in the example above, if the bowsight was moved properly down and left (error directions), the next end of arrows shot should group in or near the gold on the target face. This will occur IF the archer executes all of the other fundamental shooting skills properly. A perfect bowsight setting cannot compensate for poor shooting mechanics, mismatched tackle, or improper tackle tuning!

Concentration and intelligent analyses of the situation play an important role in the process of aiming. Archery becomes a "mental game" once the shooting fundamentals have been learned properly. The total shot must be considered; that is, each step must be performed consistently and properly leading up to the aiming step. Also, wind direction and velocity as well as other weather conditions (humidity, fog, etc.) are brought into the aiming decision. There is a subjective, kinesthetic feeling the experienced archer attains when the sight pin is being moved to and held on the gold during the aiming process prior to release. Progress is made only through intensifying your thought processes on the task at hand. Nothing must be allowed to interfere with one's concentration as the sight pin is being placed on the gold. When the fundamentals are under control, concentration regulates the aiming process and the degree of scoring success one has in target archery.

Does the sight pin always have to be absolutely fixed on the gold at the time of release? Each archer has adapted an aiming procedure based on his or her overall shooting style. Some archers do attempt perfection on every shot and they strive for precise sight pin settings on the target at the instant the arrow is released. That can add stress and increase the frustration level for some archers because it has the potential to deflate confidence when the arrow does not hit the gold.

If the aiming procedure described above does not work for you, try moving the sight pin into a *target area* instead of on a precise spot in the center of the target.

Figure 4.21
Bow string alignment used during aiming. (Courtesy of Patrick Brunhoeber)

(Keep in mind that you have a 4½ inch "margin of error" on either side of the exact center of the target in target archery.) Release the arrow properly once the sight pin is in the boundary lines of your "target area" for aiming. Many excellent archers use this aiming method with good results. It removes some of the stress concurrent with always fixating on a precise spot. Each person must define his or her target aiming areas for each specific shooting distance on the range.

One must be aware of what effect winds at different velocities and directions will have on the accuracy of arrows. Aiming rules for various wind conditions differ with the archer and tackle being used. Aiming adjustments also have to be made for other weather factors such as humidity and rain. The experience of shooting in all kinds of weather conditions is the best teacher, so practice during windy conditions, rain, extreme heat, humidity, and perfect weather. You do not get to shoot an unlimited number of sighter arrows prior to a tournament. An archer only gets 15 minutes prior to competition to make aiming decisions based on the day's weather, so you need to know what works in advance based on results from your practice sessions.

Sighting and aiming with the bow and arrow differ considerably from aiming a rifle. The rifleman tends to look down the top of the rifle barrel through a series of mounted sights. While using the low anchor point in particular, the archer does not and should not look down the shaft of the arrow. The line of sight should be through the aiming device on the bowsight toward the intended target. The bowsight is mounted above the arrow shaft to align with the archer's field of vision.

Target archery bows have unofficial rear sighting devices—the bowstrings. When the archer's head is in the correct position, the archer tends to "look through" the bowstring. The string is set toward the right side of the bow as seen in figure 4.21. This prevents the bowstring from running through the sight window of the bow and spoiling your view. The bowsight is aligned with the center of the target.

Checking the bowstring alignment becomes automatic with experience, and most of your concentration for aiming purposes must be directed toward the bowsight pin. Using the bowstring alignment as a checkpoint does place the arrow in a definite direction relative to the target. The archer must be able to maintain control of the alignment between this "rear sight" and the centered front sight if accurate aiming is to remain consistent.

Peep sights are available for use as rear sights on bowstrings. These are designed to be used with front-mounted sights as shown in figure 3.13. However, National Archery Association rules stipulate that, "A bowstring must not in any way offer aid in aiming through peephole marking or any other means." *Peep sights on bowstrings are illegal for use in target archery.* They can be used in other archery sports.

There are archery authorities who contend that the eye nearest the target should always be closed during the act of shooting. This is a fallacy! What if the eye away from the target—the right eye for a right-handed archer—is the weak eye? Should the good left eye be closed and the weak eye remain open? This could have a detrimental effect upon accuracy. Many superb right-handed archers shoot with both eyes open or with the left eye partially closed and the right eye open. Eye preference is a highly individualized matter. It is recommended that the beginner try shooting while using all combinations of eye openings and closures. Each archer should use the eye closure or opening that feels most comfortable and produces the best results. Some archers enjoy target archery without using either eye. They are blind! (See chapter 5.) Archery is truly a sport that can be adapted for everyone.

Instinctive Aiming

Many people who hunt with rifles and bowhunt use high anchor points. This allows them to partially sight down the arrow shaft and over the point if a bowsight is not used. Some bowhunters do not use a bowsight, but rely upon instinctive aiming techniques. Instinctive aiming is utilized by many field archers also. There are tournaments held in field archery for bare bow and instinctive shooters exclusively. Many excellent scores are recorded in these tournaments. The target archer can also use instinctive aiming techniques if desired, but it is not recommended. The lack of mechanical aiming devices adds to the spirit of true sport.

Each archer who uses instinctive aiming usually provides a slightly different version of how this task is accomplished. Basically, the instinctive archer must have excellent eyesight and depth perception. The term "instinct" for this style of shooting is grossly incorrect from a scientific standpoint. Through extensive practice over a long period of time, the archer increases skills related to such factors as kinesthetic awareness, conditioned responses to visual stimuli, correct reactions to wind velocities and directions, and judgment of the strengths and weaknesses of the tackle being used. These variables, and others, enable the skilled archer to adjust rapidly as he or she looks over the arrow point toward a point of aim and on toward the intended target.

As noted, the instinctive shooter makes several cognitive judgments prior to releasing the arrow. The archer perceives a space or gap between the arrow point and intended target. The bow arm moves the arrow into position for the shot. Here is where individual differences abound. Instinctive shooters approach the shot by moving the bow downward, upward, left, or right toward the target. Most, however, choose to start with the bow arm held high and move the bow downward. (This is acceptable if the range safety zone is large enough to protect people should an arrow be accidentally released before the bow arm becomes parallel to the ground.) The release of the arrow is calculated to coincide with the visual perception of the gap being closed by the arrow point coming into view of the target. Most instinctive shooters will hold the bow motionless for a second when the gap has been closed in order to implement an efficient release. This form of instinctive aiming is often called "gap shooting."

Instinctive shooting is a "pure form of shooting," and there are many expert instinctive archers. This is particularly true in field archery and bowhunting. For target archery, the bowsight method of aiming is recommended unless, of course, you are competing in a bare bow tournament.

Release and Follow-Through

Releasing the arrow properly is the most important fundamental of shooting. The key elements are: (1) relaxation and (2) concentration. The paradoxical nature of these two catalysts at this critical stage of shooting adds another dimension to the difficulty of target archery as a sport. As the reader realizes, it is extremely difficult to relax during a time of intense concentration. Both of these factors must be under complete control, however, to achieve any degree of success in archery. That is another reason people regard target archery as a "mental game," especially among elite archers.

Releasing an arrow is not the result of forceful and rapid finger extension by the target archer using an Olympic Bow. It is an act of relaxing or controlling muscular interaction within the bow hand, forearm, and shoulder girdle (trapezius muscle). When the muscles controlling flexion within the three drawing fingers release some of their tension during contraction, the bowstring will move forward as a result of the pressure brought to bear by the bow weight at complete draw. If the release is good, the extended, relaxed fingers will clear the string as it moves forward. On the other hand, if the fingers are not relaxed enough and touch the bowstring, that is a cause of erratic arrow flight. The archer does very little muscular work at the time of release in terms of consciously contracting the musculature and extending the finger joints.

As stated previously, the main problems are *relaxation* and concurrent control of hand, forearm, and shoulder girdle muscles in conjunction with maximum *concentration* on aiming prior to and at the time of release. The archer starts intense concentration prior to nocking and continues until the arrow is released. It is too late to think about the shot when the arrow is in flight! That is the time to either enjoy watching the arrow's perfect trajectory into the gold or to analyze its flight problems in hopes of avoiding them for the next shot.

How can the fingers be relaxed effectively under the tension of the Olympic Bow weight? The key to this lies in understanding the location of the muscles and their tendons that are under the greatest tension. Those muscle bellies are within your forearm, but their tendons are located on the back of the wrist and continue into the hand and fingers. These are the finger joint extensor tendons, which are stretched as the fingers flex to grip the bowstring. These extensor tendons can be palpated (touched) on the back of your hand. As you make a fist, feel the tension increase in the muscles in your forearm. This tension is increased considerably when the bow weight is being held by the three flexed fingers. When you are ready to release an arrow, relax the gripping fingers by concentrating on releasing tension within the finger extensor tendons on the posterior aspect (back) of your hand. Concentration and release mechanics are aided by having a "thought focus point" on a body segment such as this.

The use of the compound bow in target archery minimizes many of the release problems for the archer when a release aid is used instead of the traditional finger release. As indicated in chapter 3, FITA rules stipulate that a release aid can be used by the archer using a compound bow in target archery competition if the aid is not attached to the bow or does not incorporate electronic devices in its operation (fig. 4.17). There are numerous release aids on the market for use with compound bows. Some of these are shown in chapter 6. The use of a release aid in compound bow target archery removes a considerable amount of the degree of difficulty in attaining shooting accuracy.

A clicker is shown mounted on the sight window of the bow in figure 4.11. A clicker is a shooting aid that has the potential to add consistency to form and enhance scores. The arrow is placed under the clicker when nocked. If the draw is made smoothly to the established anchor point, the arrow point will pass beyond the clicker in about two seconds. The clicker will make a "click" sound against the bow, informing the archer—who should be concentrating on drawing and aiming during this time—that the release can be made. *The "click" should never be anticipated. A smooth release is executed shortly after the "click" has been heard, and the archer should never attempt to foresee when the arrow will leave the bow.*

A clicker is not recommended as a shooting aid until the target archery fundamentals have been learned. The draw and anchor point must be established. Any change of anchor point would require a clicker adjustment. When the shooting fundamentals are consistent, have the arrow point position marked on the bow at your anchor point. The clicker is then placed on the bow so only one-eighth inch of the point lies under the clicker at full draw. The "click" of the clicker is made by continuing to move the draw arm elbow backward (horizontal abduction of your shoulder joint). It is very important for the archer to understand that the drawing arm moves through its range-of-motion without interruption. The drawing elbow is moved backward by large shoulder and shoulder girdle muscles (horizontal abductors) to the point that the clicker will be heard. The release motions are started thereafter.

The archer must never make extraneous motions with the bow arm to activate the clicker. If the clicker is mounted properly and the archer's shooting fundamentals are sound, it can be a beneficial shooting aid used to: (1) enhance shooting consistency, (2) facilitate aiming concentration, and (3) assist in the timing of the release. Target archery scores have improved due to the use of the clicker.

A bow sling is recommended to help the archer during the release and follow-through phases of shooting. There are different types of bow slings available. Any

Figure 4.22
Release and follow-through positions. Watch the arrow until it hits the target before moving the arms. (Courtesy of Kathy Greene)

one of these will help the archer keep the bow from falling to the ground after release. The type chosen is a matter of individual preference. In choosing a bow sling the basic thing to remember is that nothing should *prematurely interrupt* the bow's movement toward the target after the arrow has been released. The function of the bow sling is to keep the bow from falling to the ground *after* the arrow is in flight beyond the bow. If the bow sling or the archer's bow hand grasps the bow at or immediately prior to release, arrow flight will be erratic. The archer must work to ensure that this does not occur. The bow as well as the arrow should be free to move forward at release. The bow sling should ease one's mind about what happens to the bow once the arrow is in flight. Figure 4.21 shows the use of a bow sling.

If you use a finger sling, it is placed on the thumb and index or middle finger and wraps around the back of the bow. The use of a finger sling enables the archer to release the arrow without worrying about the bow falling to the ground. Extraneous motions of the wrist joint are thereby minimized. The finger sling also supports the bow after the shot, and the archer can grasp the bow with the hand after he or she sees the arrow embedded in the target.

Figure 4.22 shows proper release form. The elbow of the bowstring arm should not extend appreciably after or during the release. The bowstring hand will usually move backward in a position relatively close to the chin or neck after release. This is a natural recoil action following release. The beginner must avoid the habit of trying to release the arrow by hyperextending the wrist—moving the back of the hand toward the forearm—or allowing the bowstring to roll off the fingertips under its own pressure. Release by "plucking" of the string is another cause of erratic arrow grouping. Also, the elbow of the bowstring arm should never be extended and the arm waved around at or following the release. Arm actions like those of orchestra conductors should be avoided in the archery release! Upon release, the drawing arm elbow remains flexed, and the bow will rotate clockwise from the pivot point during the follow-through phase (fig. 4.22).

A. Nocking

B. Drawing

C. Anchor point

D. Release and Follow-through

Figure 4.23
Nocking through release and follow-through in target archery. NEVER UNDERESTIMATE THE COMPLEXITY OF SOMETHING THAT APPEARS TO BE THE EPITOME OF SIMPLICITY WHEN PERFORMED BY AN EXPERT! (Courtesy of Kathy Greene)

To "*follow through*" *in archery means to hold the release position until the arrow is safely embedded in the target.* The following are features of a good follow-through: (1) the fingers on the bowstring hand are relaxed, (2) head and eyes are turned toward the target following the flight of the arrow, (3) the bow arm is extended toward the target, and (4) the bow hand is gripping the bow with the help of a sling. Why is follow-through important? It is absolutely essential for consistent performance and minute accuracy. Any undesired motions of the archer observed in the follow-through phase of shooting had to be initiated a fraction of a second *prior to and continued through the release phase.* Motions of that type are contraindicated as far as archery accuracy is concerned.

Figures 4.23 and 8.1 show the important phases of target archery fundamentals in sequence from nocking to follow-through. *The appearance of simplicity is very deceptive!*

Scoring

Target archery competition is conducted in *rounds.* There are numerous championship and nonchampionship rounds, some of which are discussed in chapter 5. Each round is different in terms of the number of arrows to be shot, and in the designated distances. A specific number of arrows are shot during each round before the archers are allowed to walk to the target, score, and retrieve arrows. The set number of arrows (usually 3, 5, or 6) to be shot is called an *end.* A round consists of a designated number of ends shot at various distances.

There are two target faces used for scoring purposes in outdoor target archery rounds. The 122 centimeter (48 inch) target face is used at distances of 90 meters (98.42 yards), 70 meters (76.55 yards), and 60 meters (65.62 yards). An 80 centimeter (31 inch) target face is used in rounds when distances of 50 meters (54.68 yards) and 30 meters (32.81 yards) are used. The center of the target should be 51 inches above the ground, and the target face is inclined away from the shooting line twelve to eighteen degrees.

The official target archery faces are divided into five concentric color zones. These scoring rings are each colored differently. From the center or bull's eye outward they are gold, red, light blue, black, and white. Each of these concentric colored rings is divided into two equal halves for scoring purposes. (The exact center of the gold is marked, and it is known as the pinhole.) The ten concentric rings on the target face are used for scoring as follows: inner gold, ten points; outer gold, nine points; inner red, eight points; outer red, seven points; inner light blue, six points; outer light blue, five points; inner black, four points; outer black, three points; inner white, two points; outer white, one point. The outer or nonscoring area of the target is known as the *petticoat.*

Indoor rounds are shot at shorter distances. This requires the use of smaller target faces. Distances of 18 meters (19.69 yards) and 25 meters (27.34 yards) are common indoor distances. A 40 centimeter (16 inch) target face is used at 18 meters, and a 60 centimeter (24 inch) face is used at 25 meters.

Name **Al Trombetta**

Class **Archery Techniques**

40 yards						Hits	Score
9	9	9	9	9	9	6	54
9	9	7	5	3		5	33
7	7	7	5	3	1	6	30
9	9	9	7	7	7	6	48
Distance score						23	165
30 yards							
9	9	9	9	9	9	6	54
9	9	9	9	7	7	6	50
9	9	7	7	5	5	6	42
9	9	7	5	3	1	6	34
Distance score						24	180
Total score						47	345

Figure 4.24
A sample scorecard for the
Scholastic Round.

Figure 4.25
Arrow values are given to the scorer by
the archer to whom the arrows belong.
The scorer and other archers assigned to
the target verify the scores. After all arrows
have been scored, they are removed from
the target. (Bud Clay and Linda Atwood)

Two archers on each target act as scorekeepers. Each archer tells the scorer the values of his or her arrows starting with the highest values first. Scores plus the number of hits per end are written on a score card or sheet. A sample scorecard is shown in figure 4.24. High scores are recorded first for each end.

All arrows remain in their places embedded in the target mat until they have been scored and verified by the designated scorekeepers. Pulling arrows from a target mat mounted on a tripod stand should be done with caution. First, check to see that no one is standing behind you as arrows are pulled from the target. An arrow nock in the eye can be traumatic! The arrow should be grasped near the target face and pulled by the shaft with one hand. The other hand should provide a counterforce for the pull by being placed against the target mat (fig. 4.25). This simple procedure eliminates the embarrassing and costly experience of pulling a target full of arrows onto the ground. Fiberglass arrows can be broken and aluminum arrows may be bent when a target mat is pulled to the ground.

If an arrow is embedded in the target mat up to its fletching or nock area, it should be removed by pulling it completely through the mat in the direction of its flight. That practice keeps the fletching or vanes from being damaged or torn from the shaft. If an arrow "snakes in the grass" or lies horizontal to the earth and covered with grass, it should also be removed by pulling it forward through the grass.

There are several scoring variations to account for atypical arrow hits and other unusual situations. Arrows that *rebound from the target face* can be scored in several ways if they are witnessed. The most common procedure used for class situations and competitions other than international or national tournaments is to score these rebounds as seven points. An arrow that rebounds from the petticoat area of the target is scored zero, and it is not counted as a hit. A rebounding arrow can also be scored according to where it struck the target face, *if* it is witnessed.

In the classic situation whereby one arrow impales another arrow already embedded in a scoring arrow on the target face, the last arrow is awarded the same value as the struck arrow. The "fantasy tight group" for an end of six arrows would be to have the first three arrows hit the target around the "pinhole," and the final three arrows then impale the shafts of the first three arrows. The score for this fantasy end would be 60 points. This would be one definition of perfection in the sport of target archery! The mathematical probability of that occurring during a target archery round is about the same as a score of 18 being shot by a golfer for one round of golf over 18 holes.

Arrows that strike other arrows already on the target and deflect are scored in various ways. If an arrow deflects from an arrow on the target face but somehow attaches to the target, it is scored according to the target area where it is fastened. For example, an arrow that rebounds from an arrow shaft embedded in the outer gold or yellow and enters the target in the inner light blue is scored six instead of nine points. An arrow rebounding completely off the target after hitting an arrow on the target is scored the value of the arrow hit. However, it must be witnessed, and the damaged arrow has to be identified. If both criteria were met using the example above, the rebounding arrow would be given a score of nine after deflecting off an arrow already in the outer gold ring.

After scoring, holes are marked during competition. If an arrow is witnessed as passing completely through the target mat, it is given the value of the unmarked hole on the target. This happens often in school situations when mats become worn due to excessive use and target faces are overused. One option in these situations is to score the arrow as a seven if it passed through a scoring ring on the target face and the hole could not be identified. Overused target mats with their centers shot away can cause a problem with this scoring option.

A baseball thrown by a pitcher that hits the ground in front of home plate and bounces through the strike zone of the batter can be called a ball by the umpire or be hit by the hitter. The analogous situation in archery whereby an arrow hits the ground, rebounds, and sticks in the target face does not score or count as a hit for the target archer. It is scored a miss because the arrow hit the ground first.

If an archer becomes confused and shoots an end of arrows on other than his or her assigned target during a round, the score of those arrows does not count. Zeros are recorded on the score card. Hits are not recorded for the arrows because they did not hit the assigned or correct target.

As noted on the scorecard example in figure 4.24, all legal hits are recorded. A hit is scored for any arrow receiving a score from one through ten. An arrow embedded in the skirt, or petticoat, of the target face or in the archery stand is not recorded as a hit. The recorded hits are important to break ties when they occur at the end of a round during a tournament. Three criteria are used to break ties for individual competitors: (1) the archer with the greatest number of hits is the winner; (2) if hits are also tied along with the score, the archer with the most tens wins; or (3) if hits and tens are tied, the archer with the most nines wins. If they are still tied, the Director of Shooting will declare that they were truly equal in skill for the round shot.

Common Grouping Problems: Skill Evaluation

To shoot a tight group of arrows consistently in the ten ring of the target regardless of the distance being shot is the ultimate goal in target archery. The frustration of the sport is that arrows do not always group according to the desires of the archer. The main source of help for making adjustments to improve skill should come from the individual's archery instructor or coach. However, when such help is not available, the following teaching suggestions can be quite valuable to help evaluate and improve your skill level. For the suggestions listed below to be functional, the archer should be using matched and tuned tackle.

Use of the Video Camcorder as a Coaching Aid

For skill evaluation purposes, it is recommended that the archer employ a good video camcorder to videotape his or her shooting style. (This is also recommended for use by instructors in teaching and coaching situations.) The camcorder should be mounted on a tripod for most of the filming. Videotape the shooting technique with the camcorder placed at a *right angle* to the archer on the shooting line. Some videotape needs to be taken from a rear view where slow motion would pick up the first part of the arrow flight. Videotaping from a camera angle directly above the archer is also advantageous for analysis and skill evaluation. The video camcorder can be suspended from the ceiling for the overhead angle in some indoor ranges. Views of the total body should be taken as well as close-up recordings of the fundamental sequence of nocking, bowstring finger placement, bow hold, drawing, anchor point, release, and follow-through. Close-up views of the release and follow-through are of particular importance.

Verbal comments should be made on the videotape describing such things as your perception of breathing mechanics, weather and wind conditions on the range during the videotaped practice session, reaction to how you released the arrow, arrow flight observations, the nature of flight deviations, and the exact location of the hit on the target (or miss) for each arrow released. The arrow grouping should also be videotaped after each end is shot. Shot location for each hit by number can be verified. Take videotape of several ends of arrows shot from various distances and try to determine where your consistent shooting problem(s) lie.

You should write a "shooting fault list," and make an attempt to rank your shooting problems from most to least serious. *You should only attempt to eliminate one shooting difficulty at a time; therefore, start with the one you have deemed the most serious problem on your "shooting fault list."* When progress has been made to ameliorate the most serious problem, begin working to eliminate the next shooting error on the list.

You should retape periodically to evaluate and document progress. By using two videotape recorders (VCRs) simultaneously, you can compare and contrast your shooting mechanics by using freeze frame and frame-by-frame analyses of the old and new videotapes. This procedure used in skill evaluation will objectively document and quantify the extent of improvement that has been made.

For the best results in evaluating your shooting techniques and improving your skills, analyze the videotape with a qualified archery instructor and obtain his or her reactions and suggestions. If that is not possible, use the stop action and slow motion features on your VCR so you can critique your shooting technique, determine your problems, and place your consistent shooting errors in rank order from the worst problem to minor difficulties.

You can utilize the list that follows to help document and develop your *shooting fault list.* Undertake the recommended change(s) to eliminate your shooting difficulties during subsequent shooting sessions. In addition to making physical adjustments during practice, you can also use "mental practice techniques" while doing muscle endurance conditioning exercises. Mental practice may be incorporated into the overload draw exercises described and advocated in chapter 8.

As noted, when your major shooting problem has been eliminated, move to the next highest ranked shooting error on your list and try to eliminate that problem. The skill evaluation techniques described above along with the follow-up activities will have a positive impact on your skill development in target archery. The saying that "practice makes perfect" is a myth! A person can be practicing and reinforcing all of his or her old, bad habits. *Directed practice utilizing teaching suggestions designed to eliminate specific skill problems derived from objective skill analyses and evaluations leads to perfection.* Scores will improve as a result of your efforts!

Arrows Grouping Left

1. Check your stance. You may have inadvertently rotated your spinal column slightly to the left. Place your entire body in line with the target and maintain an even weight distribution over both feet.
2. Adjust your bowsight to the left.
3. Check your bow grip. Do not involve the fingers in the gripping process; push with the bow hand; use a finger or bow sling.
4. Your anchor point may have been moved to the right. Make certain the string placement is consistently touching the same facial areas and is aligned with the center of the bow.
5. Nock with the index feather skyward in the nocking position.
6. The bow may cant to the left during aiming and release; consequently, check to see that the bow is held perpendicular to the ground instead of being rotated counterclockwise from anchoring to release.
7. Check the position of the elbow on the bow arm; the elbow should be fully extended at all times from nocking through follow-through. You may be flinching or flexing the elbow at release.
8. Check to see that you are not applying too much pressure on the nock of the arrow during the draw and release with the index and middle fingers; allow an extra space between the gripping fingers and arrow nock; adjust nock-locators.

Arrows Grouping Right

1. Check your stance; align your body with the target instead of rotating the spinal column to the right.
2. Adjust the bowsight to the right.
3. Adjust your grip to eliminate any possibility of a clockwise torque of the bow during release.
4. Check to see that your string alignment has not moved to the left; align the string to touch the middle of the nose and lips.
5. Concentrate on extension only of the distal finger (interphalangeal) joints during release. Any extraneous actions such as plucking or pushing the string inward will cause a grouping error to the right.
6. Make certain that the bow is held perpendicular to the ground and not canted clockwise.

Arrows Grouping High

1. Check your stance for an even weight distribution, as opposed to placing too much weight on the foot away from the target.
2. Adjust your bowsight upward.
3. Make certain you are not pushing against the bow grip with the entire palm or heel of the hand.
4. Keep your mouth closed; upper and lower teeth should be touching—not clenched—from the time you reach your anchor point through release; check the anchor point to see that it has not moved to a lower position on your face. The hand must maintain contact with the jaw or side of the face.
5. Make certain that a ninety-degree string-arrow nock position is attained during nocking. A low nocking point causes the arrow to go high. Adjust your nocking points; place nocking points on your serving if you do not already have them.
6. Check your breathing mechanics; do not inhale during the drawing, aiming, or release phases; breathing should be done before nocking, and you should exhale after the arrow is in the target.
7. Push through the bow at all times from drawing to follow-through; do not raise (abduct) the bow arm at release.
8. Take time to aim so your release will coincide with the bowsight intersecting the desired target spot instead of releasing above the target. Are you completely still or stable at the time of release?
9. Check the bowstring fingers to make certain that the pressure is distributed with minimal pressure on the index finger.
10. Keep the wrist of the shooting arm stabilized and extended at release so no extraneous motion occurs in that joint.

Arrows Grouping Low

1. Check your stance and make certain that weight is not being distributed over the foot nearest the target.

2. Adjust your bowsight downward.
3. Rotate the head toward the target and draw the string to your face without flexing your neck and moving the head toward the string.
4. Draw to your regular anchor point, making certain that your usual facial points are contacted with the string hand; an incomplete draw will reduce arrow velocity and cause the arrows to go low on the target or into the ground.
5. Check to see that you have not nocked above the ninety-degree angle.
6. Hold your anchor point until the arrow is in the target. Allowing the string to move forward—"creeping"—prior to release reduces arrow velocity.
7. Check your grip to make certain that you are not applying pressure to rotate the whole bow toward the target.
8. Maintain the correct bow-arm position without lowering it (adducting the bow-arm shoulder) until the arrow is in the target.

From a pragmatic standpoint in target archery, one should not overlook the value of keeping a quantitative log of competitive shooting scores for specific rounds as an integral part of the skill evaluation procedure. Also, the archer, if possible, should be videotaped shooting in competition. The archer should make subsequent adjustments based on skill analyses and evaluations as noted above. A log of scores along with a chart of placement of arrows in the target should be recorded for each round shot, and this would be included in the total skill evaluation process. The competitive shooting log (computerized if possible for statistical analyses) and videotape will also document your progress as a target archer.

Bow Tuning

If the archer understands and executes the shooting fundamentals properly and continues to have grouping problems, the bow may need to be tuned. Properly tuning a bow for an individual archer should result in appropriately spined arrows being shot accurately. Tuning is a very individualized process; that is, a bow properly tuned for one archer may not be satisfactory for another archer. The tuning process is another step in validating the reliability of your matched tackle. It may help to use a bow tuning method on several bows and ends of arrows on an archery pro shop range prior to purchase. This would help determine the tackle quality and its relationship to your style of shooting.

There are several bow tuning methods, and you might want to try more than one. The Eliason Bow Tuning Method is described below. This procedure was developed by Edwin Eliason, the senior member (age 50 plus) of the 1992 United States Olympic Archery Team. Archery manufacturers, and others, also have very good bow tuning recommendations. Observations of arrow flight patterns must be made in the vertical and horizontal planes. The grouping patterns of arrows on the target must also be made. The bow tuning process determines what adjustments are needed to your tackle to cause the straightest flight patterns of arrows.

To determine vertical plane adjustments, the archer needs to shoot several ends of his or her fletched arrows while aiming at the same spot. The shooting should be at the short distances of 10 or 20 meters. The distance would depend upon the skill level of the archer. Beginning archers should use the closer distance. Once a grouping pattern has been established, an *unfletched arrow* is shot, using the same aiming spot. The relative position of the hit of the unfletched arrow on the target to the fletched arrow group is very significant for making an accurate adjustment of your nocking point. If the unfletched arrow hits *above* the fletched arrow group, raise your nocking point until the grouping patterns coincide. Conversely, if the unfletched arrow hits *below* the fletched group, lower your nocking point.

To determine horizontal plane adjustments, follow the same shooting procedure; that is, use fletched arrows followed by unfletched arrows. You should determine the left or right deviations of the unfletched arrow hits in relation to the fletched arrow grouping. This is necessary to evaluate spine. If the unfletched arrow hits to the *right* of the fletched grouping pattern, the spine of the fletched arrows being shot is too weak. Conversely, if the unfletched arrow hits the target to the *left* of the fletched grouping pattern, the fletched arrow's spine is too stiff. The archer can make several adjustments to the tackle that will modify the spine of the arrows. If the adjustments described below do not work new arrows may have to be purchased to match your bow.

The following are possible tuning adjustments when you have found that the *spine* of your arrows is *too stiff*. Arrows may need to be lengthened, and that would require a purchase. You may want to try the following adjustments first. Heavier points and/or insert weights may be placed on the arrows. A change of arrow nocks can also have an impact on spine. The arrow plate may need to be moved to the right; or try decreasing the spring tension on a compressible pressure point if you are using one. In regard to the bow itself, adding a stabilizer system may help. Check your bowstring and decrease the number of strings to weaken spine. Decreasing the mass weight of the bow, increasing the bow weight, and/or slightly increasing the brace height may also prove beneficial in alleviating horizontal fluctuations of arrows.

The following are possible bow tuning adjustments when you have found that the *spine* of the arrows is *too weak*. The arrows may need to be shortened, or lighter points may need to be placed on the existing arrows. A change of arrow nocks may be advantageous. The arrow plate may need to be moved slightly to the left, or the spring tension on the cushion plunger being used could be increased. Try increasing the number of strands in the bowstring. If a stabilizer is on the bow, try shooting without it. Increasing the mass weight of the bow, decreasing the bow weight, and decreasing the brace height may prove beneficial.

Bow tuning helps to minimize or eliminate vertical and horizontal arrow flight deviations as well as clearance problems. It should be remembered, however, that the archer must have achieved good shooting mechanics in order for bow tuning adjustments to be effective. Bow tuning is ineffective when used in conjunction with or to help the archer rationalize poor shooting fundamentals.

Review

1. Make a list of important safety precautions to observe when on the range or critique your target archery range rules. Beside each rule indicate the chief reason for it.
2. What systems have been found effective in controlling breathing during the draw and aiming? Which one works best for you?
3. Explain brace or string height. How is it determined? What difference would it make if it were raised or lowered?
4. Name several common causes of arrows consistently grouped to each of the following, respectively: left, right, high, low.
5. In what areas of the body is the archer apt to produce considerable tension? What type of tension is contraindicated and why?
6. What is the role of the musculature within the drawing arm during the draw, and how does the skilled archer achieve the appropriate degree of tension in these muscles?
7. Why is it a misnomer to describe the bow hand as "holding" or "gripping" the bow during the draw?
8. Although the archer's head position should remain fixed as soon as the target is addressed, some novices have difficulty holding this position until their follow-through phase of the shot is completed. What can you do to solve this problem?
9. Describe the elements of a good follow-through and explain why follow-through is so important?
10. Do you think it makes for fairer competition if release aids are forbidden and why?
11. When is it appropriate in target archery for you to nock your arrow; to shoot; to stop shooting; to retrieve your arrows? Why?
12. Why should all target hits be recorded (as well as the score)?

Target and Field Archery Sports

5

The purpose of this chapter is to provide an overview of target archery and some of the other sports and activities archers pursue once they have a grasp of target archery shooting mechanics. Archery consists not only of the traditional forms of target archery competition most people associate with the sport, but of such endeavors as crossbow competition, clout shooting, flight shooting, tournaments for disabled people, and ski-archery competitions. Field archery offers a variety of activities that relate target archery to bowhunting and bowfishing. You may want to learn more about one or more of the archery sports after being introduced to them in this chapter. (See Appendix B for names, addresses, and phone numbers where further information may be obtained about archery sport organizations and their functions for archers.)

There are three principal controlling organizations for archers: (1) National Archery Association, Incorporated, of the United States (NAA); (2) National Field Archery Association of the United States, Incorporated (NFAA); and (3) Fédération Internationale de Tir à L'Arc—International Archery Federation (FITA).

The oldest of these organizations is the NAA. It was founded in Chicago in 1879. According to the NAA Constitution, "The corporation is organized and shall be operated exclusively for educational and charitable purposes and to perpetuate, foster, and direct the practice of the sport of archery in connection with the educational and charitable purposes of this corporation and to raise funds for carrying out these purposes." The NAA is recognized as the sport's governing body for archery in the United States. The NAA headquarters are located at the Olympic Center in Colorado Springs, Colorado. *The U.S. Archer* is the official publication of the NAA.

The NFAA was founded in 1939. According to the NFAA Constitution, some of the organization's major purposes are, "To foster, expand, promote, and perpetuate the practice of field archery and any other archery games as the association may adopt and enforce uniform rules, regulations, procedures, conditions, and methods of playing such games. To encourage the use of the bow in the hunting of all legal game birds and animals, and to protect, improve, and increase the sport of hunting with a bow and arrow." This organization has a strong interest in conservation as it relates to bowhunting and bowfishing. *Archery* is the official publication of the NFAA. The NFAA and NAA now have a working agreement that provides mutual participatory advantages for members of both organizations.

Table 5.1 Competitive Age and Sex Classifications for Target Archery Tournament Rounds

Males		Females	
Men	18 years old or over	Women	18 years old or over
Boys		Girls	
Intermediate		Intermediate	
	15 to 18 years old		15 to 18 years old
Junior		Junior	
	12 to 15 years old		12 to 15 years old
Cadet		Cadet	
	Less than 12 years old		Less than 12 years old

The FITA was organized in 1931, "To promote and encourage Archery throughout the World in conformity with the Olympic principles." The FITA organizes regional and world championships in target archery. Records are processed through this organization. Target archery organizations of the various countries are affiliated with the FITA; this is necessary in order to coordinate national, regional, and international competitions. The FITA determines amateur eligibility for such tournaments. The NAA is affiliated with the FITA.

Target Archery

Target archery, like competitive road running, swimming, and cycling, is divided into functional and competitive groups by sex and age. Virtually any individual, regardless of sex, age, or disability, can find opportunities to compete in target archery tournaments somewhere. Competition in target archery is available at many levels for people with all degrees of skill. The competitive classifications are shown in table 5.1. An archer may elect to shoot in a higher age classification, but may not shoot in a lower classification. As noted in chapter 3, the FITA and NAA now have target shooting divisions in target archery tournaments for compound bows as well as recurve or Olympic Bows.

To support proper archery instruction, competition, and motivation for boys and girls, the NAA has an active Junior Olympic Archery Development Program (JOAD). This program introduces archery to students in elementary and secondary schools. Its major purpose is to assist interested young archers in getting started correctly in the sport. The JOAD tournaments are very popular among young archers and their parents. Some of the world-class archers who represent the United States in national and international competitions started in JOAD.

The NAA also has a very active College Division. It promotes intercollegiate archery competition for men and women. The culmination of the college archery season is the U.S. Intercollegiate Archery Championships. College teams must be members of the NAA College Division in order to compete. Traditionally, there have been very strong intercollegiate archery programs in Arizona and California. (California has more college archery programs than any other state.) The annual

NAA Intercollegiate Ranking Program for men and women indicates, however, that excellent individual archers and college archery teams are found in community colleges, colleges, and universities throughout the United States.

If you are a college or university student, check to see whether or not your school has an intercollegiate archery team and determine what it takes to become a member. Also, check with your intramural athletic director to see when archery competition is scheduled in the intramural athletic program.

Championship Rounds

The NAA has twelve approved championship rounds designated for competitions. The James D. Easton Round is recommended as the Team Round. An archery team consists of eight archers; however, only the combined score of the best four archers from a team is calculated as the team's total score for a competition. The archer with the best overall score for any round is the individual champion even if that person competes on a team.

The outdoor FITA Round is shot twice in individual and team competitions such as the World Championships. The FITA Round distances for men and women are very demanding (see table 5.2). For men, the longest distance is 90 meters (98.42 yards), while the longest distance shot by women is 70 meters (76.55 yards). If you have never shot those distances and want to gain some understanding of the challenges of target archery, it is recommended that you set up a 122 centimeter target at each of those distances, shoot, and score thirty-six arrows. At 90 meters, the best men in the world average approximately 8.90 for each arrow shot. The best world-class women target archers average close to 9.00 for each of the 36 arrows shot at 70 meters! If you have shot from those distances, you should have gained some insight and appreciation for that caliber of scoring.

A few elite men and women archers around the world shoot *above* 1,300 for the single FITA Round—1,440 is possible. A score of 1,300 in an official FITA Round is a noble goal for many very good archers. What does it take to become a world class target archer? The FITA and NAA require *minimum* qualifying scores for Olympic Tournaments of 1,150 for women and 1,200 for men in the FITA Round. The same minimum qualifying scores are used for the girls and boys who wish to become eligible to compete for a position on a Junior World Team for the United States. As a result of these qualifying criteria, obtaining a place on a national team anywhere in the world is very competitive and challenging! (The world records for men and women for the FITA Round are considerably above 1,300. See table 5.2 for some examples of FITA Round world class scores that have been shot from the various distances.)

If you shoot a score of 1,200 for the FITA Round, as an example, that means the average value for each of the 144 arrows shot was 8.33! If you are a typical target archer struggling to improve your shooting mechanics and scoring, always remember that one fantastic thing about archery is that you do not have to average 8.33 per arrow or better to enjoy the sport. A high skill level, of course, is great! As noted in chapter 1, within the pursuit of excellence there are many values in the quest itself. There is personal satisfaction attained when you reach a realistic personal goal at any level. Therein lies part of the value and mystique of this multifaceted sport.

Table 5.2 Examples of World-Class Scores for the Single FITA Round

Distance	Total Arrows	Possible Score	Actual Score	Average Per Arrow
Ladies				
70 meters	36	360	338	9.39
60 meters	36	360	347	9.64
50 meters	36	360	338	9.39
30 meters	36	360	357	9.92
FITA Round	144	1,440	1,375	9.55
Gentlemen				
90 meters	36	360	322	8.94
70 meters	36	360	342	9.50
50 meters	36	360	348	9.67
30 meters	36	360	360	10.00
FITA Round	144	1,440	1,356	9.42

Table 5.2 is presented to show the reader a few of the actual scores that have been shot at the FITA Round distances and for the total FITA Round in international competition. These scores represent: (1) what can be accomplished in the sport, (2) a challenge to beginning and intermediate archers, and (3) potential motivation for people who like to pursue excellence! *If someone else in the world has shot these scores, why can't you?* Can you be the first person ever to shoot a perfect score in a recognized tournament from 50 meters or 70 meters during a FITA Round? Perfection was accomplished for the first time from 30 meters on June 13, 1994, by Han Seung-Hun, a male, Korean archer. He was competing in the Seoul International Archery Tournament.

Table 5.3 presents relevant information for some of the outdoor and indoor NAA Target Archery Championship Rounds. There are two variations based on the FITA Outdoor Target Round shown in table 5.3. One is called the Double FITA Outdoor Target Round where two of these rounds are shot consecutively. Secondly, there is a Half FITA Round where the archers shoot eighteen arrows only from the distances noted in table 5.3.

There is also a FITA Standard Round shot outdoors in championship competition. This round consists of shooting thirty-six arrows from the distances of 50 and 30 meters respectively. A regulation 122 centimeter target face is used in the FITA Standard Round.

Competition at the Olympic Games is handled differently for the benefit of both the participants and spectators. There are outdoor and indoor Olympic Rounds designed for team and individual competitions. These feature a Qualification Round (FITA Outdoor or Indoor Target Rounds are used except at the Olympic Games). This Qualification Round is then followed by an Elimination Round featuring the top sixty-four archers (outdoors) and thirty-two archers

Table 5.3 Selected NAA Target Archery Championship Rounds

Round		Distance	Arrows Per Distance	Total Arrows	Target Size	Total Points
Outdoor						
FITA	Men	90,70m 50,30m	36	144	122cm 80cm	1,440
	Women	70,60m 50,30m	36	144	122cm 80cm	1,440
Junior Metric		60,50m 40,30m	36	144	122cm 80cm	1,440
Cadet Metric		45,35m 25,15m	36	144	122cm 80cm	1,440
900 Metric		60,50,40m	30	90	122cm	900
Junior 900		50,40,30m	30	90	122cm	900
Cadet 900		40,30,20m	30	90	122cm	900
James D. Easton						
	(Team)	60,50,40m	20	60	122cm	600
Collegiate 600		50,40,30m	20	60	122cm	600
Collegiate 720		50,40,30m	24	72	80cm	720
Clout	Men	165m	36	36	15m	180
Intermediate Boys		165m	36	36	15m	180
Women		125m	36	36	15m	180
Intermediate Girls		125m	36	36	15m	180
Juniors		110m	36	36	15m	180
Cadets		110m	36	36	15m	180
Indoor						
FITA Round 1		18m	30	30	40cm	300
FITA Round II		25m	30	30	60cm	300

(indoors) from the Qualification Round. The outdoor Elimination Round is shot at 122 centimeter target faces from 70 meters, and indoor archers shoot this round from 18 meters. The top eight male and eight female archers from the Elimination Round advance to a Finals Round shot at the same distances. Champions are determined ultimately in what is known as the Gold Medal Match of the Finals Round. Each archer shoots four ends of three arrows from 70 meters. The two archers competing for the championship alternate their shots in this round, and they have 40 seconds to shoot each arrow. This interesting format was designed to bring the best archers in the world into competition directly with each other at the most critical times in the target archery competition in the Olympic Games.

There are annual U.S. National Indoor Championships and Regional Championships sponsored by the NAA. These competitions include all age categories and there are shooting divisions for crossbow, Olympic Bow, barebow, and compound bow shooters.

A competitive round of target archery is controlled by a Director of Shooting. Judges are assigned targets and work under the supervision of the Director. The longest distances are shot first. In order to adjust to range and environmental conditions, there is a 15 minute pre-tournament practice session. If this is not possible, archers are allowed to shoot a total of six sighter arrows prior to competition. No other trial shots in any direction are allowed on the range during the competition. The archer must be emotionally, physically, and psychologically ready when he or she steps onto the target archery range. *The mental aspects of target archery should never be minimized or underestimated!*

The Director of Shooting controls the contest by using a whistle to inform the archers when to start and stop shooting. A time limit of 2½ minutes is given to release an end of three arrows. Two blasts on the whistle is the signal for the archers to move from the waiting line to their positions on the shooting line. They address their targets. One blast of the whistle starts the 2½ minute shooting period for three arrows. Several short blasts indicate that all shooting must stop, because an emergency exists.

What type of tackle may the target archer use in competition? There are shooting divisions for archers who shoot recurve and compound bows. Compound bows may not have a bow weight greater than 60 pounds. Target archers do not compete against each other using the different types of bows. *The recurve or Olympic Bow is used exclusively in Olympic target archery competition.* The bowstring may have a serving and one or two nock locators. However, neither the serving nor the nock locators can be positioned to function as a rear sight device for the archer. An arrow rest is allowed for its specific purpose, but may not be positioned or used for aiming. One bowsight of the type shown in figures 3.9 and 3.13 is allowed. A bowsight may not include level devices, prisms, lens, or electronic gadgets. Stabilizers are approved. Arrows must be marked with the archer's name, initials, or insignia, and all arrows must have the same colors of fletching, nock, and crests. No release devices may be used or built in to finger protection accessories while using the Olympic Bow, but release aids are allowed for use by the FITA with compound bows.

Other accessories such as clickers, bracers, bow slings, and quivers are allowed. If the archer wears glasses, the glasses may not be modified in any manner to assist in the aiming process. All of these tackle items, and others, are checked by the Director of Shooting and the judges prior to the contest.

The NAA has a dress code for archers which must be followed during tournaments. White clothing is *mandatory.* According to the NAA, ladies may wear, "Dresses, skirts, slacks, culottes, or shorts with leg length not above crotch level. Suitable blouses or tops with color allowed on the upper 50 percent of exposed area. Tank tops may be worn providing the strap is at least three inches in width." Men may wear, "Full length trousers or shorts with leg length not above crotch level. Long or short-sleeved shirts with color allowed on the upper 50 percent of the exposed area." Guidelines also stipulate what can and cannot be worn in terms of the advertising of manufacturer's trademarks and logos.

Nonchampionship Rounds

Numerous nonchampionship rounds have been used for years. Some of these are excellent rounds to shoot in club, school, intramural, and class competitions (see figure 4.24). They are shot on the regulation 122 centimeter target face. A few of these rounds are listed below:

York Round

72 arrows at 100 yards
48 arrows at 80 yards
24 arrows at 60 yards

Columbia Round

24 arrows at 50 yards
24 arrows at 40 yards
24 arrows at 30 yards

Junior Columbia Round

24 arrows at 40 yards
24 arrows at 30 yards
24 arrows at 20 yards

Scholastic Round

24 arrows at 40 yards
24 arrows at 30 yards

Team Round

96 arrows at 60 yards—men
96 arrows at 50 yards—women

National Round

48 arrows at 60 yards
24 arrows at 50 yards

Junior American Round

30 arrows at 50 yards
30 arrows at 40 yards
30 arrows at 30 yards

Western Round

48 arrows at 60 yards
48 arrows at 50 yards

Hereford Round

72 arrows at 80 yards
48 arrows at 60 yards
24 arrows at 50 yards

Saint George Round

36 arrows at 100 yards
36 arrows at 80 yards
36 arrows at 60 yards

Windsor Round

36 arrows at 60 yards
36 arrows at 50 yards
36 arrows at 40 yards

Saint Nicholas Round

48 arrows at 40 yards
36 arrows at 30 yards

Albion Round

36 arrows at 80 yards
36 arrows at 60 yards
36 arrows at 50 yards

American Round

30 arrows at 60 yards
30 arrows at 50 yards
30 arrows at 40 yards

Note: To change from yards to meters, multiply by 0.9144.

As a historical note about some of these rounds, the York Round was used in national championship competitions for years in Great Britain and America. The distances are demanding. This was especially true for the type of tackle (longbows and wooden arrows) used during the nineteenth century. The American Round was

Figure 5.1
The Fourth Olympiad of 1908 held in Shepherd's Bush Stadium in London. The men shot the York Round. The central figure in the light suit is the British gold medalist, W. Dod. (From E. G. Heath, *The Grey Goose Wing*)

used to establish national men champions in the United States starting in 1911. A York Round champion was also named. For several years after 1914, the national championship was based on the combined scores of double American and York Rounds. Over the years from 1879 to 1985, the American women's championship was determined by using the Columbia and National Rounds.

The FITA Round for international competition came into vogue in 1956, and the Grand FITA Round was introduced in World and Olympic competitions in 1985. FITA Rounds are now used extensively to determine numerous outdoor and indoor championships. The new Olympic Round format noted above was approved by the FITA in 1991 and initiated at the Olympic Games in 1992.

The Olympic Games

Target archery has been included in the agenda of several Olympiads during the twentieth century. Records indicate that medals were awarded in archery at the Olympic Games in 1900 at Paris, 1904 in St. Louis, 1908 in London, and 1920 in Antwerp. The sport was not revived for Olympic competition until the 1960s. Target archery was included in the 1968 Olympic Games as a demonstration sport and it became an official gold medal sport starting with the 1972 Olympiad held in Munich. That event, highly significant to the sport of target archery, has resulted in an increased interest in target archery as an amateur sport throughout the world.

Figures 5.1 and 5.2 show some of the men and women competitors in the 1908 Olympic Games. These illustrations are interesting because they give us a chance to compare and contrast the type of archery tackle used in competition in 1908 with tackle available to archers today. The longbow is predominant in both illustrations. The use of the longbow at this level of competition today would be

Figure 5.2
The women competitors shooting the National Round at the 1908 Olympic Games. (From
E. G. Heath, *The Grey Goose Wing*)

most unusual! It is also instructive to compare and contrast the type of clothing
worn by the competitors in 1908 with the type of clothing required for archers by
the FITA. Also, the rather erratic arrow grouping shown in figure 5.2 would not
place the archer very high in contemporary competition where tight groups are the
rule rather than the exception.

Archery competition at recent Olympiads has attracted the interest of spectators.
As one example, there was tremendous interest in the sport of target archery at the
Games of the XXIII Olympiad held in Los Angeles, California. (The actual competition site for archery was Long Beach, California.) This interest was demonstrated, in
part, by the fact that the competition was observed daily by over 9,000 spectators in
a sold-out stadium (fig. 5.3). The reader should compare figures 5.1 and 5.3 to see
the difference between spectator interest in archery for the 1908 Olympic Games
and for the 1984 Olympic Games. The new Olympic Round format to determine individual and team champions in head-to-head competition was added to increase
spectator interest in archery in the Olympiads conducted after 1988.

Interest in Olympic archery has also resulted in better shooting quality as
demonstrated by the excellent scores that have been shot during the past few
Olympic Games (see fig. 5.4 for an example). The greater attention given to
archery throughout the world has produced numerous elite archers over the past
few decades especially in North America and Asia.

Figure 5.5 is provided to allow the reader to compare and contrast the clothing,
tackle, shooting stance, and equipment used by contemporary archers with that of
archers at the beginning of the twentieth century (fig. 5.1). Take-down, recurve or
Olympic Bows equipped with sights and stabilizers are used as compared with the

Figure 5.3
The shooting line and stadium at the 1984 Olympic Games. (Photo by *The U.S. Archer*)

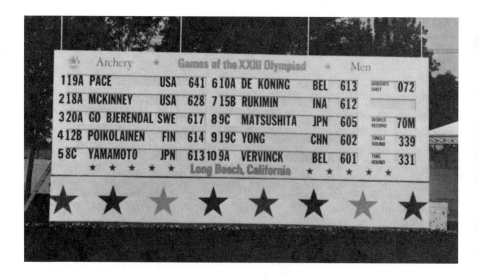

Figure 5.4
The men's scoreboard during the Games of the XXIII Olympiad showed the competitors scores in progress. (Photo by *The U.S. Archer*)

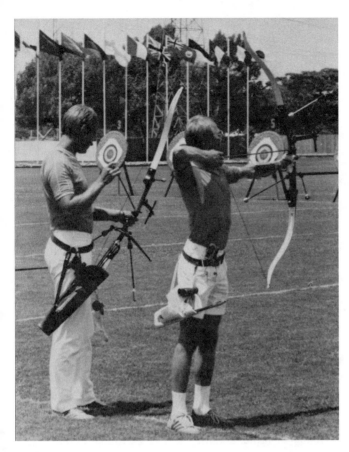

Figure 5.5
Olympic archers on the shooting line in clothing required by the FITA. (Photo by *The U.S. Archer*)

longbows used in 1908. The reader should also compare the shooting stance of the archer on the line in figure 5.1 with the stance used by the archer in figure 5.5. The stereotype of stance mechanics has changed considerably over the decades.

The NAA conducts tryout tournaments to select the men's and women's teams which represent the United States in national, World, and Olympic competitions. Archers who shoot the best qualifying scores with Olympic Bows *above* the FITA minimal Olympic standards described previously are provided coaching. Elite archers receive the benefits of having their shooting skills scientifically and technically analyzed by exercise scientists at the Olympic Center. Sophisticated analyses are made involving the archer, his or her tackle, and the interrelationships between the two while shooting.

Scientific studies of archers relate primarily to the anatomic kinesiology, biomechanics, and exercise physiology variables involved in shooting. These are all associated with the performance-related fitness of the elite archer. High-speed cinematography and videotape are utilized extensively. Physics instruments are used to measure and evaluate such elements as the forces and velocities contributing to or detracting from the archer's skill. This scientific information is communicated from the exercise scientists to the archers and their coaches with the intent of improving the technical or skill aspects of shooting. The merging of scientific theory with the technique or practice of archery has the potential to increase skill at all levels of competition. It is especially important at the Olympic level in order to provide a "competitive edge" to meet the excellent competition now seen throughout the world.

As of June 1, 1995, there is an Olympic Training Center—The Easton Archery Complex—where archers can eat, sleep, and train for world competition. This is a 150 acre complex at the ARCO Olympic Training Center near Chula Vista, California.

To determine amateur status and eligibility, the NAA is governed by the eligibility rules of the FITA and the International Olympic Committee. These rules are very specific. They cover topics ranging from the allowable maximum value of trophies or prizes retained by the archer to the uses of prescribed and over-the-counter medicines. The rules also cover the use of illegal drugs such as anabolic steroids used by some athletes. An archer desiring to be a member of an Olympic team must meet the amateur status criteria and be drug free.

Are there opportunities for professional archers? Yes. Professional archers who do not meet the amateur status criteria for Olympic competition have their own organizations. The NAA and NFAA, as examples, provide Professional Divisions for shooting activities. The Professional Archery Association of the NAA was founded in 1961.

Individuals over the age of 55 still interested in elite competition, but who are not Olympic class archers or professionals, may choose to participate in target archery each year during The U.S. National Senior Sports Classic. That event draws archers from the age of 55 years through 90 plus! It should be noted that it is possible to be over the age of 50 and still shoot well enough to be a member of an Olympic team! The United States has had an archer, Edwin Eliason, on the Olympic Archery Team who was over the age of 50. That is not too likely to happen in sports such as basketball, track, or tennis!

American archers have performed very well in Olympic competition since 1972. With good instruction, diligent practice, and "desire," the individual reading this book (YOU!) could develop into an archery competitor or champion of national and international caliber within a period of a few years. This is not impossible *if* the individual has excellent intrinsic motivation toward this type of goal. At any age (teenager, young adult, or individual 50 plus), with the proper attitude, interest, aptitude, and motivation you could possibly earn a position on the Olympic team in archery. It has been done! To represent one's country on an Olympic team is one of the highest honors an individual can achieve.

It is both fitting and proper that archery, one of the oldest sports performed by humans, is now a part of the Olympic Gold Medal Sport's Agenda.

Figure 5.6
A modern compound crossbow; one of many designs used by archers for bowhunting, field, match, and flight competitions. (Courtesy Precision Shooting Equipment, 2727 N. Fairview Ave., Tucson, AZ 85705)

Crossbows

Crossbows have been a part of the history of humankind for over 2,400 years. The Greeks developed a form of crossbow about 400 B.C., and the Chinese were using crossbows in battles as early as 341 B.C. The military use of these bows as weapons was very popular from the eleventh to the sixteenth century. They gradually declined as weapons of war with the onset of firearms. Humans remain fascinated by the crossbow today. As a result, there is a growing interest in the use of the crossbow in sport. There are opportunities to use the crossbow (fig. 5.6) in such diverse activities as flight shooting, bowhunting, field shooting, and match competition. There are several state, national and international championships organized to accommodate the interests of crossbow enthusiasts.

The Internationale Armbrustschutzen Union (IAU) is the major international controlling organization for crossbow shooting. The IAU has nineteen affiliated members representing large and small countries throughout the world. Match crossbow competitions and field crossbow shooting are controlled by the IAU and its affiliates.

The main difference between match crossbow shooting and field crossbow shooting lies in the clothing allowed to be worn by the crossbow shooters. Match shooting is also more analogous to rifle shooting. The match competitor can wear leather gloves, boots, and shooting jackets; whereas, the field crossbow archer dresses like the target archer in NAA or international competition (fig. 5.3). All field shots must be made from the standing position, and all competition is on outdoor ranges. Match competition, on the other hand, may include indoor as well as outdoor targets. The indoor targets may be as close as 10 meters.

The International Field Crossbow Round requires a standard 80 centimeter FITA target face. Ninety arrows are shot; therefore, a perfect score would be 900. Thirty arrows are shot from 65 meters, 50 meters, and 35 meters respectively. *The better men and women shooters will have scores at or above 800 for this round.* As examples, the following scores have been shot for a single International Field Crossbow Round: 856 for men (Pentti Hakkinen of Finland) and 832 for women (Sieglinde Wagner of Germany). That gives you some idea of what is being accomplished with crossbows.

The NAA conducts crossbow championships on an annual basis. Crossbow competition is usually in categories for men, women, juniors, and seniors. Most of the rules of target archery also apply to crossbow shooters, but the two different kinds of shooting always occur separately. Field shooting at outdoor targets is done with bows of 80 pounds or less. Fifty pounds is recommended for indoor competitions. No mechanical aids can be used to draw the bows unless the individual is physically disabled. *The short arrows shot from crossbows are called bolts.* The crossbow shooter cannot use a magnifying sight, but prismatic sights and level bubble sights are allowed to be mounted on the bow. Binoculars and scopes may be used to locate hits on the target.

The National Crossbowmen of the U.S.A. is the United States affiliate of the International Armburst Union. Their aim is to ". . . perpetuate the history of the crossbow and enhance its use as a sporting instrument for target shooting as well as for hunting. At times we shoot along side of, but not in actual competition with, longbow archers. Many of our members belong to archery and rifle clubs in their local areas and participate in local, state, and national tournaments. World Championships take place every two years where it is known as Field Crossbow to distinguish it from the more rifle disciplined MATCH crossbow." *The Crossbow Chit Chat* is the official publication of The National Crossbowmen of the U.S.A.

The U.S. Match–Crossbow Shooting Association is also affiliated with the IAU. Readers interested in learning more about crossbow activities are referred to Appendix B for the names and addresses of crossbow organizations. The Bibliography also contains a few references on this fascinating archery sport.

Clout Shooting

Historically, clout shooting as a sport can be traced at least as far back as the period of English archery prior to The Hundred Years' War. As noted in chapter 2, clout shooting was used as a military strategy in many wars throughout history. The archers shot great volleys of arrows into the air in clout fashion toward their opponents. This was an early and effective form of aerial bombardment. The reader can readily understand the apprehension of a soldier as a volley of arrows numbering in the hundreds or thousands suddenly and silently descended into the area. In addition to being an effective killing technique, the arrival of arrows in this fashion often caused panic among the ranks. Retreat was common following a clout shooting bombardment in an area where soldiers were densely grouped along a combat line.

The fascinating sport of clout shooting evolved from archery bombardment in war. As noted in table 5.3, the Clout Round is an official NAA Target Archery Championship Round. The circular target in clout shooting is laid out on the ground. Its outer circle measures 15 meters (49.21 feet) in diameter. It is divided into five concentric scoring zones that each measure 1.5 meters (4.92 feet) in width. The *Clout* is a brightly colored flag placed on a wooden pole 19.69 inches above the ground in the center of the target. The values of each scoring zone starting from the center outward are five, four, three, two, and one. Arrows that stick in the clout flag are given the value of five.

Target archery tackle is used for the Clout Round. As you see in table 5.3, the Clout Round distances vary based on the sex and age of the archer. The longest distance is 165 meters (180.4 yards) for men and intermediate boys, and the shortest distance is 110 meters (120.30 yards) for junior and cadet boys and girls. Women and intermediate girls shoot from 125 meters (136.70 yards). All of these distances are challenging, and the distance adds "spice" to the clout shoot. You are given only six practice or sighter arrows prior to beginning the Clout Round.

The Clout Round consists of thirty-six arrows. All arrows are shot from the single distance specified for your age and sex. A perfect score would be 180, but that is easier said than done! Clout shooting is an intriguing archery sport. If space allows for range safety to be maintained, it is recommended that a few clout rounds be shot by students taking a course in target archery. It is fun!

Flight Archery

Most people think of archery in all of its forms as placing the emphasis on accuracy. Flight archery or flight shooting may be the lone exception to that "rule." *Flight shooting places the premium on how far an arrow or bolt can be projected from a bow or crossbow.* This sport has great appeal to individuals who are fascinated by the physics of the specialized bows constructed specifically for flight shooting. The biomechanical relationship that exists between the tackle and archer is also of prime interest to participants in flight shooting. The sport demands an understanding of trajectories and aerodynamic properties of arrows and bolts. The physics involving the interrelationships between the mechanical system of the bow, its kinetic and potential energy capabilities, and the forces acting efficiently on the arrow to put it into flight are all fascinating academic aspects of this sport.

The strength of the archer to handle the forces required by his or her tackle is also of paramount importance in some aspects of flight shooting. Knowledge of the tackle of flight shooting must be integrated with the proper techniques of shooting in order to attain the desired maximum distances. Flight shooting is very unique among the archery sports!

What is the farthest an arrow has ever been shot by a human without benefit of fuel, explosive devices, or air currents in a recognized flight shooting event? As it should be, that record is held by "The Father of Flight Archery" and 1993 recipient of the J. Maurice Thompson Medal of Honor, Harry Drake (fig. 5.7). His record was set in 1988, and it would take an Olympic 1,500 meter track athlete about four

Figure 5.7
Harry Drake, "The Father of Flight Shooting," using a 25 kg flight bow in an NAA Flight Championship. (Courtesy of *The U.S. Archer;* photo by Bob Rhode)

Figure 5.8
Flight shooting includes competitive categories for women and men. Sherrie Reynolds is shown using a compound flight bow in competition. (Courtesy of *The U.S. Archer;* photo by Bob Rhode)

minutes to run and retrieve the bolt! *Harry Drake's World Crossbow Flight Record shot on a salt flat in Utah is 2,047 yards, 2 inches. That is 1.16 miles!* He has also shot an arrow from an unlimited footbow 2,028 yards, that is, 1.15 miles! In addition, he holds two other World Flight Records. Those are amazing feats for the 1974 inductee into The Archery Hall of Fame.

It should be noted that the J. Maurice Thompson Medal of Honor is only awarded by the NAA to individuals who have provided "outstanding and meritorious service to archery without expectation of reward." Harry Drake's efforts in flight shooting for over fifty years make him a worthy recipient of one of the highest awards given to archers.

As a historic footnote to support the fact that flight shooting has been around for a long time, there is a claim that a Sultan Selim had a flight shot of 972 yards in 1798 A.D. The Sultan's shot was reportedly witnessed by a British Ambassador by the name of Sir Ainslie. Harry Drake eclipsed the Sultan's record many times during the last few decades using a variety of bows.

In competition, archers shoot four rounds of flight consisting of six arrows each with broadheads and four rounds with regular flight arrows. They may use any type or weight of bow sanctioned for flight shooting during each round. If desired, a different flight bow can be used for each round.

Competitions are also held separately in flight archery involving "Regular Flight" and "Broadhead Flight." A regular flight bow may be designed with a

Table 5.4   Examples of Flight Shooting Distances Attained with Different Types of Bows

Bow Category	Archer's Name	Distance Yards-Feet-Inches
Men		
Unlimited Footbow	Harry Drake	2,028–0–0
Unlimited Longbow	Don Brown	356–1–2
50.0 lb. Primitive Bow	Daniel Perry	295–2–3
Unlimited Compound Bow	Kevin Strother	1,320–1–3
Crossbow	Harry Drake	2,047–0–2
Unlimited Primitive Bow	Daniel Perry	283–2–7
Women		
18 kg Flight Bow	Sherrie Reynolds	740–1–8
Unlimited Longbow	April Moon	244–0–0
Unlimited Compound Bow	April Moon	807–1–3
Unlimited Flight Bow	April Moon	1,039–1–1
Footbow	Arlyne Rhode	1,113–2–6

For further information on flight shooting, the reader may want to write to the NAA Flight Shooting Committee—see Appendix B.

special handle equipped with overdraw capabilities, but any recurve bow may also be used in "Regular Flight" events. The arrows are a minimum of 14 inches in length from the floor of the nock to the tip of the point. They are designed with a barrel shape, and the vanes are small. The "Broadhead Flight" competition involves the use of unaltered broadhead points as commonly used in bowhunting. There are established standards for men and women, and these specify the minimum weights of the broadheads.

Flight competition is divided according to age and sex. Men and women (fig. 5.8) categories are for people 18 years of age and older. Intermediate and Junior categories are for ages 12 through 17 years. The Cadet level of competition includes children 11 years of age and under. There are also divisions for "amateurs" and "nonamateurs" in this sport.

There are several bow classifications used in flight archery. Compound bows are divided into specific weight divisions plus an "unlimited" division for each age and sex group. In addition, there are competition classifications for crossbows and primitive bows. Broadhead flight shooting might also include recurve and longbow events.

Flight bows achieve high arrow velocities. Kevin Strother holds The World Bow Speed Record of 588 feet per second with a bow of 180 pounds draw weight. "Fastest Bow" competitions are held periodically, and arrow velocities over 700 feet per second are expected in the future.

Table 5.4 provides the reader with a few examples of the distances achieved with specific bows in flight shooting. It is a very interesting and challenging archery sport that you may want to try.

Archery for the Disabled

The people and organizations that govern archery have taken pride for many years in the fact that archery is one sport that can involve virtually everyone as participants. The NAA rules specifically stipulate that no archer with a disability shall be barred from a tournament unless his or her mechanical aids provide an advantage over the other archers or the shots cannot be made within the alloted time sequence. Archers in wheelchairs can shoot on the line from their chairs. There is also an organization for wheelchair archers, The National Wheelchair Athletic Association (see Appendix B for the address). This organization is involved with competitions in archery as well as other sports at state, regional, national, and international levels (fig. 5.9).

Archery as a sport can be adapted to meet the special needs of people with various types of disabilities. This is accomplished in many school situations and archery clubs. An archery range can also be established within the environment of a yard at home.

With some thought and ingenuity, archery tackle can be modified for use by people with all kinds of disabilities. As an example, the blind can now enjoy target archery thanks to eighteen years of effort and the creative genius of Al LeFebvre, a blind radio and sound repairman and target archer. He was blinded by diabetes mellitus. His "Sightless Sight System" for target archery was first used by blind archers in 1990 during a competition sponsored by The United States Association for Blind Athletes.

LeFebvre's system allows the blind archer to zero in on the center of the target by listening through headphones for two audible signals transmitted from the target to horizontal and vertical bars on a specially built sighting stand for the bow. When both sounds are heard simultaneously, the blind archer releases the arrow. Upon learning the location of the hit, the blind archer must attempt to make aiming adjustments just like any other archer. LeFebvre has further adapted his system to accommodate archers who are both blind and deaf. Two different levels of vibrations were substituted for the audible signals. As a result, archers who are both blind and deaf can literally feel when to release the arrows.

The National Wheelchair Athletic Association makes very few adaptations or special accommodations for the target archers in its competitions. Their events are not separated by classification of the disability except in the cases of some quadriplegics. If a quadriplegic can shoot without a mechanical release, he or she competes in regular archery rounds. If a mechanical release is needed due to upper limb weakness or some other problem, quadriplegics with common syndromes compete against one another in a separate division of each round. For shooting stability, novice quadriplegic archers who use mechanical release aids may be strapped into their wheelchairs during the first year of competition only. These archers may also receive help in nocking their arrows. All of the other challenging and difficult aspects of shooting must be met by the archer.

There are international competitive opportunities for archers with disabilities. Olympic and world competitions are held in a manner similar to the contests for able-bodied archers. Paralympic archery teams, as they are known, are chosen in

Figure 5.9
Former U.S. National Wheelchair Champion, Robert Norvelle, follows through after a shot. He has shot 2,307 for the Double FITA Round. (Courtesy of *The U.S. Archer;* photo by Raenel Jones)

each country through a trial process similar to the Olympic selection procedure for any target archer. The paralympic archer does compete in a special division based on his or her specific situation, that is, paraplegic division, quadriplegic division, or amputee division. The use of compound bows and release devices are allowed when the paralympic archers do not have use of their fingers. One competitive division requires the archers to shoot Olympic Bows as in any target archery contest. The scores are outstanding due to the devotion of the paralympic archers to the pursuit of excellence in their sport.

Many readers will remember the spectacular televised opening of the 1992 Olympics where a flaming arrow was shot to light the torch. *Antonio Rebollo, the thirty-seven year old archer who officially started the 1992 Barcelona Olympic Games by shooting a blazing arrow over but close enough to the cauldron to ignite the Olympic flame, was a member of the paralympic archery team from Spain.* His spectacular shot under pressure (181 feet from and 70 feet below the Olympic torch) was viewed that night by three billion people around the world via television and by several thousand athletes and spectators in the stadium. It now stands as one of the classic shots in archery lore throughout history. Rebollo was afflicted with polio at the age of eight months, and he started developing his archery skills at the age of twenty-two years. Now, as the lighter of the 1992 Olympic flame and a 1,300 FITA shooter, Antonio Rebollo is among the elite paralympic archers in the world.

Figure 5.10

A student with muscular dystrophy enjoying the sport of archery by using a modified bow with a mechanical release device. (Courtesy Jim Cowart, Schools of Alameda County, Hayward, CA 94501)

Jim Cowart, an adapted physical education specialist with the Alameda Schools in Hayward, California, is a professional who has modified archery tackle so his students can enjoy the sport. Figure 5.10 shows an adapted archery bow in use by a student with some neuromuscular limitations. The bow is mounted on a camera tripod, and a release aid (Stuart Hot Shot Release) was placed where the student could trigger it. The teacher or another student makes the draw and loads the string into the release aid, but the disabled student must make the all-important vertical and horizontal aiming adjustments allowed by the camera tripod. When the student has the aiming alignment desired, the release aid is triggered by the finger motion. The arrow is on its way, and the student has the pleasure of knowing that he or she has plotted its trajectory. If the arrow does not go where it was intended, the archer with a disability must go through the same mental processes and make the necessary aiming adjustments in the same manner as any other archer.

Tackle modifications can be made to handle most problems the person with a disability would have in archery. If the student cannot keep or control the arrow on the bowstring, the serving can be increased in circumference or the plastic arrow nock may be narrowed. If the student cannot keep the arrow on the arrow rest while drawing, the Bear Arro-Guide arrow rest may be modified with a strip of plastic to contain the arrow without having a negative effect on its trajectory and velocity. Jim Cowart utilized these modifications with success for his adapted physical education students.

There are opportunities for archers with disabilities to participate in virtually all aspects of archery. These include target archery, clout shooting, flight shooting, field archery, bowfishing, and bowhunting. *Archery can be a sport for everyone who enjoys it!*

Figure 5.11
A field archery club designed with a fourteen-target basic unit.

Field Archery

Field archery is different from target archery primarily in that the target course is often laid out in wooded and hilly areas. Field archers walk the course. Twenty acres make an ideal field archery course, while shooting distances range from 15 feet to 80 yards. The size and type of target are determined by the distance and type of round being shot. *A field archery course consists of fourteen targets; these are called a unit.* Two units or twice around one unit constitutes a round in field archery. Figure 5.11 is a diagram of a typical field archery club with a fourteen-target basic unit. These units are usually developed over the terrain to simulate bowhunting conditions.

The NFAA has 50 chartered associations and more than 1,200 affiliated clubs. These clubs have a membership representing over one hundred thousand archers. The clubs hold many local tournaments throughout the year for members. Each state holds a field archery championship, and these are well attended. The National Field Archery Championship Tournament draws from 500 to 1,000 competitors annually.

Figure 5.12
Interchangeable arrow for broadhead and field point use. A field archery point is being screwed into a threaded bushing at the end of the arrow shaft.

The NFAA is dedicated to bowhunting, bowfishing, conservation, the preservation of large and small game animals, and to the promotion of a wide variety of competitions. The organization of the NFAA is structured to administer to the needs of the archers interested in these areas. The NFAA and NAA now have a working affiliation between the two organizations. (See Appendix B for the NFAA and NAA addresses.)

Shooting Equipment

The type of tackle that can or cannot be used by the field archer depends upon the style of shooting done. There are six styles in field archery: (1) freestyle, (2) freestyle limited, (3) barebow, (4) competitive bowhunter, (5) bowhunter freestyle, and (6) bowhunter freestyle limited. Compound, long, and recurve bows are all used in field archery. Table 5.5 summarizes some of the major differences between shooting styles and the use of sights, release aids, stabilizers, and nocking points. Other equipment differences also exist regarding broadheads, arrow rest, clicker usage, and other equipment.

Since most field archers are interested in bowhunting and/or bowfishing, the total weight of the arrow needs to approximate the arrow weight when it is fitted with the broadhead point. Practice with broadheads or shooting with them at field archery targets can be impractical because of the damage they inflict. Field points are made to match the heavy weight of the bowhunting broadheads used by the archer. A threaded bushing can be fitted into the arrow shaft. Field points and broadheads can be used interchangeably. A single set of arrows can be used for field archery practice and hunting if the weights are matched perfectly. This setup is shown in figure 5.12. The field points are much easier to use for most regular practices. Broadheads should be used for practice before hunting season and to tune the hunting bow.

Table 5.5   Field Archery Shooting Styles and Legal Equipment

Style	Sight(s)	Release Aid	Stabilizers	Nocking Point
Barebow	No	No	Yes	Yes
Freestyle	Yes	Yes	Yes	Yes
Freestyle Limited	Yes	No	Yes	Yes
Competitive Bowhunter	No	No	One	Yes
Freestyle Bowhunter (5 points & peep)	Yes	Yes	One	Yes
Freestyle Limited Bowhunter (5 points & peep)	Yes	No	One	Yes

Divisions of Competition

Age and sex divisions are established in field archery to provide equitable competition. In addition, the NFAA has a sophisticated handicapping system designed to be an equalizer for archers with different abilities. The divisions for competition plus the handicap system make competitions very interesting for all field archers.

The Adult Division is for men and women archers 18 years of age and older. The NFAA Junior Division is divided into three groups. The Young Adult Group is for archers 15 through 17 years of age. The Youth Group is for archers ages 12 through 14. Cub competition is for archers under 12 years of age. NFAA Junior archers shoot freestyle, freestyle limited, and barebow styles. A FITA Junior division is also provided for archers of both sexes under the age of 18 who shoot the FITA Recurve Styles of freestyle and barebow. There is also a Professional Division for men and women 18 years of age and over. All of these divisions of competition and the styles of shooting noted provide opportunities for competition at the sectional and national tournaments. To complete the range of NFAA age group competition, an additional division is added for archers 55 years of age and over at national tournaments. This is known as the Senior Division. The Senior Division is optional at sectional and state competitions.

In addition to these divisions of competition, the NFAA has a program to accommodate the needs and interests of young people under the age of 18 who shoot with compound bows. This activity is known as the NFAA Junior Bowhunter Program. It provides a special award system plus competition for junior compound shooters. It is designed to help interested and motivated young archers get into competitions at the state, sectional, and national levels. Guidance is also provided for young people who want to develop their bowhunting skills or who desire just to pursue the sport of field archery.

The Junior Bowhunter Program offers Indoor and Outdoor Field and Animal Rounds. These are the Freeman Bowhunter Round, Indoor Round, Animal Round, and Field Round. Achievement level scores for patches and awards are established for each of these rounds based on the shooting styles: (1) barebow, (2) freestyle limited, or (3) freestyle. What may or may not be used with these styles of shooting is outlined for you in table 5.5. The NFAA Junior Bowhunter Program helps the young archers get started in the sport correctly, and that is an important factor.

Official NFAA Rounds

The number of arrows shot, targets, shooting positions, rules, and scoring differ widely between field archery rounds. There are thirteen official NFAA Rounds. Eight of these are shot outdoors, while the remaining five are indoor rounds:

Outdoor

1. Field Round
2. NFAA Expert Field Round
3. Hunter Round
4. Animal Round
5. 15 Target "300" Field Round
6. 15 Target "300" Hunter Round
7. 15 Target "300" Animal Round
8. NFAA International Round

Indoor

1. NFAA Indoor Round
2. NFAA Indoor Championship Round
3. NFAA Freeman Round
4. Freeman Bowhunter Indoor Round
5. Flint Bowman Indoor Round

Generally, the target faces used for most of the outdoor rounds are 65, 50, 35, and 20 centimeters in diameter, based on the distances to be shot. Targets for the various rounds have different configurations, and the animal rounds use animal targets only. There are three-dimensional, life-size animal targets. These targets are placed in four diminishing size groups. Animals such as elk and moose are in the largest group, while ducks and jackrabbit targets are in the smallest group. The diversity of the outdoor rounds and their placement within the shooting unit help make field archery challenging and fun.

The indoor rounds have targets of various sizes and designs. They are 40, 35, 20, and 16 centimeters in diameter, depending upon the round. Animal targets may be used instead of the 40 centimeter target face in the Freeman Bowhunter Indoor Round. Twenty yards is the greatest distance shot in the first four indoor rounds listed above. Thirty yards is the greatest distance shot in the Flint Bowman Indoor Round. These distances make indoor shooting popular among field archers.

Awards

Any effective organization has a system to recognize the efforts of its members. The NFAA has a good awards system ranging from NFAA Membership Pins to the Compton Medal of Honor. The latter award is the most highly esteemed honor in all archery. The NFAA bowhunters gain recognition by qualifying for the following game awards: (1) Art Young Big Game Awards, (2) Art Young Small

Game Awards, (3) Bowhunter Pin, (4) Expert Bowhunter Pin, (5) Master Bowhunter Medal, and (6) the Diamond Buck Award for the largest deer based on antler measurements.

If a field archer telescopes an arrow shot during a round into the shaft of an arrow already lodged in the highest scoring area of a target, he or she is eligible for entry into the Fellowship of Robin Hood. And, on a less prestigious note, a field archer who commits an unwitting error or "boner" while bowhunting is eligible to enter The Order of the Bone! Recognition is also given in the NFAA Bowfisher Program to those archers taking the largest rough fish during the year. The NFAA Bowfisher Program is discussed in chapter 7.

Field archery, like other archery sports and activities, is a challenging and fulfilling endeavor. It can be enjoyed throughout a lifetime from "Cub" through "Senior" Division status.

Ski-Archery

Ski-archery (Ski-Arc) is a relatively new and developing archery sport. As a historical note, The First Annual United States Ski-Archery Championship was held at Park City, Utah, on January 16, 1993. The Second Annual National Ski-Arc National Championship and Novice Event was held in 1994 in the White Mountains at Bretton Woods, New Hampshire (figures 5.13 and 5.14). Skill development clinics for Ski-Arc are being held around the United States for archers interested in learning more about how to compete in this intriguing sport.

Ski-archery is a combination of archery and cross-country skiing much like the current Winter Olympic biathlon which combines cross-country skiing with rifle shooting. The Ski-Arc course for men is 12 kilometers in length—three 4 kilometer loops. The Women's and Junior (under 18 years of age) course covers 8 kilometers. This course has two 4 kilometer loops for the competitors to traverse.

The archers shoot four arrows from 18 meters following each 4 kilometers (2.48 miles) of cross-country skiing. The target faces are 16 centimeters for Olympic Bow and longbow shooters and 12 centimeters for compound bow archers. The second end of arrows is shot from the kneeling position. Bows are carried by the archers in a harness, and the arrows are kept at the shooting range. Winners are determined by combining the fastest skiing time with the best shooting accuracy. Awards are based on factors such as age, sex, and the type of bow one uses during the competition.

The challenges of Ski-Arc are numerous. First, as a winter sport, the weather conditions can be unpredictable for outdoor shooting and cross-country ski practice. The athletes must be ready to perform in all kinds of weather. Also, the courses can present unique conditioning problems in high altitude mountain environments, especially if the athlete resides at a low elevation. Furthermore, the cross-country skiing aspect of the competition requires the athlete to develop and maintain an excellent level of cardiovascular endurance (see training guidelines in chapter 8). Your level of cardiovascular endurance is measured by the

Figure 5.13
Starting line at the Second Annual Ski-Arc National Championship, 1994, held in the White Mountains at Bretton Woods, New Hampshire. (Courtesy Marcia Wyman, New England School of Archery, 109 School Street, Concord, NH 03301–2923.)

Figure 5.14
Shooting line at the Second Annual Ski-Arc National Championship in 1994. (Courtesy Marcia Wyman, New England School of Archery, 109 School Street, Concord, NH 03301–2923.)

maximal oxygen consumption test. You should be aware of the fact that the best maximal oxygen consumption values ever measured on human beings are from testing Olympic level cross-country skiers. So, the training for the skiing phase of ski-archery can be physiologically demanding.

The unique target archery shooting challenge in this sport comes at the end of each 4 kilometers when the archer must be absolutely steady in order to execute the skill to shoot the four arrows as accurately as possible. (In conventional target archery competition, keep in mind that the archer does not have to run 2½ miles as fast as possible immediately before addressing the target and shooting!) If the individual's level of performance-related fitness is not excellent, factors such as dyspnea (shortness of breath) and even small tremors in the antigravity muscle groups, shoulder girdle muscles, and bow arm musculature—described in chapter 8—will adversely influence archery accuracy. The shooting phase of Ski-Arc is more difficult than the Winter Olympic Biathlon where a rifle is used.

Since the Ski-Arc athlete must shoot with precision and ski the course as fast as possible in order to win, one can readily understand some of the demands inherent in this sport. Therein lies some of its challenge to the human spirit, potential values, and intrigue for competitors. The interest in Ski-Arc competition will gain momentum in forthcoming years due to all of these factors. Opportunities for competition will increase in time and include state, regional, national, and international levels. Ski-Arc could evolve into a Winter Olympic archery sport early in the twenty-first century.

Review

1. What are the full names of the two organizations for archers in the United States, and what are the titles of their official publications?
2. What is the bow weight restriction for a compound bow used in target archery competition? What equipment and tackle modifications are legal in target competition?
3. How does the NAA contribute to the development of archers for the Olympic Games?
4. How does a field archer qualify for the Fellowship of Robin Hood and The Order of the Bone?
5. What is the NAA dress code for tournament competitors?
6. By what process and by whom are archery teams chosen to represent the United States in national, world, and Olympic competitions?
7. During a round in target archery, what do several short blasts on the whistle by the Director of Shooting indicate?
8. Name the several types of competitive events for which the crossbow may be used.
9. Describe the differences between match and field shooting with crossbows.
10. How do target scoring values for clout shooting differ from target archery? Are there also differences in the tackle used for target archery and clout shooting?

11. What distances are attained in flight shooting with the various types of bows? What is the longest distance ever recorded for an arrow shot from any type of bow? How long would it take you to run that distance to retrieve the arrow?
12. Describe the feat performed at the 1992 Barcelona Olympic Games by a paralympic archer.
13. The current World Speed Record for Flight Archery is 588 feet per second. What arrow velocities are anticipated in the future?
14. How did the sport of clout shooting originate? How do target scoring values differ between clout and target shooting?
15. What are the six shooting styles used for competition by the NFAA?
16. Describe the sport of Ski-Arc, and on what does the archer's score depend?

Bowhunting

6

Bowhunting should be pursued AFTER you have developed a very good level of archery skill; a thorough knowledge of stalking; a genuine understanding of the habits of the animal being hunted; and cognizance of which shots should or should not be taken when a game animal is close enough for a shot. Leaving an animal such as an elk wounded in the field with an arrow stuck in his rump, for example, is an inexcusable act by an incompetent bowhunter! BE A RESPONSIBLE BOWHUNTER: STUDY, PRACTICE, AND LEARN ABOUT THE SPORT BEFORE YOU EVER SET FOOT IN THE FIELD TO ACTUALLY BOWHUNT.

The sport of bowhunting has become increasingly popular in the last few years. Its gain in popularity is documented by the escalating numbers of archery hunters who register for licenses and permits with the official wildlife agencies located in each state (see Appendix A). According to *Archery Business,* it is estimated that there are three million licensed bowhunters in the United States. That indicates a significant increase in bowhunters over the past decade.

Let's look at a historical overview of deer bowhunting data from the Missouri Department of Conservation. The trend in Missouri tends to typify the growth in this sport elsewhere in the United States. Permit sales for bowhunting for deer was initiated in 1946. *Seventy-three permits were sold in 1946, but no deer were harvested.* In fact, although permits were sold each year, only 8 deer were shot by bowhunters in Missouri over an eight year period from 1946 through 1953! By 1956, permit sales had risen to 2,075 and 33 deer were shot by archers that year. After another decade passed, permit sales had increased to 11,878 with 458 deer being harvested statewide in 1966. The year 1976 saw a deer harvest in Missouri of 1,973 with 31,281 bowhunters in the field. Permit sales more than doubled by 1986 with 69,265 sold, and 5,832 deer were harvested by bowhunters. This upward trend for bowhunting continues in Missouri. *Bowhunters with permits to hunt for deer in Missouri in 1994 totaled 97,441, and 16,848 deer were harvested!* That means only 17 percent of the bowhunters with permits were able to harvest a deer. Bowhunting is popular, but it is not an easy sport.

A lottery system for permits has had to be established in some states due to the popularity of bowhunting. This allows state wildlife agencies to control the amount of game animals harvested in each area of the state. Another trend of the future may also be a state requirement that each bowhunter must first obtain a Bowhunter Education Card before he or she is allowed to hunt. This will be more than the ordinary hunter education card. Attaining a Bowhunter Education Card would also require testing to prove that the bowhunter is knowledgeable and skilled in the sport. If that trend is followed in popular bowhunting states, it would minimize the number of incompetent bowhunters who seek game. It also has the potential of reducing the number of wounded animals that are not recovered after they are shot by bowhunters. Some states are now requiring bowhunters to have a Bowhunter Education Card.

There are numerous reasons given by hunters for using the bow and arrow as their primary hunting weapons. One of the most common is that the inherent challenge of bowhunting has rewards that cannot be met by any other hunting method. The bowhunter is limited to close shooting ranges. Furthermore, the animal's habits and the environment must be known for the hunter to be successful. Stalking is an integral part of bowhunting. Seasons set by state game and fish departments are generally longer for archery than for firearms. This gives the archer a chance for more time in the field. Also, there is a wider variety of small and large game animals that can be harvested, and this makes the sport more attractive than gun hunting. Finally, many archers indicate that they prefer the relatively uncrowded conditions found in the field during the bowhunting seasons. Unfortunate hunting accidents are not likely to occur during bowhunting seasons; however, they are fairly common during firearm seasons.

There are over thirty thousand members and seven hundred clubs associated with the International Bowhunting Organization (IBO). The address and phone number are listed in Appendix B for readers interested in learning more about the activities, purposes, and functions of the IBO. This not-for-profit organization was formed in 1984: "To support, foster, and promote the sport of bowhunting." The official publication of the IBO is *Bowhunting World* magazine.

With more people participating in bowhunting, there has been a corresponding increase in the refinements of archery tackle. Competition between the archery manufacturers has resulted in a wider selection of fine bowhunting equipment. With the large number of specialized hunting products on the market, the process of selecting equipment can become a confusing task. It is necessary to have a basic understanding of what constitutes good bowhunting tackle. That will help in making the correct purchasing decisions. It is recommended that bowhunting tackle be purchased from a professional archery tackle shop where people understand how to accurately match bows to arrows and archery tackle to the needs of the bowhunter.

With modifications, good bowhunting tackle can also be used for some other archery sports. As examples, bowhunting tackle can be modified for use in field archery and bowfishing. The principles for purchasing bowhunting tackle are almost the same as those for buying target archery tackle discussed in chapter 3. There are, however, major differences between target archery and bowhunting tackle. *The individual who wants to participate in bowhunting exclusively should purchase tackle designed specifically for bowhunting purposes.*

Hunting Bows

Modern hunting bows are different from bows wielded by the ancient people of Europe or the bows used by American Indians in the last few centuries. Bows that have provided food and protected primitive people for centuries look like toys when compared to current bowhunting tackle. Though the primitive hunting bows

Figure 6.1
A hunting compound crossbow camouflaged and ready for use with a broadhead on the bolt.
(Courtesy Precision Shooting Equipment, 2727 N. Fairview Ave., Tucson, AZ 85705)

were not as efficient, the individuals who used them possessed excellent hunting skills. Their very survival attests to that fact. Those people had a key motivational factor that most bowhunters today do not have—HUNGER!

Bows used commonly for modern hunting include the crossbow, straight bow (longbow), recurve, and compound bow. Each step in the progression from longbow to compound bow represents an improvement in the ability of a bow to transfer its potential energy into kinetic energy to project the arrow. While it is virtually impossible to make a bow that is 100 percent energy efficient, the best designs of today's bows are reaching an energy storage efficiency in the range of 80 to 84 percent.

Crossbows

The crossbow is one of the legendary weapons of archery. The saga of *Wilhelm Tell* helped romanticize the crossbow. Most people have read about crossbows, but they have never seen or held one. A quality crossbow camouflaged for bowhunting is shown in figure 6.1.

The use of the crossbow as a legal hunting weapon has gained momentum in the past several years. Some states now allow its use for a few of the larger game animals as well as for the so-called "varmint critters" (coyote, bobcat, fox, etc.) and bird hunting. As with recurve and compound bows, specific criteria are established by state game and fish commissions for hunting with the crossbow. They specify the poundage of the crossbow, length of the bolt, and size of the broadhead. In Arizona, for example, a hunting crossbow must have a minimum draw weight of 125 pounds and shoot at least a 16-inch bolt. The bolt must be tipped with a broadhead that has a metal cutting edge of at least ⅞ of an inch in width.

If you are interested in bowhunting with the crossbow, keep in mind that state regulations vary regarding the legal use of this weapon. You must contact

Figure 6.2
A state-of-the-art modern longbow designed for use by bowhunters interested in retaining more sport in bowhunting. (Courtesy Black Widow Custom Bows, Inc., 1201 Eaglecrest, P.O. Box 2100, Nixa, MO 65714)

the appropriate wildlife agency in the state where you wish to hunt *prior* to going into the field. They will supply you with the latest rules and regulations pertaining to crossbow hunting. (See Appendix A.)

The crossbow has gone through several design changes in recent years. The newer generation of crossbows of the type shown in figure 6.1 use the same mechanical devices as compound cam bows for increasing arrow velocity. They also use modern construction materials that can withstand the added stresses on the bow limbs. These factors make the crossbow highly efficient for use in both target archery and bowhunting.

Longbows

Longbows can be used for hunting, however they are currently used only on a limited basis. The reason lies in the fact that they are not as mechanically efficient as recurve and compound bows. The differences between these bows were discussed in chapter 3. The limitations of the longbow, however, are viewed as advantages by some bowhunters who value true sport and adventure in their hunting.

If you use a longbow for hunting, the emphasis must be placed on the terms *hunting* and *sport*. The bowhunter who uses the longbow must be an excellent stalker and hunter with considerable knowledge of the game being sought. Some legendary archers from the past such as Howard Hill, Dr. Saxton Pope, and Art Young used the longbow effectively in the field. It can still be done today. If you desire "true sport" while bowhunting, the longbow may be the bow for you.

Figure 6.3

A take-down recurve hunting bow equipped with a covered bow quiver, brush buttons, and string silencers. (Courtesy Black Widow Custom Bows, Inc., 1201 Eaglecrest, P.O. Box 2100, Nixa, MO 65714)

Because the longbow places more demands and challenges on the human being as a hunter, some bowhunters are returning to it as the bow of choice for the hunt. As a result, some bow manufacturers have designed and are now producing a modern and more efficient type of longbow for bowhunting as can be seen in figure 6.2.

Recurve Bows

Recurve design principles have been known by bowyers for a long time, but recurve bow efficiency was not fully realized until modern materials were developed. Plastics and adhesives have made it possible to laminate layers of material that will remain intact under the stresses that a bow is exposed to during the shooting process. The tips of a working recurve bow will point away from the archer when the bow is unstrung. However, when the bow is braced, the tips are pulled back and will usually point upwards with the string contacting the belly of the bow for at least two inches. That adds to the leverage and energy potential of the bow. If the string does not contact the bow in this manner, the bow will not work to its best mechanical advantage. It will perform like a longbow. A take-down recurve hunting bow is shown in figure 6.3. The bow is equipped with a covered bow quiver, brush buttons, and string silencers.

The conventional recurve bow will stack its draw weight as the string is drawn to the anchor point. The peak weight of the bow increases during the draw, and there is added pressure on the drawing hand fingers. (Release aids do minimize this problem, and they are legal in bow hunting. See figures 6.13, 6.14, and 6.16.) You hold the complete bow weight for your arrow length at anchor point when using a recurve bow. This can be a problem for some people. (That is one of the major differences between recurve and compound bows, and it is one factor that motivated H. W. Allen to invent the compound bow.) Most people begin with draw weights that they can handle comfortably and then grow into higher poundage equipment. It makes no sense to purchase a bow that is too heavy in terms of bow weight. This will only cause bad habits resulting in accuracy and technique errors, and learned shooting problems are difficult to unlearn.

Famous bowhunters such as Fred Bear, Doug Kittredge, and Jim Dougherty used the recurve bow extensively in years past and added to its popularity. Recurve bows in the hands of expert archers like these have taken the largest and most dangerous animals found in the world. The recurve bow was the primary choice of most bowhunters until the mid-1970s. Compound bows are currently the bows of choice for most bowhunters. However, some bowhunters surveyed indicated that they were returning to the recurve bow after using compound bows for several years. The general observation was that the recurve bow made hunting more of a sport than using the compound bow, especially on smaller game animals. Some expert bowhunters who are using the recurve bow again believe that the modern compound bows are being built with too many "mechanical gadgets" on them. That takes some of the sport out of the hunt.

Compound Bows

As noted, the compound bow is by far the most popular hunting tool used by modern bowhunters. A check of recent entries into the Pope and Young Records for trophy class animals shows that most were taken by this type of bow. The two-wheeled compound bow seems to be the most popular. An example of a two-wheeled bow and the terminology for the compound bow are shown in figure 6.4.

As discussed in chapter 2, the compound bow was invented in January, 1966, by H. W. Allen of Billings, Missouri. He wanted to make a more efficient bow for hunting that would shoot arrows at a higher velocity, reduce "stacking," and minimize bow weight held by the archer at full draw. One of his early models is shown in figure 6.5. The reader can gain some understanding of the engineering evolution of the compound bow by comparing and contrasting figure 2.11, which shows the original Allen Bow (now housed in the Smithsonian Institution), with other compound bows shown in this chapter and on today's market.

The compound bow generates greater foot-pounds of energy than composite bows due primarily to its eccentric pulley system which can be seen on the bows in figures 6.4 and 6.5. The mechanical principles utilized by these pulleys allow peak bow-weight poundage at mid-draw. This effect has two advantages: (1) There is no stacking effect in a compound bow at full draw. The peak poundage is at mid-draw, and (2) At release, the poundage increases to peak, and this gives a major increase in foot-pounds of energy for application to the arrow. Arrow velocity is increased.

The compound bow, when drawn, has a "peak" weight and a "let-off" weight. In most cases, compound bows, because of their eccentric wheel design, will have a

Figure 6.4
A two-wheeled compound bow with bow terminology. (Courtesy Precision Shooting Equipment, 2727 N. Fairview Ave., Tucson, AZ 85705)

Figure 6.5
An early model (c. 1970) of the Allen Compound Bow. (Courtesy of Allen Archery, 201 Washington Street, Billings, MO 65610)

"let-off" weight of approximately 30 to 65 percent. This means, for example, that if you shoot a 60-pound compound bow with a 65 percent "let-off" factor, the actual weight held on the fingers at full draw will be 21 pounds. This has its advantages in a situation, for example, where the hunter must hold in a fully drawn position at the anchor point for a prolonged period of time waiting for the best shot. Due to advanced engineering, some of the compound bow manufacturers now have bows available with let-off weights approaching 80 percent.

The newer cam-wheel compounds have a change in wheel designs. Instead of a round wheel at the tip, there is a cam-shaped device. These bows generally produce faster arrow velocities than eccentric compounds and recurves of the same bow weight. The advantage in this faster cam-type bow lies in the arrow trajectory. When arrow velocity is higher, the amount of arrow drop in flight is less. This means that your "margin for error," due to arrow drop, is decreased. The estimation of distances at close ranges is not as crucial with a cam compound as it is with a recurve bow. An error of 5 yards in estimating distances of 30 yards or less will usually result in a kill shot. This same judgment error with a longbow, recurve, or compound bow of lower arrow velocity may result in a missed shot or a wounded animal.

There has been a shift by compound bow manufacturers in recent years from using magnesium for the bow risers to using aluminum. Aluminum tends to be more sensitive than cast magnesium when used in these bows. That feature can mean better accuracy when the compound bow is used by a competent bowhunter. Progress in the engineering, research, and development of new bow designs and materials is an ongoing process by archery manufacturing companies. Those processes hold exciting prospects for the bowhunter.

Bow Weight

Hunting bows have higher draw weights than their target bow counterparts. While draw weights used for target bows are set by personal preference, the *minimum draw weights* for bowhunting are established by state game and fish departments. Generally, a bowhunter must use a minimum bow weight of 40 pounds. This ensures that arrow penetration is sufficient for killing game. Most experienced archers use higher draw weights than this for hunting. It is recommended that bow weights of 45 to 60 pounds be used on game animals up to the size of deer, and bow weights ranging from 60 to 80 pounds be used for larger game animals such as elk, bear, and moose.

Bowhunters, like target archers, need to select and shoot bows they can handle. The choice of bow weight will depend on several things: (1) bowhunting experience, (2) muscular strength, (3) the type of game you plan to hunt, and (4) state game laws. When selecting a hunting bow, you should choose the heaviest weight you can handle with ease and comfort for several consecutive shots. If you are comfortable with a 40-pound bow, then that is the bow you should shoot. Do not make the common mistake of purchasing a bow that has excessive poundage for your strength level. It will be especially difficult to shoot when you are tired and cold out on the hunt. Start with a lighter bow and work up as you become stronger and more experienced. Use the conditioning guidelines outlined in chapter 8 for developing your strength and endurance.

The Archery Manufacturers Organization (AMO) recommends for personal safety purposes that people who use compound bow weights heavier than 60 pounds with draw lengths longer than 30 inches should utilize arrows heavier than 6 grains per pound of peak bow weight. Those who use compound bow weights lighter than 60 pounds and draw lengths shorter than 30 inches can use arrows lighter than 6 grains per pound of peak bow weight. (Total arrow weight includes the combined shaft weight, point and insert weights, and the weight of fletching plus the nock.) These recommendations were made because bowhunters tend to overstress their compound bows in an attempt to increase arrow velocity. That is a safety problem! The AMO considers the maximum safe arrow velocity for compound bows under these guidelines to be *270 feet per second.* Keep these facts in mind when purchasing bowhunting tackle.

Bow Length

The length of the bow for hunting is a very important consideration. Some archers believe that a short bow length is most desirable in the hunting situation. Their argument usually centers around the fact that the shorter bow is less cumbersome in heavily wooded and foliaged areas. This may be true, but how many times does a good bowhunter confine himself or herself to hunting in heavy brush? In these circumstances, it is virtually impossible to shoot accurately with any length bow. The arrow will strike limbs or leaves. As a result, the arrow will not find its mark because of deflections and loss of velocity.

A more important reason for not using a shorter bow is the sharp angle created for the archer against the bowstring and arrow. The angle at the nocking point tends to compress the fingers of the bowstring hand so tightly that a smooth release is difficult when using the conventional three-finger grip. A longer bow, 64 inches, has longer limbs and a longer bowstring; consequently, the angle created at the nocking area at full draw is greater than the same angle for a shorter bow. This allows a smoother release when using the traditional three-finger grip with a recurve bow.

The use of release devices is legal in bowhunting, and this negates some of the argument for greater bow length related to finger release techniques. The fact remains, however, that the most common and best lengths for hunting bows range from 58 to 64 inches.

Hunting Arrows

The arrow is the single most important piece of tackle when the bowhunter considers accuracy. Many beginning bowhunters make the mistake of purchasing a good bow and then trying to shoot arrows that are not matched specifically for the bow. This only leads to frustration as shots are missed because of inconsistent arrow flight. Most beginners will do better by starting with a lower quality bow and shooting matched aluminum or graphite arrows than they will with a top-of-the-line bow shooting a quiver full of arrows that have different fletching, spines, broadheads, and weights. Exact matching of arrows to each other and to the bow that will shoot them is essential for any type of bowhunting success.

The fiberglass arrow became popular when it came on the market years ago because it offered improvements over the older, wooden arrow shafts. Aluminum and graphite arrows are now being produced, and they are far superior to any fiberglass arrows one can purchase for bowhunting. *Very few bowhunters use fiberglass arrows today. Aluminum has been a very popular material used for years in making hunting arrows, but carbon arrows are also now used by many bowhunters.* It is recommended that the serious bowhunter look at both types of arrow shafts when purchasing new hunting arrows. This should include shooting arrows made of both materials and equipped with your broadheads from your own hunting bow. The arrow material that gives you the best accuracy should be the purchase choice. Most professional archery shops have a target range available where you can use tackle before purchase, and that is highly recommended.

Bowhunters choose aluminum over wood or fiberglass because it offers excellent accuracy. This is accomplished because aluminum and aluminum-carbon arrows are aerodynamically sound and can be matched exactly for such factors as spine, shaft weight, length, shaft size, peak bow weight, straightness, and other variables related to your specific shooting style and other tackle.

Aluminum arrows can be purchased to match any type of bow or bow weight. The manufacturers have developed charts to assist you with arrow selection using the variables of draw length, bow type (recurve or compound), bow weight, and let-off. These shafts are made of high strength tubular aluminum that comes in different diameters and wall thicknesses. By varying the diameter and wall thickness of a shaft, different spines can be obtained. (Aluminum shafts usually have four numbers imprinted on them that indicate the diameter and wall thickness. For example, an aluminum arrow that has the number 2216 tells you that the shaft diameter is 22/64ths of an inch with wall thickness 0.016 of an inch.) In most cases, the bowhunter will have several shaft sizes to choose from when using any particular bow weight.

Archers are so concerned with accuracy that most do not mind the extra cost of purchasing aluminum or graphite arrows. One of the major annoyances is that, unlike fiberglass, aluminum shafts often bend when they deflect off a hard object. If the bend is not too drastic or close to either end of the shaft, the arrow can be straightened by using an arrow straightener. Most archery pro shops have this tool and will straighten arrows for a minimal charge. Many serious bowhunters, who use aluminum or aluminum-carbon shafts, will invest in a precision arrow straightener. This provides the convenience of being able to straighten bent arrows in the field or at home. Also, an arrow straightener will pay for itself if a person does much field practice or bowhunting.

The hunting arrow used while shooting a crossbow is known as a *bolt* (fig. 6.1). Bolts are shorter than regular hunting arrows, but they are usually shot at much higher draw weights. This is evident when looking at the minimum allowable draw weights used for hunting. Most states set *minimum draw weights* for recurve and compound bows at 40 pounds as compared to crossbow minimums of 125 pounds. The rationale for setting the higher draw weights for crossbows lies in the relationship between the speed of the bolt and its weight. A lighter projectile (crossbow bolt) shot at a higher velocity should penetrate as well as a heavier object shot at a slower speed. Here again, the concern is for good arrow penetration so a properly placed shot will result in a successful kill—not a wounded animal!

Arrow Fletching

Fletching material is generally made of either turkey feathers or plastic vanes. Most hunters choose the plastic variety simply because they are more durable and re-silient in poor weather conditions. A plastic vane subjected to a rainstorm will continue to the target with good accuracy. Also, plastic vanes do not make as much noise during arrow flight. This reduces the probability of "spooking" the animal during the critical moment between arrow release and impact.

Turkey feathers are still used by bowhunters who favor a natural material over a synthetic substitute. Some people claim that shooting turkey-fletched shafts will give a faster arrow flight and flatter trajectory due to better clearance from the bow. The chief drawbacks to using turkey fletching are that moisture affects them, and they do not wear as well as plastic vanes. Wet turkey feathers will alter the flight of the arrow.

Another consideration in dealing with arrow fletching is the length. In most cases, the fletching used for hunting is longer than that used for target archery shafts. This is due to the differences in the total weight of the arrow. Since a hunting arrow is heavier due to its broadhead point, it needs longer fletching to stabilize it during flight. Fletching used for hunting arrows range from 4 inches to 5½ inches in length, depending on the number of vanes and total weight of the arrow. Most hunters experiment with these factors to determine which combinations work best for them. (See fig. 3.3.)

The number of vanes placed on an arrow shaft has aroused considerable debate among archers. Some individuals prefer a three-vaned arrow, while others like four vanes. The proponents of the three-vaned arrows claim that this arrangement results in more efficient arrow stabilization during flight. An arrow that utilizes three vanes usually has two set at 120 degrees and the other at 90 degrees out from the bow. The odd vane is called the *cock feather* and is usually of a different color. When nocking an arrow to the string, it is essential to make sure that the cock, or index feather, is facing out; otherwise it can brush against the arrow rest or riser section of the bow and throw the shot off. Hunters who use the four-vaned shafts usually do so because they do not want to have to concern themselves with making sure that the cock feather is pointing outward before taking a shot. This is an advantage in a situation where the bowhunter does not want to drop the eyes from the target in order to nock an arrow. The four-vaned arrows are glued to the shaft at 75-degree and 105-degree angles.

There are several other types of fletching used by bowhunters. One of the most common is the flu-flu. A flu-flu (fig. 3.3) utilizes oversized fletching material in order to create wind resistance and shorten the arrow's flight distance due to drag resistance. This makes them effective at close ranges, but their velocity drops off very fast as distance increases. Bowhunters use these arrows on small animals such as squirrels where shots are taken at distances of under 20 yards. A missed shot at a tree squirrel with normal fletching usually results in a lost arrow. The chance of arrow recovery with flu-flu fletch is much greater.

Vanes are glued to the shaft in two ways: helical and straight. It is recommended that hunting arrows use the helical fletching because it helps to increase the velocity of the spin of the arrow around the longitudinal axis of the shaft. That helps stabilize the heavier hunting arrow in flight.

Figure 6.6
A Navajo Indian and his bowhunting tackle.
(From E. G. Heath, *The Grey Goose Wing*)

Figure 6.7
Indian arrow and spear points from the collection of Loyd Howell. These artifacts were found in Clark County near Wyaconda, Missouri.

Just as with all other aspects of archery, the type of material, length, weight, and number of vanes used on the arrow shafts should match precisely. Mismatching any of these can cause accuracy problems not directly related to the shooting ability of the bowhunter.

Bowhunting Points Past and Present

Let us digress and evaluate some of the bowhunting tackle of the American Indian. These people were highly successful hunters. Their survival over thousands of years in wilderness and hostile environments is evidence of their skill. Satisfying hunger as well as obtaining skins and furs for clothing and shelter were the major motivating factors for developing bowhunting skills. Protection against human enemies and predators were also significant reasons why the Indians worked at maintaining a high level of archery skill. The art of tackle making was passed from generation to generation. An Indian child learned archery skills at a very young age as an integral aspect of play. As seen in figure 6.7, some of the tackle made by adult Indians was modified to accommodate the skill development of their children.

Figure 6.8
Popular bowhunting broadheads. (Courtesy Precision Shooting Equipment, 2727 N. Fairview Ave., Tucson, AZ 85705)

Figure 6.9
Close-up view of a modern three-bladed insert type of broadhead. Broadheads must be RAZOR SHARP!

The Navajo Indian drawing his bow in figure 6.6 would have had less trouble obtaining game if he and other Indians had had bows like those shown in figures 6.3 and 6.4. Broadheads like those shown in figures 6.8 and 6.9 instead of the Indian arrowheads seen in figure 6.7 would have also contributed more game to the tribe for consumption. The outcomes of tribal wars also would have been different if one tribe had had modern tackle and the competing tribe depended upon the type of tackle shown in figure 6.6.

The Navajo Indians, as one example, developed effective composite bows made with a backing of layers of animal tendons or sinew. By using this type of connective tissue, the strength and durability of their bows were increased. Tendon has a tensile strength value of 20 kilograms per square millimeter, which is approximately four times greater than using wood only. The Apache Indians, in contrast, preferred to use green mulberry branches to form their single and double arc bows. These were allowed to dry into the desired shape. The single arc self bow, longbow, design was preferred by the Apache. The Apache discovered that it was easier to brace and draw arrows from a single rather than a double arc bow. The use of sinew was also common among Indian bowyers in the construction of bowstrings.

The development of the composite bow probably evolved by trial and error over several centuries in the United States by Indian bowyers. American Indians had no way to know that sophisticated composite bows had been developed centuries before by other bowyers elsewhere in the world.

The arrowheads, or points, used by American Indians differ appreciably from those used by contemporary bowhunters. Metal points were made when that material became available, but stone was the material of choice for centuries. Stone Indian points were made primarily from white flint. However, some wooden arrows used for hunting were simply sharpened to a point. It is interesting to note that the Apache arrow makers also designed a four-crosspiece point for bird hunting analogous to the contemporary bird point (fig. 6.11). The Navajo and Apache Indians mounted their arrow points on shafts made either of cane or desert broom (*Baccharis sarothroides*). Those arrow shaft materials are very inefficient in contrast to the sophisticated graphite and aluminum alloys used by archery manufacturers today. The Indian's favorite fletching came from the red-tailed hawk, but they also used feathers from doves, quails, flickers, and turkeys.

If the reader takes time to compare and contrast figure 6.7 with figures 6.8 and 6.9, the differences between Indian and modern hunting points will immediately become apparent. Figures 6.8 and 6.9 show popular broadhead points used by contemporary bowhunters.

Figure 6.7 features Indian arrow and spear points that were found in the northeast corner of Missouri by Loyd Howell. Indian tribes inhabited the Clark County area of Missouri for hundreds of years prior to the nineteenth century. Some individuals would assume that all of the points shown in figure 6.7 are arrowheads, but that is not the case. The point on the extreme right in figure 6.7 and the point on the extreme right of the upper row are both spear points. The large, 4¾-inch-long "beaver tail" point on the right side of the picture was used on a shaft of a spear. The point in the upper right of the figure is 3¼ inches in length.

The remaining points in figure 6.7 are arrow points ranging in length from ¾ inch to 3 inches. These were attached to the ends of wooden arrow shafts. The small, ¾-inch-long arrow point, in the lower row on the left side, is called a *bird point*. One theory about bird points specifies that they were made and used by smaller children who used them with light pulling bows and shot them at birds. In other words, these small points may have been functional toys used by Indian children learning to shoot the bow and arrow.

The arrow without a notch in the upper row of figure 6.7 is a war point. These arrows were shot into enemies. When the shaft was pulled, the war point (2½ inches in length) remained within the body of the individual who was shot. If the penetration by the arrow itself failed to kill the individual who was hit, the infection

Figure 6.10
Blunt bowhunting points used for killing smaller game animals with impact force.

caused by having this large foreign object in the body would ultimately be the cause of death. There were no medical corpsmen, antibiotics, or M.A.S.H. units with the Indians to help take care of their wounds!

Today, bowhunting points or broadheads are designed in all shapes and sizes, depending on the intended purpose. Many bowhunters incorporate inserts with their arrows, thus allowing them to change a point by simply screwing one out and putting another point in its place, as seen in figure 5.12. There are several devices on the market for changing and inserting points.

Field tips commonly used in field archery are utilized for bowhunting practice and on some small game animals. They come in various weights and shapes. Most bowhunters try to match the weight of their field tips to the weight of their broadheads in order to make target practice a more functional exercise. Field tips are much easier on target faces and mats. It is best to practice with tips that are of the same weight as your broadheads because it makes the aiming process more functional.

Blunts, as seen in figure 6.10, are favorite tips for bowhunting for small game. They are made of rubber or metal, and usually slip on or screw into an insert on the arrow shaft. These tips kill by impact force. As a result, they do not destroy edible meat on the small animal. (A broadhead such as the one in figure 6.9 does incredible damage to an animal the size of a rabbit or squirrel!) The shocking power of a blunted arrow is usually enough to cause death instantaneously to smaller game animals.

There are other types of arrow points, manufactured or homemade, used for bagging small game. Some incorporate field tips that have a piece of wire brazed through them, others use spring wire protruding in four directions. These tips also work on force of impact and are efficient for bagging small game. Another reason for using wire protruding points is that they usually snag on brush and do not travel far from the intended target. This makes them easier to locate when the animal is missed.

Figure 6.11
Bowhunting for birds requires a special arrow point with wire loops. These loops increase the probability of hitting the bird in flight. (Courtesy *Bow and Arrow Magazine*)

Bowhunters who try to shoot very elusive birds have developed a tip that has four wide loops of wire. A loop can clip a bird in flight. By looping the wire, a wider circumference is created in which the bird can be hit as the arrow passes. A direct hit is not necessary to bring down the bird with this kind of tip (fig. 6.11). (Other tackle adaptations and practice techniques for bowhunting for pheasant and quail will be discussed later in this chapter.) A wire loop impacting with a bird's wing in flight will usually cause it to drop to the ground. As noted, the Apache used a similar design to bring down birds in flight.

Broadheads are the only legal hunting points that can be used on large game species. Most state game and fish departments require broadheads to be at least ⅞ of an inch in width and have metal cutting edges. The key to the broadhead's effectiveness is its *sharpness*. SINCE A BROADHEAD KILLS BY HEMORRHAGING, IT IS ABSOLUTELY ESSENTIAL THAT THE CUTTING EDGE BE KEPT RAZOR SHARP (fig. 6.9).

It is important to remember that penetration by a dull arrow point will not always kill a large animal. The blood vessels will not be lacerated enough to allow a steady, unobstructed blood flow. The dull arrow point will tear tissue instead of making a surgical type of laceration. A torn blood vessel's smooth internal musculature will constrict to act as its own protective mechanism against hemorrhage. The bowhunter attempting to kill his prey does not want this to occur. The animal struck in this fashion tends to continue moving and become lost to the bowhunter. The American Indian had the problem of dull arrow points while bowhunting with the type of tackle shown in figures 6.6 and 6.7. However, the

American Indian was better at trailing and finding the stricken animal in various types of terrain and under all kinds of weather conditions. He also was not under the same time constraints as modern bowhunters, for example, vacation's over and there is a pressing need to get back to the job. Bowhunting for food and clothing was a major part of the Indian's way-of-life!

A bowhunter shooting a dull arrow must strike the heart or lungs most of the time to kill the game animal. This is not necessarily true if a razor-sharp arrow is used. Such a hit in a large muscle group, for example, will clearly sever arteries, veins, capillaries, and other blood vessels in the area. This will cause hemorrhage sufficient and fast enough to result in death rather quickly. The bowhunter merely waits a while and then follows the trail of blood from the stricken animal to where it collapses from asphyxiation.

One way to tell a novice from a serious bowhunter is by the sharpness of the latter's broadheads. Knowledgeable bowhunters will not step into the woods with broadheads they could not shave with! It is the responsibility of the hunter to see that this critical factor is not overlooked.

There are two basic types of broadheads, the ones that need to be hand sharpened and the ones that use razor blade inserts. If you do not know how to hone an edge to razor sharpness, it is recommended that the insert type be used so you will be assured of effective cutting edges (fig. 6.9).

If you prefer to hand sharpen your broadheads but have had difficulty getting the desired edge, the following suggestion is one way to make the task easier. The tools needed for this sharpening job include: two files, one cowhide strop, and some jeweler's rouge. The strop is made from a piece of leather, rough side out, securely glued to a 10- to 12-inch piece of 2 × 4 board by means of contact cement. The sharpening process is started by putting a rough edge on the broadhead with a 10-inch mill bastard file. Once the edge is formed and the tip chiseled, it is reworked lightly with an 8-inch mill bastard file. The final step puts the desired cutting edge on the broadhead. It consists of putting jeweler's rouge on the cowhide strop and moving the edge away in long strokes. This is repeated until the edge is sharp enough to shave with. Sharpening your blades does add a personal touch to the bowhunting experience.

There are many quality broadheads on the market today, and most of them are more than adequate for bringing down game as long as they are sharp and hit a vital area. It is recommended that you talk to as many experienced bowhunters as possible to learn their preferences before making your first choice.

Finally, transporting and storage of bows and arrows when they are not in use is very important. Putting your tackle in cases designed for those purposes as seen in figure 6.12 is highly recommended. There are cases designed specifically for longbows, take-down recurves, one-piece recurves, and arrows. Utilization of these cases eliminates loss and damage to bows and arrows when moving from place to place or when storing them between bowhunting practice sessions and seasons. This beats hanging the bowhunting tackle on racks in closets or trucks. Prior to placing each piece of tackle into its case, it should be inspected

Figure 6.12
Proper care and storage of bowhunting tackle when not in use is very important. Cases are available for longbows, take-down recurves, one-piece recurves, and arrows. (Courtesy Black Widow Custom Bows, Inc., 1201 Eaglecrest, P.O. Box 2100, Nixa, MO 65714)

and cleaned thoroughly. Damaged items should be repaired or replaced. If that procedure is followed, your tackle will be ready for use the next time you are ready to practice or bowhunt.

Bowhunting Accessories

A quick look into any well-stocked archery pro shop will reveal many different devices available to bowhunters to improve their chances of a successful hunt. Some of these accessories can be used for both bowhunting and target archery. Devices discussed in chapter 3, such as finger tabs, arm guards, and arrow rests, fall into this category. Bowhunters, however, need some additional tackle specifically for hunting. This includes such items as special quivers, mechanical releases, string silencers, overdraw systems, and hunting sights.

The arrow quiver is one of the most necessary accessories in terms of safety and convenience. There are three common quivers in use today: (1) the hip quiver, (2) the shoulder quiver, and (3) the bow quiver. The hip and shoulder quivers are sometimes used during field practice where the archer does not have to be concerned with brush or other obstacles. *The bow quiver is the most popular and recommended method of carrying arrows in a hunting situation* (fig. 6.3). It is attached directly to the bow by means of springs or screws. Bow quivers come in different models capable of carrying

Figure 6.13
A release device (c. 1970) for use with lighter bow weights. This release utilizes a strap and thumb pressure. (Courtesy Wilson Brothers, Route 1, Elkland, MO 65644)

Figure 6.14
The Allen Hunting Release designed for use with compound bows. (Courtesy Allen Archery, 201 Washington Street, Billings, MO 65610)

from four to sixteen arrows. Each individual should decide what capacity quiver will fit his or her needs. If you are going to use a bow quiver during the hunt, be certain to mount it on your bow for use during practice sessions.

The single most important safety consideration for a bow quiver is that the broadheads be covered and tightly secured. Some of the early clip-on bow quivers did not shield the broadheads. As a result, serious accidents occurred when archers inadvertently touched these razor-sharp points while reaching for an arrow. Falling on an uncovered bow quiver or one of your broadheads could be fatal while in the field. They are designed to cause hemorrhage in all animals including humans!

Release aids are used by some bowhunters to eliminate elements of human error caused by the fingers when releasing the arrow. These are designed in many shapes and have evolved through several steps. Some of the first releases were made of a piece of rope or strap, which was wrapped around the string and held with pressure from the thumb (fig. 6.13). These were very useful on recurve bows of lower draw weights, but they are difficult to handle on higher weighted compound and recurve bows. Other releases, like the one in figure 6.14, were developed to handle this problem.

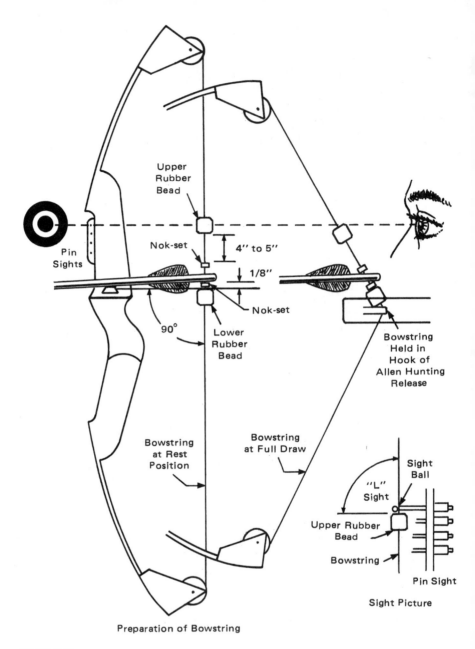

Upper
Rubber
Bead

Nok-set

4″ to 5″

1/8″

Nok-set

Pin
Sights

90°

Lower
Rubber
Bead

Bowstring
Held in
Hook of
Allen Hunting
Release

Bowstring
at Rest
Position

Bowstring
at Full Draw

"L"
Sight

Sight
Ball

Upper Rubber
Bead

Bowstring

Pin Sight

Sight Picture

Preparation of Bowstring

Figure 6.15
Aiming and using the Allen Hunting Release with a compound bow. (Courtesy Allen Archery, 201 Washington Street, Billings, MO 65610)

Figure 6.16
A release aid (c. 1990) designed for use with heavier compound bows. (Courtesy Precision Shooting Equipment, 2727 N. Fairview Ave., Tucson, AZ 85705)

Figure 6.14 shows a hunting release device for a compound bow. The front hook is attached to the bowstring. The release is held in the palm of the hand, with the draw pressure distributed over the heel of the hand on the rear butt plate. Vigorous gripping is not needed, and the thumb is placed below the release. The index finger is placed on the trigger. After the draw has been made, the forward end of the release is placed on your anchor point. (Fig. 6.15 can be used as a reference for using the type of release shown in fig. 6.14.) There are two rubber beads mounted on the bowstring, along with the nock-sets. At full draw, slide the upper bead to the line of sight across the top of the bead to the point where the sight ball appears as shown in the "sight picture." When the proper alignment is made and the sight pin is on target, the arrow is released by squeezing the trigger with a steady force. There must be *no motion* of the bow at the instant the arrow is released.

A newer type of release aid is shown in figure 6.16. This type of mechanical release is popular for use with compound bows, especially those with higher bow weights.

Although release aids remove human error and can improve accuracy, it is important to realize that arrows may be accidentally released while using these devices before the archer is ready. Common sense dictates that you thoroughly familiarize yourself with the release device and be especially aware of where the tip of the arrow is pointing as the bow is drawn.

String silencers serve one function, and that is to dampen the sound of release. There are many variations to choose from. The type seen in figure 6.3 are commonly referred to as "cat whiskers," and they are used by many hunters. Other common types include rubber buttons, yarn strands, or rubber burrs. The cost is nominal. The silencer is valuable, because it allows the bowhunter a chance at a second shot by not spooking the animal.

Figure 6.17
A pin-type bowsight used by bowhunters. The sturdy guard is needed to protect the pins while in the field. (Courtesy Precision Shooting Equipment, 2727 N. Fairview Ave., Tucson, AZ 85705)

The majority of bowhunters view the bowsight as a vital accessory. The hunting bowsight is usually calibrated in 5- to 10-yard increments, starting at 10 yards and moving out to as much as 60 yards depending upon the skill level of the archer. While 60-yard shots at a game animal are not unduly difficult for experienced bowhunters, it is highly recommended that beginners limit their shots to distances of 40 yards or less.

Archers who use bowsights for hunting are commonly called "pin-shooters." The reason is that pin devices are used as target locators. An example of a pin bowsight is shown in figure 6.17.

The pins on a bowsight can be adjusted up and down or left and right to meet the requirements of each archer. Pin spacing will differ from bowhunter to bowhunter depending on the type of tackle used, shooting technique, and anticipated shot distances while on the hunt. The majority of your practice sessions should be at those distance settings.

"Sighting in" a bowsight for accuracy at various distances is not difficult. *You must remember to move the pin in the direction(s) of the miss.* For example, when target shooting at 20 yards, your arrow hit high and right from where you aimed.

Figure 6.18
Example of an overdraw system. The arrow rest on the right is moved toward the bowhunter to increase draw length. (Courtesy Precision Shooting Equipment, 2727 N. Fairview Ave., Tucson, AZ 85705)

Your corresponding adjustment would be to move your "20-yard pin" up and to the right. After a few adjustments and assuming your shooting mechanics are good, you should be hitting the center of the target with your pin setting established for 20 yards. Each pin on the bowsight must be adjusted in this manner for accuracy at a specific distance chosen by the bowhunter.

Bowhunters who use pins for aiming must practice judging distances. Bowsights are useless unless the person shooting the bow can make good distance estimates and execute proper shooting fundamentals. There are no distance markers out in the mountains or deserts where the game animals live! How you can practice judging distance without mechanical assistance is discussed later in this chapter. *There are mechanical aids on the market known as "range finders" that assist bowhunters in making distance judgments.* These do tend to minimize some of the sport inherent within the bowhunt.

The overdraw is another accessory that has gained popularity with bowhunters in the last few years. A compound bow equipped with an overdraw system allows the archer to move the arrow rest closer to the shooter (fig. 6.18). The overdraw accessory allows the bowhunter to shoot a shorter and lighter arrow at a higher velocity. The resulting flatter trajectory makes errors in judging distance less critical. As a result, accuracy is enhanced. The overdraw accessory appears to be most important to bowhunters who use pin-type bowsights for aiming.

Camouflage clothing and paint are considered necessary items for bowhunting. The very nature of archery demands that the hunter move extremely close to the quarry before releasing an arrow. The ideal shots are usually less than 30 yards in

Figure 6.19
Camouflage helps conceal Dave Brilhart on his tree stand while bowhunting.

Figure 6.20
Blending in with the surrounding environment during any season of the year is the objective of camouflage for the bowhunter.

distance. To do this, the human shape must blend into the surrounding terrain to such a degree that the animal cannot discern you from other objects in the area. A bowhunter is camouflaged on a tree stand in figure 6.19.

Camouflage clothing is made in many patterns and color variations. The bowhunter should consider both the time of year and the type of terrain when choosing the color of camouflage. Also, the good bowhunter will have camouflaged clothing heavy or light enough for both cold and warm climates.

To be totally camouflaged means that all reflective surfaces and exposed body areas must be dulled so that large color patterns are broken up. This can be accomplished by applying "camo paint" to face and hands. The reflective surfaces of the bow can be covered by using paint or tape that does not cause glare. Some bowhunters even paint leaf patterns on their bows to make them blend into the surrounding vegetation. The archers in figures 6.19 and 6.20 are suitably camouflaged for the lighting, foliage, terrain, and season of the year.

Techniques

Preparation for a bowhunter must begin long before the opening day of the hunting season. Game laws need to be studied. All tackle must be checked and organized for the trip. It is recommended that the bowhunter have an ongoing physical conditioning program such as that presented in chapter 8. Shooting practice should be held on a regular basis throughout the year. The bow should be kept tuned. If possible, trips into the area to be hunted should be made prior to the season to scout for intended game. All of these preparations take considerable time, study, thought, money, and effort. It is a worthy use of leisure time for those who place value on the sport of the hunt.

Although shooting techniques for the bowhunter are very similar to those outlined in chapter 4, the information in this section is primarily delimited to recurve and compound bowhunting.

One of the main differences between target archery and bowhunting is the choice of the anchor point. Most bowhunters will use a side-of-the-mouth anchor or a high anchor point, as seen in figures 4.18 and 4.19. Some people like to anchor with the arrow at eye level so they can aim down the shaft in a manner similar to aiming with a firearm. The anchor point ultimately chosen is a matter of personal preference established during practice. It is highly recommended that the bowhunter's choice of anchor point should not be changed prior to the hunting season as this can cause accuracy problems. Any anchor point adjustment must be made during off-season practice sessions.

Target practice is absolutely essential on a regular basis for several weeks prior to the hunting season. For serious bowhunters, it is recommended that shooting be an ongoing practice throughout the year. If the archer has been shooting with target or field points, a switch must be made to the heavier broadheads or hunting points for preseason target practice. Flight trajectories of arrows equipped with broadheads differ considerably from trajectories of arrows equipped with target or field points. The reason for this lies in the fact that the arrow spine changes due to the increased length of the bowhunting arrow. During this preseason target practice, bowsight adjustment for hunting distances will have to be made as noted. Traditionally, these are for the shorter distances of 10, 15, 20, 25, and 30 yards.

The good bowhunter practices on both target ranges and field archery units by taking shots while in unusual stances and positions. Three-dimensional targets are available for numerous animals, and they help make these practice sessions more realistic. Competitions are held periodically by archery clubs using these targets strategically placed on field archery units. These events put the archer in practice situations similar to those encountered during the bowhunt. Archers should practice taking shots at these targets using a variety of stances that may be necessary to use during the bowhunt. An example of this is shown in figure 6.21, where the archer is taking a shot from a kneeling stance at a 3-D deer target.

Figure 6.21
A three-dimensional animal target tournament on a field archery unit allows the bowhunter, Dave Brilhart, the opportunity to practice stance adjustments that may be used later during the hunt.

Figure 6.22
Larry Rogge, an Arizona bowhunter, utilizes a hay bale for target practice in his back yard.

Figure 6.23
The Rob Davis "Bow-Skeet," a plastic bottle throwing device, designed for use during bowhunting practice for pheasant and quail. (Courtesy J. Robert Davis, 32191 Spearin Road, Salisbury, MD 21801)

Figure 6.24
Rob Davis preparing to practice bowhunting for birds by activating his "Bow-Skeet" device. The trajectory of the released bottle simulates a pheasant or quail rising in flight from a field. (Courtesy J. Robert Davis, 32191 Spearin Road, Salisbury, MD 21801)

All shots made in the field will not be like shots on the target range. Consequently, it is a good idea to practice periodically before the bowhunting season starts on a field archery unit where the targets are at varying distances in a wooded and/or hilly area. If possible, you should also set up a hay bale range on your own property with the common distances of your hunting shots marked. The hay bale (fig. 6.22) is ideal for handling field point impacts. Removal of broadheads from a hay bale, however, is more difficult. There are special targets on the market designed for easy removal of broadheads.

The 3-D animal target tournaments sponsored by archery clubs are of great value because they help archers become aware of weaknesses in their techniques or inaccuracies in the estimation of yardage between them and the target. Once a problem is known, it can then be remedied with intelligent practice before the season starts. And, these competitive club shoots are fun!

If you plan to bowhunt game on mountains or hills, you should practice shooting both at uphill and downhill angles. Shooting in hilly terrain presents entirely different problems than shooting over a flat surface. The arrow will tend to rise above the line of sight when it is shot from an extreme angle either above or below the imaginary level line of horizontal sight. The greater the degree of angle away from the horizontal level, the greater the amount of rise of the arrow. *In shooting situations, this means that you have to take off yardage for uphill and downhill angles depending on the steepness above or below the horizontal plane.* The degree to which this is done depends on the archer and the tackle being shot. So, if you are going to bowhunt in hilly terrain, it is best to practice in hills and become accustomed to making the necessary aiming adjustments.

Your bowhunting practice sessions should always be specific for the game you are going to hunt. This principle is not too difficult to follow in terms of preparing to bowhunt for animals such as deer and elk, but how do you practice to bowhunt for pheasant or quail? Rob Davis is an inventive, expert bowhunter from Maryland. He answered that question for himself several years ago by developing a bottle throwing rig (fig. 6.23). The Rob Davis "Bow-Skeet" device will throw an old, empty detergent bottle 8 to 10 feet into the air. That action simulates the approximate size and flight angle of a pheasant as it rises into the air from the field ahead of the bowhunter.

How is the Davis "Bow-Skeet" device triggered? As can be seen in figure 6.24, the bowhunter stands at the ready behind the throwing rig. A release string is attached to the bowhunter's waist and to the throwing rig. The bottle is released by simply taking a step backwards. His "bird target" (plastic bottle) is projected into flight, and a practice shot can be released at the bottle as it moves away from the bowhunter.

While practicing to bowhunt for birds as well as actually bowhunting for them, it pays to modify the fletching of your arrows to reduce flight distance. If you do not do this, you will lose many arrows. The addition of a spiral feather to the top of any arrow is a good idea. This is shown in figure 6.25. This will slow a regularly fletched arrow so it will only fly about 50 yards, and flu-flu fletched

Figure 6.25
Spiral feathers attached to flu-flu as well as regularly fletched arrows reduces flight distance and the number of lost arrows while bowhunting for birds. (Courtesy J. Robert Davis, 32191 Spearin Road, Salisbury, MD 21801)

arrows will fly less than that if your target or bird is missed. This makes the probability of retrieving your arrows much higher than shooting arrows without the spiral feather attached or by using flu-flu fletching only.

The bow also needs to be checked to make certain it is properly tuned. (Bow tuning is discussed in chapter 4.) A bow is out of tune when arrows shot by a skilled archer do not fly in a straight line. Any porpoising or fishtailing of the arrow shaft in flight is generally an indicator of a tuning problem. The arrow spine could be incorrect for the bow. Clearance and flight problems usually derive from cushion plunger, nocking point, draw weight, bowstring, improper arrow nock placement on the arrow shaft, and/or arrow rest irregularities.

Generally, movement of the arrow to the left and right during flight (fishtailing) is an indicator that a cushion plunger adjustment is needed. If the arrow flight motion is up and down (porpoising), the nocking point needs to be adjusted. Bow tuning procedures are slightly different for recurve and compound bows. There are several tuning procedures available from archery tackle manufacturers. The reader should refer to chapter 4 for the Eliason Method for tuning recurve bows. Also, the tuning procedures published by Easton Aluminum are recommended for both compound and recurve bows.

Shooting a bow and arrow when fatigued is vastly different from shooting when rested. It is entirely possible that the bowhunter may get the best shot of the year when he or she is near the point of fatigue while out in the field. The conditioned archer can handle this situation much better than the individual who is "out of shape." Regardless of physiologic condition, anyone can become tired considering the type of physical exertion one experiences while in the field on some hunts. Consequently, bowhunters should know how to compensate during shooting for the feeling of being tired. The best way to accomplish this is to practice shooting when fatigued as well as when you are rested. It is recommended that some shooting practices *follow* conditioning workouts such as described in chapter 8.

The bowhunter should practice judging distances constantly throughout the year. This can be accomplished almost anytime. As an example, while walking get in the habit of choosing a sign, tree, person, or object you are moving toward. Estimate the distance in yards from your position to the object chosen. Count your steps (stride length is approximately one yard for most people) as you move toward your chosen goal. Judgment of distance will improve steadily through such practice. Why is this important to the bowhunter? If a bowsight is used as recommended, practice will help you gauge distances more precisely when in the hunting environment. Thus, the bowsight setting can be used more accurately and this can lead to more game. Instinctive shooters can also benefit by knowing distance.

Like the American Indian of yesteryear, the bowhunter must become very familiar with the game being sought. The bowhunter should be aware of the habitat, eating, and drinking habits of the animals being pursued. If possible, go into the hunting area on foot a few weeks prior to the hunting season to study or scout intended game. As an example, a deer herd may be scrutinized for several days. Their eating, drinking, and bedding habits can be observed if the individual is an excellent stalker. Some people who live in rural environments are so good at this that they actually choose the deer to be shot prior to the opening day of the season. This takes considerable patience, knowledge, and hunting skill. Many "hunters" of the "instant hunting school" are in such a hurry to kill their game that they fail to enjoy the hunt. Hunting from an ATV or spotlight-equipped 4 × 4 truck cruising up and down country roads is illegal and not considered sport in any way, shape, or form!

An important part of any hunt is the fine art of stalking or seeking out game animals. This is more critical in bowhunting than gun hunting because the bowhunter must get very close to the game animal to make the kill. Most deer, for example, are killed with the bow and arrow at distances ranging from 10 to 35 yards. Gun hunters, on the other hand, routinely kill deer with high-powered rifles equipped with powerful scopes at distances of 100 yards or more. If a person is a marksman, it does not take much true stalking or hunting ability to kill a large animal with a powerful rifle at distances up to 300 yards or more. Hunting should be "sport" whether one uses a bow or a rifle.

The good bowhunter takes his or her shot at a deer while the animal is motionless. To obtain that type of shot, the bowhunter must be an excellent stalker with an intimate knowledge of both the animals and their environment. In addition, the bowhunter must understand such factors as habits of the animal, common noises and scents in the area, wind direction changes by time of day and type of terrain, animal camouflage techniques, and animal movements. This helps in positioning oneself for the shot either on the ground or from a tree stand.

The bowhunter must also face one fact prior to stalking game animals. Regardless of cleanliness, the human body has odors atypical to those in the hunting area. These odors come from orifices at both ends of the alimentary canal, skin, and hair.

Human habits with unusual odors, such as the use of tobacco and liquor, also perk up the animals in the area. If the bowhunter does not walk *into* the air currents, the chance for success will be diminished. Every animal will know that a predator, a human being, is in the locality.

The bowhunter should try to eliminate all odors of civilization. This can be accomplished, in part, through a study of wind patterns. Wind patterns differ depending upon the time of day and nature of the terrain. These should be studied, preferably prior to the opening of bowhunting season. If this is not possible, it will take some very astute observations to note these patterns while in the process of hunting.

Odors should be minimized by using soap without scent. Burping and flatus should be limited to the "bull sessions" around the campfire. Finally, keep in mind that the use of tobacco and alcohol places odors on one's clothing and breath that will be carried out of camp and into the field where the sensitive noses of game animals will smell them.

There is a great sport associated with bowhunting that depends upon specialized noise. This sport is known as *varmint calling*. Noise is used to attract predatory animals. The predator hears the noise made by the bowhunter and thinks it is an animal in distress. The game animal becomes the stalker, and the bowhunter becomes the hunted object. This can be very exciting. How does a bowhunter know he or she is an excellent varmint hunter? According to Tim Atwood, National Field Archery Association Bowhunting and Conservation Chairman, you attain that status after accomplishing the *Varmint Grand Slam*. That means you have taken a coyote, bobcat, and fox using varmint calling techniques. These are difficult animals to lure by calling.

The varmint caller uses a hand-built or commercially-built device to attract the predator. The sound of the call is not like any emitted by a particular animal; however, the pitch resembles the common squeal of many small animals in distress. The noise attracts the predator because the animal associates the distress sound with previous experiences while on a hunt. The motivating drive for the game animal is hunger. When the predator gets within a few feet of the area where the bowhunter is camouflaged, the hunter releases the arrow. This is seen in figure 6.26. The distance of the shot depends upon the species and size of the predatory animal stalking the bowhunter, the extent of the bowhunter's intestinal fortitude and courage and the ability to shoot accurately under pressure. It can get exciting waiting and watching that predatory animal circling and stalking you looking for a kill!

Wounded rabbit calls are very effective on predators such as coyotes, bobcats, foxes, and occasionally the mountain lion. This type of call, when used correctly, can also be used to attract adult javalina by imitating the sound of their young in distress (fig. 6.27). Other types of calls are used on game as small as quail and as large as bull elk. Turkey calling has become very sophisticated over the years.

Some cities have game calling clubs that meet periodically to practice and exchange ideas on the art of calling. Some organized competitions are held for game callers. Many of the people in the clubs are experts who have pursued this hobby for years, and they are usually more than happy to share their experiences and skills with others. It is a good place for the interested novice to learn more about game calling and hunting.

Figure 6.26
How close a predatory animal gets to a varmint caller before the shot is taken depends upon several characteristics of the bowhunter! (Courtesy *Bow and Arrow Magazine*)

Figure 6.27
Bowhunting for javalina is a popular pastime for patient archers in the Southwestern desert area of Arizona. (Courtesy Jerry Day, Arizona Game and Fish Department)

In many situations noise can be used to the bowhunter's advantage. Many bowhunters believe that they should be absolutely quiet at all times on the hunt, but it is virtually impossible to be quiet in all hunting situations. Stepping on and snapping a dead limb on the ground, for example, is not unusual noise in the woods. Animals are accustomed to that type of noise periodically. They will become alert, look in the direction of the sound, and they could move away from the sound. The hunter should remain still for a period of time and then move in the same direction as the game animals.

Sounds not typical of the environment should be avoided as much as possible when stalking. However, noise can be used to drive game out of thick, brushy areas where a shot would be unwise. The animals can then be stalked to a better area where a good shot may be more feasible.

Any noises from your bow during the critical drawing and release phases of the shot should be eliminated during the tuning process prior to the hunt. Noise at the decisive time of the shot is undesired and results in many misses out in the field. (Devices that attach to the bowstring to avoid noise were discussed earlier.) The reason you do not want this noise lies in the fact that any sound from your bow will travel at 1,100 feet per second toward the keen hearing mechanism of the game animal. That is approximately 850 to 900 feet per second faster than your bow will propel the arrow through the air! The velocity difference between your undesired bow sounds and the arrow in flight only amounts to a fraction of a second over the typical 20- to 30-yard hunting shot distance in the field. But, this infinitesimal amount of time is great enough for a wild animal such as a deer, antelope, or javalina to react and move. This motion by the animal causes many carefully aimed shots to miss their marks.

Noise can also be used to flush birds from their hiding places in high grass or bushy areas. This is common practice in bowhunting for birds such as quail and pheasant (fig. 6.11). Hitting a bird on the wing even with an arrow equipped with a wire loop point is a real challenge!

It may seem obvious, but the bowhunter must know how to see the animal being hunted. This takes considerable practice and experience. In their natural habitat, animals are capable of hiding or camouflaging themselves effectively. The untrained eye can miss seeing a potential shot. Some animals, especially birds such as pheasant and quail, depend upon their cover and camouflage for protection even more than on their movement abilities. They are difficult to see!

There are no secrets for spotting game animals. A bowhunter should know the coloring of the animal being sought and how these colors change with the seasons. You should also know how the colors blend with the foliage in the environment where the hunt will take place. Anytime a bowhunter walks through the desert, forest, or a wooded area, he or she should practice this skill by trying to observe every detail in the area. This practice will help develop field awareness while on the hunt. (You should also listen to the natural sounds of the area where you hunt.) A good set of binoculars will help in locating game; these are considered essential by most bowhunters.

A bowhunter who has located and stalked an animal to within bow range must know how to distinguish a good shot from a poor one. It is essential to know where to place an arrow so it will penetrate a vital area. Many an animal has been lost because of an archer's ignorance of the anatomy of the animal being hunted. (It is recommended that animal targets—with the vital organs of animals outlined—be used for some practice sessions prior to the hunt.)

Knowing the anatomy of the hunted animal is important because the most effective shots put the arrow in the lung and heart vicinity. Bowhunters should also familiarize themselves with the locations of major bones, arteries, liver, stomach, and kidneys. A razor sharp broadhead shot into or through the chest cavity will cause severe bleeding, easy tracking, and almost always result in a successful kill and retrieval. That is very important.

Once the shot has been taken, the bowhunter has to make some judgments regarding whether or not the arrow hit its mark. Exactly where was the animal hit? The answers will dictate the plan of action for tracking. Most archers look for blood or try to recover the arrow to help give them the answers to these kinds of questions.

The color of blood can tell the archer if the arrow severed a vein or an artery. Blood that comes from a vein is dark red in color, whereas oxygenated blood from an artery is bright red. *If it is known for certain that the chest area was penetrated, the plan of action is to wait for at least 30 minutes to one hour before trailing.* The animal will usually bed down a short distance from where it was hit and die. Some beginning bowhunters make the mistake of trailing too soon and end up chasing the wounded animal all over the woods for hours!

If the shot went through the intestinal area of the animal, the plan of action would be much different. Even though this type of shot is always fatal, the animals are hard to trail and they take much longer to die. *In this situation, the archer should wait an hour or longer before following the animal's trail.* A "gut shot" animal that is pushed can travel miles before it is exhausted enough to bed down.

There are several situations where the best plan of action is to follow the animal immediately. These include muscle hits, leg hits, and situations where darkness or bad weather is approaching.

Before following a trail, be sure to mark the spot from which the shot was taken and the spot where the animal was hit. Blood is easy to follow, but sometimes the flow stops. In that case, the archer will have to rely on other clues such as prints, scuffmarks, and broken vegetation. Be patient and do not overlook any signs, because trailing can take hours of tedious searching and concentration. One should not give up the trailing task until all possibilities have been exhausted.

When an animal has been recovered, it needs to be field dressed as soon as possible so the meat can cool. This helps keep it from spoiling, especially in warmer climates. Special care should be taken during the field dressing process because there is always the possibility of cutting one's self.

For information regarding bowhunting, legal game, season dates, license fees, lottery systems for various species, and other matters, the official state wildlife

Figure 6.28
The successful completion of an antelope hunt shows on the face of Jack Frazier, an expert bowhunter. (Courtesy of Jack Frazier)

agency where you plan to hunt must be contacted. Addresses are listed in Appendix A. There are all kinds of exciting species to hunt, which can bring satisfaction to the bowhunter. One example is shown in figure 6.28.

Table 6.1 includes several examples of game taken with the bow and arrow in the United States, Mexico, and Canada.

The Pope and Young Club is one organization responsible for maintaining, recording, and determining the authenticity of the Bowhunters Big Game Records of North America (see Appendix B for the address). This club appoints and maintains official measurers across the North American continent. These highly qualified people score outstanding big game animals taken with the bow and arrow. The scoring procedure is based on well-established criteria. It is a challenging task to qualify a game animal you have taken with the bow and arrow for a Pope and Young documented big game record. The Pope and Young Club is open to bowhunters who have proven themselves in the field over the years, accepted the challenges, and adhere to the principles of fair chase. Beyond documenting game records, the members have a keen interest in maintaining the integrity of the wildlife heritage.

The Pope and Young Ishi Award is given only to bowhunters who bring in very outstanding trophy animals in North America. It honors Dr. Saxton Pope and his legendary Yahi Indian friend, Ishi (see Bibliography). The award was started by the NFAA and Pope and Young Club in 1962. Due to the demanding criteria established for this honor, an Ishi Award is only given about every two to three years.

The Boone and Crockett Club is another organization that keeps records on game animals taken primarily by gun hunters. There is a very good display of ranked trophy animals in The Boone and Crockett Gallery located in the Cody

Table 6.1 Examples of Game Animals Taken with Bow and Arrow in the United States, Canada, and Mexico

Alaska Brown Bear	Javalina
Alaska-Yukon Moose	Mountain Caribou
Antelope	Mule Deer
Barren Ground Caribou	Musk Ox
Bighorn Sheep	Polar Bear
Bison	Quebec-Labrador Caribou
Black Bear	Rocky Mountain Goat
Canada Moose	Roosevelt Elk
Columbian Blacktail Deer	Sitka Blacktail Deer
Coues Deer	Stone Sheep
Cougar	Whitetail Deer
Dall Sheep	Woodland Caribou
Grizzly Bear	Wyoming-Shiras Moose
Jaguar	Yellowstone Elk

Firearms Museum within the excellent Buffalo Bill Historical Center in Cody, Wyoming. The Boone and Crockett Club publishes a comprehensive record book (see Appendix B for the address).

For the individual who views hunting as a true sport, bowhunting can occupy many leisure hours. The game animals can be as small as a quail or as large as an elk. The environment can range from the wilderness of the Canadian Rockies to the deserts of the southwest area of the United States. Bowhunting is for the adventurous individual who respects nature, ecology, sport, conservation principles, and is a lover of the great out-of-doors and wilderness areas.

Review

1. What are the several types of bows commonly used for hunting and what is their order of energy storage efficiency?
2. In purchasing hunting tackle, which is more important, the quality of the bow or the arrows? What are the advantages and disadvantages of the various types of hunting arrows?
3. How can the bowhunter learn to compensate for the effects of fatigue on performance?
4. Describe the use of the pin-sight commonly used by bowhunters. What techniques can the archer use to enhance his or her judgment in estimating distances?
5. Why do state game and fish commissions specify minimum rather than maximum draw weights and bolt lengths for bow hunting?
6. Assume that you are planning a bowhunt. What preparation is necessary in regard to tackle, conditioning, practice, site of the hunt and quarry?

7. In which direction should the tips of a working recurve bow point when the bow is unstrung and when it is braced?

8. When shooting in hilly terrain rather than on level ground, how must you adjust your aim?

9. Is arrow velocity greater with a round wheel or a cam device at the bow tip? Why does greater velocity reduce error in the arrow trajectory?

10. What is "varmint hunting" and how does it differ from deer hunting with the bow and arrow?

11. Familiarity with the intended game animal and its habitat are important to success in bowhunting. What factors should be noted during a scouting trip prior to the hunt?

12. The compound bow can generate more foot-pounds of energy than composite bows, and it is now the most popular hunting tool of the bowhunter. Why are a few hunters returning to the use of longbows and the recurve bow?

13. Why does the modern bowhunter need to be more concerned about using dull arrows than was the American Indian?

14. Why is stalking more critical in bowhunting than in gun hunting?

15. How long should you wait to trail an animal if your shot has penetrated its chest, and how long if the intestinal area has been struck? Under what circumstances should you trail a shot animal immediately?

Bowfishing

7

The purpose of this chapter is to introduce the reader to the exciting sport of bowfishing. There are many challenges to be met in this sport, and there are numerous aquatic animals that can be taken with bow and arrow. These range from small goldfish (carp) to rather large and violent sharks. It can be exciting!

Bowfishing is a sport with considerable appeal for people who enjoy archery and angling. It is a wholesome mixture of both sports with some aspects of harpooning or gigging added. Bowfishing is not new. Primitive people used the technique for years to acquire fish, frogs, and other aquatic animals to supplement their diet. However, as a sport, bowfishing is relatively new as compared to target archery and many of the other archery sports. It is gaining in popularity as people discover that the sport exists.

The National Field Archery Association has encouraged and supported bowfishing for many years. Recognition of prize fish and articles on bowfishing appear periodically in the official NFAA magazine, *Archery*. The number of people who bowfish for avocational purposes is growing. This fact prompted the formation of the Bowfishing Association of America (BAA) in 1990. The official publication of the BAA is Wilbur Corley's *Bowfishing Digest*.

Bowfishers can ply their skills on rivers, lakes, ponds, marshes, and oceans. The size of the "rough fish" sought adds to the excitement of the sport. On average, the species legalized for bowfishing are much larger than most game fish taken with rod and reel. The smallest of the common "rough fish" approved for bowfishing are the bowfin and shortnose gar; these fish average about 5 pounds as adults. Saltwater fish are among the largest sought by bowfishers. Sharks often exceed 200 pounds, and the giant sunfish found in the Pacific Ocean range in weight from 50 to 1,000 pounds.

The largest of the "rough fish" sanctioned for bowfishing outside of ocean water is the alligator gar. The largest alligator gar ever caught by any method weighed 302 pounds, and it was over 7 feet in length. The record alligator gar for bowfishing was taken on June 29, 1993, by bowfishers Donnie Powell and Jerry Hester on Toledo Bend Lake in Louisiana. It weighed 215 pounds, 2 ounces! It measured 7 feet 3¼ inches in length, and it had a girth of 3 feet, 11 inches. The best time to bowfish for gar is between the middle of May and into June.

If you bowfish and land an alligator gar that weighs more than 100 pounds, you can be proud of the struggle. The BAA will award you a citation for your efforts. Figure 7.1 will give you some idea of how large a gar in that weight range can be! The fish in figure 7.1 weighed in at 140 pounds, and it was taken by bowfishers Chris Cockrill, Collin Cockrill, and Todd Wachman at Choke Canyon State Park in Texas.

Figure 7.1
Collin Cockrill weighs a 140-pound alligator gar taken while bowfishing in Texas by Chris Cockrill, Todd Wachman, and himself. (Courtesy Backwater Bowfishing, 36 W. Parnell, Denison, TX 75020; photo by Chris Cockrill)

If you fish with rod and reel, remember the excitement the last time you landed a 10-pound game fish. Now, imagine having your bow-propelled arrow hooked into an alligator gar the size of those mentioned above. Or, ponder the action when you have a 200-pound shark on the line! Think of the challenge of landing a fish of that size safely (fig. 7.2).

As another example, the smallmouth buffalo is another popular freshwater fish sought by bowfishers. If you want to bring in a record for smallmouth buffalo, you would have to boat one that weighs more than 105 pounds! Kenneth Harvey landed a 105-pound smallmouth buffalo while bowfishing on Harris Brake Lake in central Arkansas in 1994. As indicated in the above examples, the size and variety of legal game fish add to the adventure and intrigue of bowfishing.

If you are an angler, the process of obtaining bait can be rather dull. Simply stated, you dig for earthworms or purchase your bait in a variety of forms from a store. In contrast, obtaining bowfishing bait for sharks can be very exciting! Some people use stingrays as bait to bowfish for shark. They shoot the bait first and then go after the big stuff! Figure 7.3 will give you some idea of the difference between this type of "bowfishing bait" and the typical bait used by traditional anglers!

Figure 7.2
Three brown sharks landed by Robie Davis and his father, J. Robert Davis. The sharks were taken while bowfishing the bays on the Maryland coast. (Photo courtesy of J. Robert Davis, 32191 Spearin Road, Salisbury, MD 21801)

Figure 7.3
Bill Johnston and Robie Davis with a 100-plus-pound southern stingray taken off the Del Mar Va Peninsula in Maryland. Rays are used as bait for shark. (Courtesy *Bowfishing Magazine*, P.O. Box 2005, Wausau, WI 54401)

As emphasized specifically in chapter 4 and throughout this book, if you are interested in any archery sport, the first step is to perfect your target archery shooting mechanics. Those shooting skills serve as your foundation for becoming a good bowfisher. Some modifications in shooting technique are necessary as you switch from target to bowfishing tackle, but the drawing and release mechanics remain the same. If you are accurate during target range practice, you will increase the probability of taking more pounds of fish once you get into the bowfishing situation. Ideally, practice should progress from standard target archery targets to moving, simulated fish targets submerged beneath the water.

Bowhunters are turning to bowfishing as an "off-season" activity. The summer is not a game animal season, but it is a good time of year to go after many of the "rough fish" on rivers and in lakes. The hunter can keep the skills honed as well as enhance his or her leisure time through the sport of bowfishing.

"Rough fish" such as carp, gar, and buffalo are usually relegated to "garbage status" by gourmets. Game fish such as trout, bass, and bluegill are preferred eating. The resourceful bowfisher can learn many ways to prepare, cook, and eat the carp, gar, and other fish that have been caught. These fish can be a valuable and savory food source. They may be prepared for frying, broiling, smoking, and canning. Due to the large number and pounds of fish that may be taken by the bowfisher in most states, the "rough fish" can supplement the diet. The food budget for the family can benefit if a taste is acquired for "rough fish." (Table 7.1, later in this chapter, shows the wide variety of legal species for bowfishing throughout the United States.)

Conservation departments in the various states look at the harvest of "rough fish" by bowfishers at the present time as a positive conservation practice. These fish are large, as noted, and they tend to be prolific reproducers. As a result, they can disturb the ecological balance in the waters that they inhabit, especially in those areas where few, if any, predators exist for the "rough fish." As bowfishing increases in popularity, however, even the rough fish populations will have to be monitored carefully by state conservation departments. There could be a significant depletion of the numbers of rough fish on the rivers and lakes across the country that generate the most interest to bowfishers. That would have a negative impact on the bodies of water in which they live and on the sport of bowfishing.

Tackle

Any bow can be rigged for bowfishing. However, hunting bows—recurve and compound—are most commonly used and best suited for this purpose (see figs. 7.4 and 7.5). The draw weights for hunting and fishing bows tend to be higher than target bows. This is an important consideration when going after the larger species of fish or trying to propel an arrow through a few feet of water. Minimum bow weights of 50 pounds are recommended for bowfishing. This will produce an adequate amount of arrow projection force to handle most situations. Lighter bow weights, however, can be used with success when bowfishing in shallow water or when shooting fish

Figure 7.4
A hunting recurve bow rigged for bowfishing with a spinning reel and short rod mounted on the back of the bow. (Courtesy Black Widow Custom Bows, Inc., 1201 Eaglecrest, P.O. Box 2100, Nixa, MO 65714)

barely submerged. The archer who cannot handle higher bow weights should rig his or her bow for bowfishing and go fishing. There will be numerous opportunities to shoot. If a dorsal fin is seen or the fish is swimming a few inches below the surface, shooting skill and not bow weight becomes the critical factor. Bowfishing gets exciting at that point regardless of the strength, age, or sex of the participant!

An excellent Black Widow recurve hunting bow is rigged for bowfishing in figure 7.4. The bow has a short rod and bow reel adapter rod mounted on the back of the bow. The bow reel adapter screws into the stabilizer hole, and the rod fits into the adapter. The adapter is needed to hold the spinning reel, as shown in figure 7.4. As noted previously, this type of rod and reel setup, as compared to the older hand-wrap reels, has made bowfishing easier. The rod provides better leverage for playing the fish, and, with the spinning reel, line tangle is minimized. There is good line retrieval on missed shots and better recovery of fish once they are shot.

Another type of popular bowfishing bow, the Oneida Aero-Force X80 compound bow, is shown in figure 7.5. This bow can be outfitted and used for bowfishing or bowhunting. It is the bow of choice of recent BAA World Champion Bowfishers (see fig. 7.17). Some of the features of the bow in figures 7.5 and

Figure 7.5
The Aero-Force X80 Aquaflage Bow. A popular and efficient bowfishing bow used by several recent Bowfishing Association of America World Champions. (Courtesy Oneida Labs, Inc., 8 Jason Drive, P.O. Box 68, Phoenix, NY 13135)

Figure 7.6
The Aqua Launcher Bowfishing Rest designed for accurate shooting of the heavier bowfishing points. (Courtesy Oneida Labs, Inc., 8 Jason Drive, P.O. Box 68, Phoenix, NY 13135)

7.17 include: up to 80 percent let-off capacity, arrow velocity to 241 feet per second, and excellent draw control. These are highly desired features in a quality compound bowfishing bow.

The bowfisher will find that some modifications even to the best bows may be needed to make bowfishing more efficient. For example, the arrow rest and/or shelf may have to be altered to handle the larger bowfishing arrows and avoid line entanglement upon release of the arrow. Figure 7.6 shows a specialized arrow rest designed to handle the heavy bowfishing arrows. This arrow rest is made from aluminum and can be fitted to a bow riser as shown in figures 7.5 and 7.6. Anything you learn about your bow during practice that interferes with accurate arrow flight should be modified or tuned prior to getting on the water to bowfish.

The changes in reel designs in recent years have helped make bowfishing more popular. Bowfishers have used all types of ingenious gimmicks in the past to attach line to the bow and arrow and crude reels to bows. Hand-wrap reels were improvised and mounted on bow backs. Hand-wrap reels (see fig. 7.13) were eventually manufactured and placed on the market. These remain popular with some bowfishers. The

Figure 7.7
A cable mounted on the arrow for attaching the bowfishing line eliminates the problem of too much line laying on the shooter's arm while drawing. (Courtesy Ron Skirvin, Shure Shot, P.O. Box 748, Stevens Point, WI 54481)

spin-cast reel attached to a short bowfishing rod that mounts on the back of the bow has become very popular (fig. 7.4). The Retriever Reel is another popular string retrieval system used by many bowfishers. The Retriever Reel stacks the line in a plastic bottle rather than winding it on a drum. This reel is mounted on the bow. These newer types of reels, and others, have minimized some of the line handling and tangling problems for bowfishers.

Solid white fiberglass or aluminum arrows are recommended for use by bowfishers. Fiberglass arrows are durable, and the heavier mass weight is needed to increase accuracy as the arrow penetrates the water on its way to the fish. Some fiberglass arrows warp over time and cause flight problems. You may also want to try shooting a high quality aluminum arrow before making a final choice of which arrows to purchase for bowfishing. Aluminum arrows do have the disadvantage of having less mass weight. The arrows should be at least 30 inches in length to keep the line away from the bow hand.

One way to ensure keeping the line away from the bow hand is to connect a cable to the arrow as shown in figure 7.7. The line attaches to the swivel that runs the length of the cable. This means that only a few inches of line is off the reel, that is, the distance from the reel to the front of the bow or arrow rest. That eliminates the long length of line that could lay across the shooter's arm as the arrow is drawn. That is a problem the bowfisher encounters when using some of the other line attachment procedures. This type of line problem can interfere with shooting.

Rubber fletching may or may not be used on bowfishing arrows. Arrow flight is minimal in bowfishing, so the aerodynamic stability purpose of fletching is nullified to a great extent. White is the desired color of arrows for visibility reasons. It is recommended that several extra arrows be taken on each trip because nocks and points do break. Extra nocks and points should also be taken while bowfishing. Some repairs to broken tackle can be made on the boat.

There are several bowfishing arrow points on the market. Which of these points is "best" depends on personal preference, and that may change, depending

A.

B.

C.

Figure 7.8
A retractable "sting-a-ree" bowfishing point: (a) shooting position, (b) open position to gaff the fish, and (c) point adjustment to remove the arrow from the fish.

Figure 7.9
The Shure Shot point with one-piece rotating barb design. (Courtesy Ron Skirvin, Shure Shot, P.O. Box 748, Stevens Point, WI 54481)

Figure 7.10
Ron Skirvin, 1994 NFAA Bowfisher of the Year, with a 43-pound bigmouth buffalo. (Courtesy *Bowfishing Magazine,* P.O. Box 2005, Wausau, WI 54401)

upon the species of fish being sought. All of the bowfishing points are barbed; some of these barbs are retractable, allowing for easy removal, while others have stationary spring steel barbs. There are also four-pronged "gig points" for shooting those huge bull frogs found in various parts of the country.

The retractable barbed arrow points are usually preferred over the nonretractable variety; they are much easier to recover. One barbed arrow is shown in figure 7.8. This is a heavy point that helps penetration through the water and into the fish. It opens to 2¾ inches across the tips to provide holding power during fish retrieval. The point is removed by simply twisting the shaft counterclockwise. The point is kept within the fish as the shaft is rotated, and the barbs reverse their position while still inside the fish. The arrow can be removed easily without disrupting the line. These barb positions are shown in figure 7.8. This type of point is recommended for fish with "soft skin" such as the suckers and bowfin.

Another type of arrow point is shown in figure 7.9. This is a newer design made of steel with a one-piece rotating barb. This eliminates the need to remove the point from the arrow once the fish is landed. The barbs rotate forward by unscrewing the point three-fourths turn while holding the arrow. A spring lock washer between the point and adapter prevents accidental release. This point attaches to a threaded adapter epoxied to the arrow shaft. Figure 7.10 shows a rather large bigmouth buffalo taken by Ron Skirvin, an NFAA Bowfisher of the Year Award Winner, with the arrow point shown in figure 7.9.

Bowfishing line is made of braided nylon or monofilament. The choice of which to use lies with the archer. The most commonly used line, however, is braided nylon. The poundage test of the line is important, with choices usually ranging from 50- to 100-pound test line. The poundage used depends upon the size of the fish one expects to encounter. If you go out with line too weak and large fish are found, the trip could be a great disappointment. However, it can be an adventure and test of your bowfishing skills to land heavy fish on relatively light test line. It is recommended that 50- to 70-pound test line be used in one reel and a second reel be loaded with heavier or lighter line, depending upon the anticipated size of the fish known to inhabit the locale being fished.

Maximum line length for the reel being used is important. Fish will "run" upon arrow impact, and line length is important to enable the bowfisher to control the extent of this movement. Control of the fish after the arrow has struck is where some of the bowfisher's skill is tested. There are times when it is better to use lighter and longer line rather than heavier and shorter line. Line should also be examined periodically for damage caused by friction against such things as abrasive skin, teeth, or boat hulls. Weak lines will snap, and fish are lost.

The line is usually attached to a leader of heavy braided nylon by a strong swivel. The leader should be about 30 inches long. The heavier leader, not the fishing line, should be held as the fish is being lifted into the boat or dragged toward the shore. It is recommended that the line be tied as close to the back end of the arrow as possible. This helps flight accuracy by avoiding lateral tension on the arrow shaft as you release the arrow.

Plan ahead for all contingencies on a bowfishing trip, and your disappointments will be minimized. This means that your tackle box and boat should be packed with extras of most everything that will break. Furthermore, you should include tools and other items needed to repair your tackle while on the trip. It is frustrating not to have such small things as pliers and glue to repair or replace nocks and points. Those oversights can ruin a trip, so overstock your tackle box before you leave home.

Major Accessories

Bowfishers can use some of the same "minor accessories" as the target archer and bowhunter, for example, finger tab, arm guard, bow sling, and so on (fig. 7.4). In addition, they must have some "major accessories" to place them close to the fish being sought. The largest financial expenditures are for wading gear and a boat.

Some of the best and most interesting bowfishing can be done while walking in rough marshlands, shallow edges of lakes and along rivers, swamps, and flooded fields. Boats either cannot enter these areas or are difficult to handle in those situations. Also, boats can be noisy and create greater water disturbance than a man or woman moving slowly through the shallow water. Chest waders are an absolute essential for bowfishing in these elements. Wading will be productive for bowfishers during the spring spawning time. In addition to the excitement of

Figure 7.11
Landing a carp from an unstable boat NOT designed for bowfishing can be dangerous.
(Courtesy *Bow and Arrow Magazine*)

shooting the fish, there is always the added adventure provided by water snakes, deep and unseen holes, insects, sunshine, and rapidly developing thunderstorms. You have to love it! For safety purposes, the bowfisher must be a swimmer if he/she wants to wade while bowfishing!

If a bowfisher plans to pursue the sport frequently on rivers and lakes, a modified, flat-bottomed boat will prove to be a valuable asset. It can also be used for other recreational pursuits by the individual and family. Bowfishing on rivers and lakes can be accomplished in a variety of boats ranging from canoes to rowboats. However, boats of that type and like the one shown in figure 7.11 *are not recommended.* Canoes, kayaks, and regular keeled small boats tend to be unstable. As a result, they sway too much and can tip when the archer stands to shoot and bring in the fish.

A bowfishing boat should be stable, that is, set relatively low in the water to minimize sway when the archer stands on the bow or stern to shoot. The archer must stand to visually hunt for the fish to be shot, to execute the shooting fundamentals, and to obtain the correct shooting angle to hit the fish. These actions cannot be performed properly while seated.

An example of a boat redesigned and modified for bowfishing is shown in figure 7.12. This boat was the idea of Jim West. He started with a standard Lowe "Husky John" Boat and gradually built a specialized boat for bowfishing. Its features include the following:

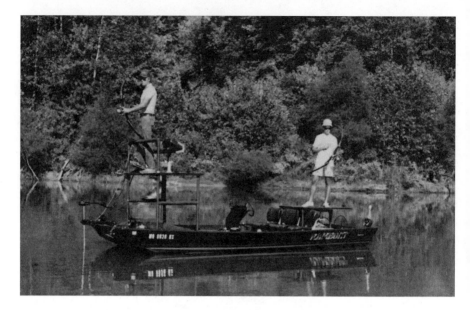

Figure 7.12
Jim West (*left*) and Michael Shore aboard Jim West's customized bowfishing boat—Ramboat. (Courtesy *Bowfishing Magazine,* P.O. Box 2005, Wausau, WI 54401)

1. 18 feet long, 7 feet at the beam, and 24-inch high sides.
2. Welded aluminum hull.
3. Two stable shooting platforms; the forward platform is 5 feet above the water—highly desired in terms of shooting angles.
4. Holders for extra arrows attached to each platform.
5. Nine built-in storage compartments:
   a. Two for storage for camping gear.
   b. Two for bowfishing equipment.
   c. One for wiring.
   d. One is a tool box.
   e. One for life jackets and fire gear.
   f. One live well.
   g. One for food cooling.
6. V-8 Chevrolet engine bored to 406 cubic inches.
7. Dominator jet pump for propulsion—navigation is possible in as little as two inches of water.
8. Depth finder, videocamera setup, AM/FM radio with cassette tape player.
9. Burglar alarm system.

Any reader interested in more details regarding this boat should read the articles by Paul T. Shore listed in the Bibliography.

In addition to the above features, the bowfisher should also consider each of the following as possible additions to his or her boat. A good bowfishing boat needs a trolling motor. A propelling fan and motor may be needed if bowfishing is done often on shallow waters. The boat should also be equipped with halogen lights for night bowfishing. Recommendations include 2,200 watts of 110v halogens and 400 watts of 12v halogens. Many bowfishing tournaments are conducted at night. The lights require that a functional generator be placed on board. You will also find that butt-high support seats placed on one or both shooting platforms come in handy for rest purposes on those long bowfishing excursions. For safety and communication functions, a citizen band (CB) radio or cellular phone can be of use at times on your bowfishing boat. Finally, a functional trailer to haul and launch the boat is an absolute necessity.

Bowfishing on the ocean requires a seaworthy ship, but most bowfishers are not wealthy enough to afford that type of craft as a "fishing accessory." However, ships can be chartered by groups or individuals directly or through travel agencies for ocean bowfishing trips. The travel and charter costs are not inexpensive, but the money spent can provide considerable excitement when one contemplates landing shark, rays, or sunfish. Sighting, shooting, and landing a large shark or sunfish on an ocean vessel bobbing up and down on the water is a challenge, and it can add excitement to a vacation.

Legal Species for Bowfishing

Because of extensive environmental, political, and ecological differences between states, bowfishers should never assume that a specific species is legal. A license is required in most states to bowfish, and each state clearly defines the species for legal bowfishing. It is the responsibility of the archer to know that list and the fishing limits. These laws change, so the individual desiring to fish in any given state should know the current game laws and obtain a license. One should never assume that a species legal in one state will be legal in another state. As one example, Colorado allows trout to be taken by bowfishers, while New Mexico, its neighbor to the south, allows only gar, carp, buffalo, and bullfrogs to be taken in its waters. Carp are probably the most common fish taken by bowfishers (fig. 7.11).

Most of the areas in the United States and Canada restrict the legal species to the so-called rough fish. The most common are the following:

Alligator gar	Bowfin	Shortnose gar
Bigmouth buffalo	Carp	Smallmouth buffalo
Black buffalo	Longnose gar	Spotted gar

Table 7.1 is provided simply to show the reader the diversity of legal species that may be taken in the United States. The species listed are not found in all states nor are they legal in all states. If you are planning to bowfish or hunt in a specific locale in the United States or Canada, you are advised to contact the official wildlife agency where your trip will take you. Ask them to mail you the latest game regulations. *The names, addresses, and phone numbers of the official wildlife agencies in the United States and Canada are listed in Appendix A.*

Table 7.1 Legal Species for Bowfishing Throughout the United States

Aholehole	Gar (Spotted)	Quillback
'Ama'ama	Gasperpou	Rays
Awa	Goldeye	Redhorse
Bass (Largemouth)	Goldfish	Salmon (Atlantic)
Bass (Smallmouth)	Hardhead	Salmon (Kokanee)
Blackfish	Herring	Saugeye
Blowfish	Kala	Shad
Bowfin	Lamprey	Sharks
Buffalo (Bigmouth)	Ling	Skates
Buffalo (Black)	Manini	Squawfish
Buffalo (Smallmouth)	Minnows	Stingrays
Bullhead	Moanu	Suckers
Burbot	Moi	Sunfish
Carp	Mullet	Toads (Oyster)
Catfish (Channel)	Muskellunge	Trout
Catfish (Flathead)	O'io	Tullibee
Chub	Omilu	Turtle (Soft-shell)
Ciscoe	Opelu Kala 'Opakapaka	Turtle (Snapping)
Drum	Paddlefish	Uha
Eel	Papio	Uku
Frogs	Perch (Rio Grande)	'Ula 'ula
Gar (Alligator)	Pickerel	Ulua
Gar (Longnose)	Pike (Northern)	Weke
Gar (Shortnose)	Pike (Walleye)	Whitefish

State game laws must be checked annually to determine legal species for each state.
See Appendix A for names and addresses of official wildlife agencies.

Technique Suggestions

This section describes some of the more important shooting fundamentals for bow-fishing. Some suggestions for making the experience more rewarding are also presented. Bowfishing, like any archery skill practiced outdoors, has many variations. These are learned only through study, directed practice, and experience.

The nocking, drawing, anchoring, releasing, and follow-through shooting fundamentals are the same as those practiced in target archery. Obviously, the stance for the bowfisher must be modified, depending upon the position of the fish in relation to the archer. The release cannot be hurried in the excitement of the moment. The three fingers relax and extend as in target archery to let the bowstring move forward in a straight line without causing unnecessary deflection of the arrow. This appears to be easy, but the excited bowfisher who has sighted a "big one" will periodically try to help the bowstring move by plucking it or pushing the bow at release. One must refrain from these types of extraneous motions. (Some bowfishers prefer to use a release aid rather than the traditional three-finger bowstring grip and release. The release aid reduces some of the "sport" found in bowfishing.)

Target practice plus experience in the field help to minimize undesired release reactions. Target practice on land should be performed with field points that weigh the same as your fishing points. Hay bales make good target mats for field points. It is highly recommended that the bowfisher also prepares by practicing with his or her bowfishing tackle while using an underwater bowfishing target. Underwater fish targets are available on the market, and these can be adjusted to any water depth desired.

Aiming presents unique problems in bowfishing. From the standpoint of physics, water and air are both fluids. But, looking at a target through water presents a different set of problems than looking at a land target through the air. A land target does not appear distorted; the distance to a target is either known exactly as in target archery or can be readily estimated by an experienced bowhunter. The bowfisher, on the other hand, must deal with the refraction of the sun's light rays as they penetrate the water in the immediate area of the fish. (It is best to wear good sunglasses to increase visual acuity, especially on bright days.) *It is difficult to evaluate the depth of the fish in the water, because light rays have a tendency to bend downward. This means that the fish will be closer to you than it looks.*

As a result of these visual factors, aiming is difficult in bowfishing because you cannot aim directly at the fish. *Your aim must be at a theoretical point below the fish.* The aiming point below the fish is dependent upon (1) the depth of the fish in the water and (2) the distance the bowfisher is away from the fish at the time of the shot. Ken Brown, an expert bowfisher from Oklahoma, recommends that one inch be allowed for every five feet of distance between the archer and the target, and the archer should allow an additional one inch for each foot the fish appears to be below the surface of the water. For example: for a side shot from 15 feet when the fish is one foot deep in the water, the aiming point would be four inches below the fish, that is, three inches for the distance factor plus one inch for the depth of the fish. Fortunately, most shots by good bowfishers are made at relatively short distances.

You may hit the fish if you follow the aiming directions, though certainty is not guaranteed. Fish simply will not hold still for any predictable length of time to allow time for a good shot. The bowfisher has problems with the water, with aiming, and with moving fish, but these difficulties help to make bowfishing a challenging and exciting sport. The archer can derive considerable personal satisfaction when these problems are overcome and the fish is landed.

In figure 7.13, satisfaction and pride of accomplishment can be seen on the faces of two expert bowfishers, Rob Davis and Bob Alexander. They have landed a 212-pound lemon shark that measured 8 feet 11 inches in length. They fish the bays between the barrier islands and the mainlands of Delaware, Maryland, and Virginia from May until September. They hunt stingrays (fig. 7.3) to use as bait to

Figure 7.13
Rob Davis, a former NFAA Bowfisherman of the Year, and Bob Alexander, appear pleased after landing a lemon shark that weighed 212 pounds and measured 8 feet 11 inches in length. (Courtesy J. Robert Davis, 32191 Spearin Road, Salisbury, MD 21801)

draw the sharks close for a shot. Shark and rays are exciting game. Aiming and shooting a large fish is only half of the excitement. What you do with a fish with sharp teeth that weighs more than you do is the other half!

It is not a good idea to drag live large fish with sharp teeth, such as those shown in figures 7.2 and 7.13, into your boat. They can cause serious problems, including capsizing small boats. If they are brought on board alive, their violent movements can cause loss of equipment, damage to gear on board, and trauma to the bowfishers. Therefore, it is best to make certain the fish is dead prior to bringing it aboard the boat. In the case of sharks, it is best to haul them alongside the craft and beach them rather than trying to lift them into the boat. J. Robert Davis, an expert bowfisher, recommends the following procedure for hauling sharks to shore: utilize an innertube as a flotation device attached to the line and arrow. This shark rig is reinforced with steel cable to help control the shark in the water and drag the fish on land. This improvised rig is seen in figure 7.14.

Once the fish has been landed or dragged to shore, the problem is what to do with it? The fish legal for bowfishing are edible, but one may have to develop a taste for the meat. There are many ways to prepare them for human consumption. The most popular edible rough fish is probably the carp. If you land a "big one" of any species, it could make a nice trophy mounted on the wall of your den to document the fact that not all big ones get away. Finally, fish not eaten make excellent fertilizer for home gardens. *The rough fish you land should never be left on the bank to rot.*

Figure 7.14
A steel cable rig attached to a fishing arrow and innertube flotation device used in fishing for and safely landing sharks. (Courtesy J. Robert Davis, 32191 Spearin Road, Salisbury, MD 21801)

Bowfishing Activities

Besides the bowfishing activities of individuals, there are numerous organized activities conducted each year. These activities are sponsored by local archery clubs, national archery organizations, and manufacturers of archery tackle. Bowfishing tournaments are conducted in many states and throughout the world.

National Field Archery Association Bowfisher Program

The NFAA Bowfisher Program is designed to promote bowfishing as a sport and to recognize the accomplishments of bowfishers throughout the country. To be involved in this program, you must be a member of the NFAA. Patches are given to participants in the NFAA Bowfisher Program, and there are patch awards to indicate the type of fish taken. Recognition is also given to bowfishers by printing a Top Ten List each year of the carp, shark, gar, and rays taken by bowfishers. In addition, photographs are published of bowfishers with their fish in *Archery*, the official magazine of the NFAA. Carp and gar are the most popular approved species, but records are also kept for shark and stingrays.

The NFAA Bowfisher of the Year awards (plaques) are presented to the individuals who document that they have landed the largest fish. There are awards for carp, gar, shark, and stingrays. Winners are determined by weight of the fish, and the catch must be fully documented to the satisfaction of the NFAA Bowfisher Committee.

Figure 7.15
Wilbur Corley, an expert bowfisherman, with a 123 pound 6 ounce alligator gar he landed on a river in south Texas. (Courtesy Wilbur Corley, 727 Holiday Lane, Claremore, OK 74017)

The NFAA, with its annual Shark Derby, has hosted a different type of bow-fishing event for several years. The Derby is held at the Elkhorn Slough located near Gilroy, California. This event usually results in the taking of a small number of blue, shovelnose, leopard, and sand sharks along with a few bat rays. Plaques are awarded to the bowfishers who bring in the largest fish in each of the various species. This event has been of some concern to conservation organizations such as the Sierra Club, but the California Department of Fish and Game has indicated that the Shark Derby has had no negative impact over the years on the species taken from the slough during the event.

Bowfishing waters should be monitored by professional biologists to determine whether or not the area is being overfished by bowfishermen. Eliminating or greatly reducing the fish species in any area should be deemed undesirable by anyone who enjoys being in natural environments, and this includes bowfishers.

The NFAA also maintains ongoing records of who has taken the largest carp or gar while using bowfishing techniques. To hold a NFAA Bowfisher Record, you must be a member of the NFAA. Record keeping and review of the records are completed annually. If no records are broken during the year, the old records stand for the next year. The NFAA has an established procedure for documenting catches and fish weights.

NFAA Bowfisher Program Records are as follows: CARP: 51 pounds, Lance Sullentrop of Missouri; SHARK: 130 pounds, Donald R. Walter of California; GAR: 185 pounds, William Nicar of Texas; RAY: 103 pounds, Ron Skirvin of Wisconsin.

Table 7.2 Bowfishing Association of America Citation Program Standards

Fish Species	Minimum Weight (Pounds)
Freshwater	
Alligator gar	100
Bowfin (grindle)	10
Buffalo	35
Carp	32
Gaspergou (freshwater drum)	15
Goldfish	3
Longnose gar	30
Paddlefish	35
Shortnose gar	7
Spotted gar	8
Sucker	5
Tilapia	4
Saltwater	
Cownose ray	50
Flounder	5
Mullet	43
Shad	2
Shark	100
Sheepshead	10
Stingray	75

Bowfishing Association of America

The Bowfishing Association of America (BAA) was formed in 1990 to promote and protect the sport of fishing with a bow and arrow. The main goals of the BAA include: (1) protection of the natural resources used by bowfishers, (2) national organization of bowfishing tournaments, (3) administration of an annual World Championship in bowfishing, (4) establishment of a point system to objectively qualify bowfishers to a championship team via a World Championship, (5) selection and recognition of the Bowfisherman and Junior Bowfisherman (sixteen years of age or younger) of the Year, and (6) recording and presentation of Bowfishing Citation Awards to members. The official publication of the BAA is *Bowfishing Digest* published by Wilbur Corley.

The BAA has continued a tradition started by Paul T. Shore of recognizing individuals who land quality size fish while bowfishing. The BAA accomplishes this through their citation program. The minimum weights for specific species are listed in table 7.2. These weight standards are an excellent idea. Based on the criteria outlined in table 7.2, if you land an alligator gar that weighs 123 pounds 6 ounces, for example, you know that your catch is something special (see fig. 7.15)!

Figure 7.16

Weighing the fish for "largest fish" prize consideration always creates considerable interest at a BAA World Bowfishing Championship. This was a 28-pound buffalo taken during the 1993 Championship at Lake Dardenelle in Arkansas.

Citations are awarded by the BAA to any member who catches fish—with bow and arrow—at or above the minimum weight for each species listed in table 7.2. Certification procedures must be followed to document the catch date, weight, and other anthropometric data for each fish.

Bowfishing Tournaments

There are numerous bowfishing tournaments for rough fish held throughout the world annually. And, as examples, there are other bowfishing fun events such as the Shark Derby held in California and the Stingray Hunt conducted in Maryland each year. People of all ages and both sexes enter these events for prizes such as cash, tackle, clothing, trophies, boats, motors, or just for the fun of it. Prizes are provided through entry fees and corporate sponsors. Awards are given for such things as the largest fish taken in each species available during the tournament, greatest total fish weight caught during the hours of the tournament, and/or the largest number of fish shot during the tournament. There are competitive opportunities for teams as well as individuals. Currently, bowfishing tournaments are growing in numbers similar to the way bass fishing tournaments have evolved over the past few decades in the United States.

Tournament officials make arrangements for the disposal of the fish shot during these tournaments. The fish are usually given for human consumption to low income families, the homeless, and other people in the area who want them. As noted, these rough fish are edible. They can be prepared for frying, broiling, and smoking. Many people do acquire a taste for eating fish such as carp, buffalo, and gar.

Bowfishing tournaments sanctioned by the Bowfishing Association of America have been held in several states since 1990. The states where these tournaments have been held include Alabama, Arkansas, Florida, Georgia, Indiana, Kentucky, Louisiana, Maryland, Michigan, Mississippi, Missouri, Montana, New York, North Dakota, Oklahoma, Oregon, Pennsylvania, South Carolina, Tennessee, Texas, Washington, and Wisconsin. These tournaments will continue to increase in popularity in the future, and they will be found ultimately in most states that have rough fish. As a historic note, the First Annual BAA World Championship Bowfishing Tournament was held in 1991 at Mobile Bay, Alabama.

The bowfishing tournaments described below are examples of competitions where overall champions were determined by (1) the number of fish shot and (2) the overall weight of the fish taken during the hours of the tournament.

The 1993 BAA World Championship Bowfishing Tournament was held at Lake Dardanelle, Arkansas. This championship was a two-person team affair involving fifteen hours of bowfishing overnight. This was an example of a tournament where the team champions were determined by the number of fish shot instead of the total weight of the fish. Individuals who shot the heaviest carp, gar, buffalo, and bowfin were given cash or merchandise prizes (fig.7. 16).

The 1993 World Bowfishing Champions were Bob Brown and Danny Nichols (fig.7.17). *They shot a total of 306 fish during the fifteen hours of the tournament!* To put their achievements into perspective, that means they shot and put a fish in their barrels every 2.9 minutes during the tournament! This was accomplished despite the fact that the lake water was muddy due to rain before and during the competition. One competitor colorfully described the bowfishing conditions as, ". . . like shooting through a chocolate milk shake at night!" You can not have many misses under those conditions and become World Champion Bowfishers. It is a challenging sport.

The Annual Bowfishing Championship held at Clear Lake in northern California is an example of a tournament where the winning team is determined by the overall weight of the fish shot during the time allowed. This is a carp shoot with cash and merchandise prizes presented to the winners. It is a two-person team event. A winning team has taken as much as 847 pounds of carp during the two-day competition! A cash prize is also awarded to the individual who lands the largest carp. The California Department of Fish and Game authorizes this type of tournament because carp tend to multiply prolifically, grow very large, and upset the ecologic balance in the waters of Clear Lake if they are not harvested by bowfishers and other fishers.

The Great Lakes Bowfishing Championship at Lake Huron is another event where the champions are determined by total weight of the fish they shoot. This tournament has produced amazing weight results for carp and other rough fish. In a recent tournament involving 230 two-person teams, *81 tons of rough fish were taken by the 460 bowfishers over a two-day period!* It can get exciting!

Figure 7.17
Bob Brown and Danny Nichols shot 306 fish in fifteen hours overnight to become the 1993 BAA World Bowfishing Champions! Archery skill, quality tackle, and a good boat all contribute to accomplishments of this calibre. (Courtesy Oneida Labs, Inc., 8 Jason Drive, P.O. Box 68, Phoenix, NY 13135)

Bowfishing, like other archery sports, can be satisfying as an individual endeavor and/or as a social activity enjoyed with family and friends. It is an archery sport that can provide many hours of recreation throughout a lifetime for the active participant who enjoys combining archery, fishing interests, and a love for being in a natural environment in all types of weather conditions.

Review

1. Why do conservation departments approve of bowfishing for "rough fish?"
2. Describe the aiming techniques that have proved successful in bowfishing.
3. Which of the species listed in table 7.1 are currently legal for bowfishing in your state and what are the fishing limits?
4. When selecting and outfitting a boat for bowfishing, what are the essentials for safety and communication?
5. Compare and contrast recurve and compound bows in bowfishing.
6. In addition to regular target practice, how should you practice specifically for bowfishing?
7. What programs are available to recognize the efforts of bowfishers, and how do these programs operate?
8. Why does aiming in bowfishing present problems not encountered on land?
9. What would be your aiming point for a side shot at a fish from a distance of 30 feet when the fish appears to be 3 feet below the surface?
10. The fish encountered on a bowfishing trip may be smaller or larger than expected. What can you do to minimize this problem?

Physical Conditioning for the Archer 8

Archery, like most sports, places specific anatomical and physiological demands on the individual. The athlete must be ready to meet these exigencies. *Excellent physical conditioning increases the probability of success for the skilled athlete in any sport. Participants in the archery sports are not exceptions to this axiom.* Competitive target archers, field archers, and ski-archers are athletes, and they must prepare to meet the challenge of competition. Bowhunters also need a conditioning routine throughout the year. Their regular workouts should be vigorous enough to prepare them for the physical exertion required for stalking, shooting, and retrieving game animals.

The purpose of this chapter is to provide physical conditioning guidelines for serious archers. Health-related fitness guidelines are presented. Exercises are provided and described with some anatomic detail. The archer needs to know what muscular exercise can and cannot do for you. Therefore, the exercises are described to show the archer how they should be performed; which muscles are most involved to produce the joint motions for archery skill; how those muscle groups relate to archery performance; what outcomes can be expected through use of exercise at properly prescribed intensity, frequency, and duration levels; and what energy expenditure levels are required to attain a good level of performance-related fitness for archery.

Specificity of conditioning is unique for each sport. The conditioning for an archer differs considerably from exercise programs designed, as examples, for long distance runners or basketball players. Each sport places distinctive physiologic demands on various body systems. *Different muscles are not used from one sport to the next, but the muscle groups that cause joint motions are used differently.*

Skilled motions of limbs or body segments in terms of their velocities, degrees of motion, and dynamic stability vary between athletic specialties, and these even differ from one position to the next in team sports. A baseball pitcher, as one example, must be conditioned to move his throwing limb at maximum velocity at precise angles in order to be effective and minimize trauma to the joints of the throwing limb. In contrast, prescribed conditioning for a baseball catcher involves a completely different process because the throwing and other demands on the catcher differ considerably from those of a pitcher.

The target archer's sport has distinctive performance criteria. He or she must develop the strength to draw the arrow to the anchor point, keep the major joints of the body extended and stable, hold the bow and drawing arm units at maximum steadiness at full draw, and control extrinsic hand musculature under considerable force to perform a perfect release through finger extension. The archer must be prepared to perform this procedure consistently over the several hours each day required for tournament shooting. Logan and McKinney's SAID Principle (Specific Adaptations to Imposed Demands) applied to specificity of training deems that each of the aforementioned athletes (pitcher, catcher, and target archer), as examples, should be conditioned differently for them to achieve their potentials in competition.

Muscle Analysis of Shooting

This brief muscular, or myological, analysis of shooting is presented for two reasons: (1) to help the serious archer gain a better understanding of precisely what parts of the anatomy need to be conditioned and (2) to reinforce the learning of the shooting mechanics presented in chapter 4. It is highly recommended that the reader refer to chapter 4 and figure 8.1 as needed. This will help you associate the motions and skill techniques of the stance, bow arm, drawing arm, and release to the muscle functions described below.

Stance

In the conditioning considerations for the stance of target archers, field archers, and bowhunters, there are more similarities than there are differences. It is understood that the bowhunter's stance must be modified according to the terrain, foliage, and so on, while the target archer's stance remains constant. The common bond is that archers in each of the archery sports must develop good levels of muscle strength and endurance in the large muscle groups that maintain the body in its upright or shooting position against gravity.

The muscle groups that perform the function of extending the major joints at the ankles, knees, hips, and spine are called the *anteroposterior antigravity muscles*. These are shown in figure 8.2. Strength development in these antigravity muscles is indispensable for the archer because steadiness in the stance from anchoring through release is the foundation for shooting accuracy. Slight tremors or deviations of the extended body and bow arm segment will adversely affect arrow flight and accuracy. *Therefore, developing the anteroposterior antigravity muscles for optimum strength should have the highest priority in a conditioning program.* Good levels of strength and muscle endurance in the anteroposterior antigravity musculature will increase the probability for success on the target range or in the field.

The shooting stance is described as a bilateral, weight-bearing position. The major joints within the legs and spine are kept extended. This can be observed in figure 8.1. As a result, the static stability of the stance is maintained by a combination of the weight-bearing force and modest muscle contractile force within the antigravity musculature as needed to maintain equilibrium and steadiness (figure 8.2).

A. Nocking

B. Drawing

C. Anchor Point

D. Release and Follow–through

Figure 8.1
The shooting sequence in target archery. (Courtesy Patrick Brunhoeber)

Figure 8.2
The anteroposterior antigravity muscle groups form the foundation for stance stability.
(Courtesy Justin List, Mr. Teenage Arizona)

The *triceps surae* are the large posterior calf muscles (*gastrocnemius* and *soleus*). These muscles extend, or plantar flex, your ankle. The *quadriceps femoris* muscle group on the front of the thigh consists of four large muscles that extend the knee against gravity. The large buttocks muscle (*gluteus maximus*) extends the hip. The spinal column is maintained in the erect, or extended position, by the deep back muscle group known collectively as the *erector spinae*. If an archer has a tendency to lean backwards, or hyperextend, the spine while in the stance, the six large *abdominal, or stomach, muscles* act reflexively as antigravity muscles. They counteract the slightest posterior motion of the spine and move the trunk back to the extended position. The *erector spinae* muscles will extend the spine of the archer if he or she has a tendency to lean forward or flex the lumbar-thoracic spine. Those two large muscle masses located anterior and posterior to your spine provide constant force-counterforce to maintain a stable and extended spine required in the stance.

Fortunately, the antigravity muscle groups do not need to work maximally to maintain the erect shooting stance. That would lead to fatigue. They do contract as needed to maintain alignment of your body segments over each other and above the base of support (feet). Your equilibrium is maintained in this manner. The antigravity muscle actions are monitored and directed through several central nervous system mechanisms including those in the middle ear. Keeping the antigravity muscle strength levels above average help to make stance stability and equilibrium more efficient for the archer.

The antigravity muscle's strength and muscle endurance are most significant for those last few arrows shot during a target archery tournament when you need to be in the gold to be a medalist, or for the hunter's shot at a trophy animal after he or she has been hiking and climbing in the mountains for several hours. Fatigue can have a negative effect on accuracy at such times. The conditioned archer prevents or delays the onset of fatigue and increases the chance for success.

There is an old saying in athletics indicating that, "You make your own breaks." Being in good enough condition to delay or eliminate fatigue as a factor in competition or hunting is one way to make your own breaks in archery. *An excellent level of performance-related fitness is the most important fundamental for an athlete participating in any sport!* The performance level of all other fundamental skills of a sport is highly correlated to the physical condition of the athlete.

The Bow Arm

For the functions of the bow arm segment and drawing arm, the conditioning needs are basically the same for the target archer, field archer, and bowhunter. Bowhunters on average draw greater bow weights than target archers, so they need to develop more strength for the greater effort during the draw. However, strength and muscle endurance development in the arms, shoulders, and shoulder girdles should greatly exceed the demands of the bow weights used by all archers. *One should always over prepare for the strength requirements demanded in competition.*

Some of the arm, shoulder, and shoulder girdle musculature used to hold and draw the bow are shown in figures 8.3 and 8.4. These are the superficial muscles, that is, those you can palpate, or touch, on yourself or a cooperating adult. It is recommended that you find a consenting adult archer to collaborate with and feel these muscles as they contract during the draw and while holding prior to release. This will help you understand your own drawing process and the need for conditioning specific muscle groups.

The bow arm segment (left arm and shoulder for the right-handed archer) is vital to accuracy in archery. The muscles must be strong enough to eliminate motion in this arm prior to and at the time of release. Furthermore, the muscle endurance must be good enough to allow you to shoot efficiently for long periods of time, for example, 144 arrows during one FITA Round.

As can be seen in figures 8.3 and 8.4, the bow arm segment is held stable with the elbow and wrist extended. After nocking, the bow arm is raised from the side

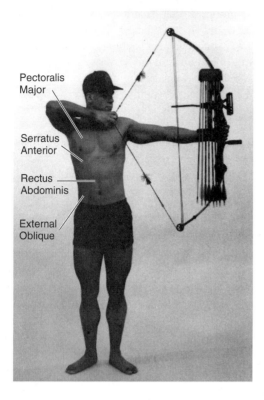

Pectoralis
Major

Serratus
Anterior

Rectus
Abdominis

External
Oblique

Figure 8.3
Anterior, superficial muscles during the drawing process. (Superficial muscles are those that can be palpated or touched.) (Courtesy Justin List, Mr. Teenage Arizona)

(shoulder joint abduction) about 90 degrees, as seen between figure 8.1A and B. That motion is accomplished primarily by contractile force of the large shoulder (*deltoid*) muscle. The deltoid, plus the underlying smaller muscles that help move the bow arm into shooting position, must have the strength and muscle endurance to repeatedly perform that function. More importantly, the deltoid must contribute considerable stabilizing force for the shoulder joint. It must help to hold the literal weight of your arm as well as the mass weight of the bow in space from the draw through the follow-through. Any deviation of the bow arm segment just prior to or at release will have a negative effect on accurate arrow flight. Both left and right deltoid muscles must be strong and have a good level of muscle endurance.

The *triceps brachii* on the posterior side of your upper arm is also a very important muscle within the bow arm segment, because it must keep the elbow in the extended position shown in figures 8.3 and 8.4. Maximal contraction of the muscles in the bow arm is contraindicated. That would tend to produce fatigue and tremors in these important muscles. As indicated in chapter 4, the skilled archer "relaxes" as much musculature as possible. As a result, the *triceps brachii* and *deltoid* muscles in the bow arm exert only enough contractile force to maintain the proper elbow and shoulder positions.

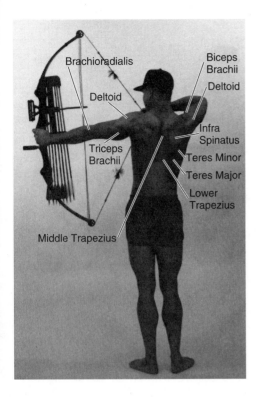

Figure 8.4
Posterior, superficial muscles during the drawing process. (Courtesy Justin List, Mr. Teenage Arizona)

There are thirteen muscle tendons surrounding the wrist joint. These are your *extrinsic hand muscles.* The bellies of these muscles make up the mass of your forearm, and they help keep the wrist extended by contributing some stabilizing contraction as the archer moves the bow arm during the draw and holds the anchor position through the follow-through. It is a serious mistake to maximize static or isometric contraction of these bow arm muscles in your forearm. That would result in slight tremors in the muscles after several arrows were released. Relaxation is the key. One must take advantage of the external forces provided by the bow weight during the draw to assist in maintaining extensions of the wrist and elbow joints. As noted in chapter 4, the wrist is kept extended during the shooting process. The wrist never flexes, hyperextends, or moves in any other direction. Your forearm (radioulnar joint) remains stable in the midposition (handshake position) between supination and pronation throughout the entire shooting sequence.

The Drawing Arm

The drawing arm segment (right arm and shoulder for a right-handed archer) must have adequate strength and muscle endurance to handle the archer's bow weight during numerous draws, for example, 288 times during a double FITA Round competition. From a competitive perspective, it is very important to the archer that the last draw feel as easy as the first draw. The key to this is to condition the muscles most involved in the draw, and learn how to relax all of your remaining muscle groups as much as possible throughout the competition.

The key point to remember regarding the draw is: *the major contractile force and ultimate control of the draw lies in the larger shoulder joint and shoulder girdle musculature and not in the smaller muscle mass of the arm.* The arm tends to be the focal point because it is the moving segment. The *biceps brachii* on the anterior aspect of your upper arm and other elbow flexors do contribute some force during the draw. The draw, however, results mainly from contractions by the musculature within your right shoulder joint and right shoulder girdle. The drawing arm segment transfers those muscle forces to the bowstring as the hand is drawn to the anchor point. Scientifically, the total motion of the drawing arm is the combined result of muscle contractile forces for the following: (1) elbow flexion, (2) horizontal abduction of the shoulder joint, and (3) shoulder girdle adduction or retraction.

The muscle force that causes horizontal abduction of the shoulder is provided by concentric contraction of the *posterior portion of the deltoid, infraspinatus*, and *teres minor* muscles. These superficial muscles are shown in figure 8.4. Because of the posterior location of these muscles, some archery instructors advise students to utilize a "focal concentration point" on "back muscles" instead of "arm muscles" during the draw. This is a good idea. The force to cause the right shoulder blade or scapula to move toward your spinal column during the draw (shoulder girdle adduction) is caused by contraction of some of the superficial *trapezius* muscle fibers on your back, as shown in figure 8.4. The deep rhomboid muscles attached to the shoulder blade *beneath the trapezius* also move the scapula during the draw.

If you feel a consenting adult archer's back during a draw, you can palpate the superficial drawing muscles described above and better comprehend their roles. Use this area on yourself as a *concentration focal point* during the draw. This will give you better perception and kinesthetic awareness of your draw. Also, palpate the biceps brachii in the upper arm of another archer to feel its involvement in the drawing process. It will be tense, but its force contribution is not as significant as the larger muscles most involved in the draw.

In compliance with the SAID Principle, conditioning for the draw arm segment must be designed to develop adequate strength and muscle endurance levels in the very important "back muscles" of the shoulder girdle and shoulder joint. In addition, the elbow flexors need specific work to provide their force contribution to the draw. Exercises are described later in this chapter.

As the drawing arm moves the bowstring and hand toward the anchor point, the shoulder blade (scapula) is being rotated upward to accommodate the head of the humerus of the arm at the shoulder joint. This rotary motion of the scapula is the result of muscle contractions by the *serratus anterior* and parts of the *trapezius*. Once your hand reaches the anchor point, the serratus anterior stabilizes (fig. 8.3) or holds the scapula in a firm position. Muscular stability of this type is very important in order to maintain steadiness during the shooting process. The muscle stabilizers in this body segment and elsewhere also need specific exercise during your daily workout schedule.

The Release and Follow-Through

The key muscle force component of the release is the final one-eighth inch movement of your arrow through the clicker prior to release. This very important motion is accomplished through intense concentration on your "middle back muscles." Specifically, the middle fibers of your trapezius muscle are conditioned to contract and *gently* move your shoulder blade toward your spinal column (scapular adduction). That moves the arrow past the clicker. When the "click" is heard, the joints of the string fingers are ready to extend, allowing the bowstring to move forward and the arrow to release.

As mentioned in chapter 4, the extension of your finger joints (interphalangeal joints) *is not* the result of forceful finger extensor muscle contraction by musculature in your forearm and hand. *The external force for release is caused by the bowstring as you relax the tension within the finger musculature, that is, relax the "three-finger hook" around the string (fig. 8.1D).* The bowstring should be released to move forward directly toward the target. The extending fingers should clear the string smoothly without any lateral pressure exerted on it.

During the follow-through phase of shooting, you simply watch the arrow flight to observe any erratic flight motions such as porpoising or fishtailing. You may exhale and inhale at this time and watch the arrow until it strikes the target. There will be a slight "recoil motion" of your draw arm, and the bow arm may drop a few degrees. Your sling keeps the bow from falling to the ground, and you regrasp the bow *after* the arrow is in flight or in the target.

Fitness Guidelines

Health and performance-related fitness include four important parameters that must be evaluated for each athlete. They include: (1) flexibility, (2) strength, (3) muscular endurance, and (4) cardiovascular endurance. If possible, each of these parameters should be measured for the individual prior to starting a conditioning program. That would quantify a fitness profile and help in writing the exercise prescription and goals for conditioning.

Flexibility

Flexibility is the degree to which a joint can move through its maximal normal range of motion.

Flexibility guidelines and exercises are not presented in detail. Due to the nature of the sport of archery, total body flexibility is desired, but it is not a high priority fitness factor for success. An athlete in gymnastics, for example, must consider total body flexibility as a prime fitness objective in order to meet the skill demands of that sport. The joint range-of-motion requirements needed to be highly skilled in archery are not as general, and they are much less demanding than in a sport such as gymnastics.

Full range-of-motion flexibility for archers is desired in the joints and body segments directly involved in the drawing process. Lack of flexibility in the drawing shoulder and shoulder girdle could be a problem, but this is observed in only a very small percentage of archers. The nature of the draw (a slow stretching process followed by a hold at the anchor point) tends to increase flexibility in the noncontractile tissue (tendons, ligaments, fasciae, etc.) of the drawing shoulder and shoulder girdle; therefore, a functional range-of-motion for the archer is maintained to some degree through the shooting process.

Drawing the bow can be used as a specific flexibility exercise when bow weight is held for 20 to 30 seconds *beyond* the anchor point at the completion of the total range-of-motion for the draw. *The 20 to 30 second static hold at the end of a joint's range-of-motion is an integral part of any flexibility exercise.* This type of flexibility exercise can be included and is recommended as a part of the "overload draw" procedure using an older, overweight bow. Overload drawing exercises are described later in this chapter.

Rapid or ballistic movement of a limb or body segment through a joint's range-of-motion is medically contraindicated. That can lead to lacerations of the noncontractile tissue which supports your joints. (A negative application of the SAID Principle.) As one example, many people are traumatized as they perform what they believe to be "flexibility exercises" to music. This involves rapid joint or limb motions during aerobic activities that are actually designed to improve cardiovascular endurance!

Strength

A functional definition of strength is the ability of an individual to overcome resistance by the use of internal force developed through muscle contraction. A strength development program for archers is included in this chapter.

In order to elicit the neuromuscular changes in the body needed to produce strength, the following scientifically-based guidelines are needed to define the workload:

1. INTENSITY: The weight load should be great enough to limit the number of repetitions to eight for each exercise, i.e., maximum weight load for a maximum of eight repetitions for each joint motion. When strength improves to the point that more than eight repetitions can be performed, add enough weight to return to the eight repetition level. Breathe during the difficult portion of the exercise. This keeps the glottis open in the throat and reduces the probability of herniation and undesired shifts in blood pressure. Maximum weight loads for less than eight repetitions should be avoided.
2. FREQUENCY: Strength workouts should be performed a *minimum* of four days per week in order to obtain the best results. Daily workouts may be performed without ill effects by individuals who are already strong and highly motivated as weight trainers. Workouts should be spaced 24 to 36 hours apart.
3. DURATION: The average strength workout should consume approximately one hour. A series of exercises such as those described later in this chapter should be selected to work the desired musculature. One series of weight training exercises is called a *set*. Three sets constitute a strength workout following the intensity guideline outlined above. *Perform the exercises slowly through the complete range-of-motion of the joint.* The one exception to that rule is knee joint flexion when exercising from the standing position. "Deep knee bends" are not recommended as an exercise

due to the potential for trauma to your knee ligaments and cartilages. If these strength guidelines are followed, the archer will acquire strength. It usually takes four to six weeks for the initial strength changes to be "felt" subjectively. Some natural muscle stiffness due to a residual of acid metabolites following muscle contraction will occur in the beginner during the first two weeks of weight training but will not be a problem as you continue with your workouts.

The term "neuromuscular changes" was used above for good reason. The most significant anatomic and physiologic changes to increase strength will be a result of *Specific Adaptations* of central nervous system (CNS) anatomy to the *Imposed Demands* of strength training outlined above. (This is another positive example of Logan and McKinney's SAID Principle related to changes in the human organism due to conditioning.) You become stronger by making the interrelationships between the muscle and central nervous systems more efficient. Muscle mass and tone increase in many people as a result of strength work, but the most important changes for increasing strength occur within the neural pathways in your CNS. Some "lean" people become very strong due to maximizing the efficiency of the CNS, and they have very little change in muscle mass.

Muscular Endurance

Muscle endurance is the ability of a muscle group to perform repeated contractions against relatively light resistance. Muscle endurance is needed when a performer must repeat joint motions numerous times during competition. The repetitive shooting procedure used in target archery tournaments is one example; therefore, the muscles most involved in the shooting process need a good to excellent level of muscle endurance.

To elicit the physiologic changes in the body to increase muscle endurance, the following workload guidelines must be followed:

1. INTENSITY: *The weight load to produce muscle endurance should be established to allow the performer to complete a minimum of twenty repetitions.* More repetitions may be performed at each workout station as time allows. The physiologic changes associated with this level of intensity will enhance aerobic metabolism for energy production.

2. FREQUENCY: *Muscle endurance workouts should be performed a minimum of four days per week.* Daily workouts may be performed without ill effects by people who already have a good level of health-related fitness. Individuals produce excellent results working six or seven days per week. It is recommended that a person alternate strength and muscle endurance workouts. That is functional, and boredom is reduced by not performing the same workload or activities on a daily basis.

3. DURATION: The average muscle endurance workout should consume approximately one hour. Three sets of exercises constitute one workout. The maximum number of repetitions at each exercise station per set may need to be adjusted periodically as a time consideration. *Perform all exercises slowly through the complete range-of-motion.* Avoid "deep knee bends" (full knee flexion) from the standing position as noted earlier.

An individual who starts a conditioning program must be patient. The anatomic and physiologic adaptations may not manifest themselves for weeks. You must also establish realistic goals and expectations for yourself. If you anticipate fast results, you will be frustrated. You must remember, for example, that muscular endurance development involves cellular as well as central nervous system adaptations. Time is required to produce the sophisticated modifications of muscle cells and organelles within cells responsible for increasing aerobic respiration and endurance. Using the guidelines above, you will begin to notice increases in your muscular endurance level in four to six weeks. Persistence will pay off!

Specific recommendations regarding strength and/or muscle endurance exercises for the various muscle groups used by archers are presented in detail in this chapter. Priorities will be established for strength and muscle endurance intensities during workouts.

Cardiovascular Endurance

Good to excellent levels of cardiovascular endurance require a high level of physiological efficiency of the heart, lungs, and the circulatory system to transport oxygen and other fuels to the organism during prolonged periods of physical exertion. This is the most important of all the fitness parameters. The best measures of cardiovascular function are cardiac output, the electrocardiogram, and maximal oxygen consumption.

Generally, the principal conditioning difference between target archers, field archers, and bowhunters is in the extent of cardiovascular endurance required to execute the skills. The average target archer does not need to develop more than an average or functional level of cardiovascular endurance. The nature of the sport does not place unusual maximal oxygen consumption demands on the archer. It is recommended, however, that the serious target archer perform enough aerobic exercise on a regular basis to maintain a good to excellent level of cardiovascular fitness.

There is one notable exception to the above for target archers. If you plan to be a serious competitor in the sport of ski-archery you will need to place a high priority on cardiovascular endurance conditioning. The most cardiovascularly fit athletes tested in past Winter Olympic Games are the cross-country skiers. Cardiovascular endurance is measured by the maximal oxygen consumption test. *Maximal oxygen consumption is the greatest volume of oxygen taken into the body, delivered to the lungs, and circulated to the cells for metabolic purposes per minute.* This is most commonly expressed in milliliters of oxygen consumed per minute per kilogram of your body weight (ml/kg/min). The higher the better! Cross-country skiers at the Olympic level have been measured as high as 94 ml/kg/min on this test!

It is recommended that serious ski-archers, who must shoot with accuracy following each circuit of four kilometers of cross-country skiing, should have maximal oxygen consumption values of at least 60 ml/kg/min for men and 55 ml/kg/min for women.

Field archers and bowhunters should analyze the physical exertion demands they can expect while in the field. As an example, if a hunt will take the bowhunter into wilderness country to walk and stalk for extended time periods, in cold or hot environments, over hills or into high altitudes, and with the possibility that you might have to pack out heavy game (e.g., a field-dressed elk), the hunter should give considerable thought to maintaining or developing cardiovascular endurance to meet these increased demands without difficulty.

Why is conditioning important? It is a tragic fact that a few hunters, usually age 35 (that is middle age!) and beyond, die of myocardial infarctions in the field. They were not capable of handling the added stress of their physical exertion in hot or cold environments in deserts, hills, or mountains. It pays to be prepared in terms of your cardiorespiratory mechanisms!

There are other, less traumatic, problems observed more frequently in unconditioned bowhunters. Much money is spent on tackle preparing for the hunt. Time is devoted to developing shooting skill and tuning tackle for the hunt. People go to the trouble to enter game animal lotteries and spend large amounts of money traveling to high mountain country for their prey. After spending all that money, time, and effort, some bowhunters are not capable of meeting the physiologic challenge of the hunt on foot through rugged terrain at high altitude in the cold. Surprisingly, this tends to happen among younger people who are not fit but "talk a good game" with a beer in hand. *If they pack in, their hunting partners often have to pack them out!*

The full preparation of the archer should include concurrent development of shooting skill and cardiovascular conditioning. An archer who wishes to increase his or her cardiovascular endurance should first be evaluated by a physician to determine whether or not the circulatory and respiratory systems are normal. The scientifically based guidelines below should help interested bowhunters, field archers, and target archers exercise at the energy expenditure levels required to maintain or develop cardiovascular fitness.

1. INTENSITY: To improve your cardiorespiratory capacity, intensity of exercise is measured according to two criteria: (1) A heart rate during exercise sufficient to produce positive aerobic training effects. That level of exercise intensity is known as your *threshold heart rate* or *THR*. (See table 8.1 for THR levels according to age and general condition status.) (2) *Energy expenditure* during workouts for men should be above 3,000 kilocalories per week (kcal/week), and women's physical exertion level should be over 1,800 kcal/week.

How do you determine what your exercising or threshold heart rate should be? Use table 8.1. Your maximum and resting heart rates play a key role in establishing your THR. The heart rate needs to be monitored in the morning while you are lying in bed. This measurement will provide your *resting heart rate*. Take a one-minute reading by gently palpating your radial artery at the wrist with your index and middle fingers. Such a reading is noted in *beats per minute* (BPM). Generally, if you are in average cardiovascular condition, your resting heart rate will be 55 to 75 BPM. Better conditioned people usually have more efficient cardiac function and slower heart rates. This is an exercise-induced slow heart rate (bradycardia), which should not be confused with pathological forms of bradycardia observed in geriatric patients.

Imagine, as an example, that you are 19 years of age with a good resting heart rate of 46 BPM. Table 8.1 will inform you that your heart rate intensity (THR) during exercise should be kept between 152 and 168 BPM. Your target heart rate number to keep in mind during cardiovascular or aerobic workouts should be 160 BPM.

Table 8.1 Threshold Heart Rate Intensity Levels for Cardiovascular Endurance Development

Age Group	Max HR*	Morning Resting Heart Rate Above 75 BPM	Morning Resting Heart Rate 55-75 BPM	Morning Resting Heart Rate Below 55 BPM
15–19	200	114 (120) 126	143 (150) 158	152 (160) 168
20–24	195	111 (117) 123	139 (146) 154	148 (156) 164
25–29	190	108 (114) 120	135 (142) 150	144 (152) 160
30–34	185	105 (111) 117	131 (138) 143	140 (148) 156
35–39	180	102 (108) 114	128 (135) 143	136 (144) 152
40–44	175	99 (105) 111	124 (131) 139	132 (140) 148
45–49	170	96 (102) 108	120 (127) 135	128 (136) 144
50–54	165	93 (99) 105	116 (123) 131	124 (132) 140
55–59	160	90 (96) 102	113 (120) 128	120 (128) 136
60–64	155	87 (93) 99	109 (116) 124	116 (124) 132
65–69	150	84 (90) 96	105 (112) 120	112 (120) 128
70–74	145	81 (87) 93	101 (109) 116	108 (116) 124

*The variability for maximum heart rate is ±10 BPM.
Note: This table should read as follows: A 22-year-old person has a maximum heart rate of 195 BPM ±10 BPM. If this individual's resting heart rate is 62 BPM, the threshold heart rate (THR) *during exercise* should average 139–154 BPM. The *target number* for THR would be 146 BPM for this person during aerobic activities to produce cardiovascular training effects.

How do you monitor THR intensity during an aerobic workout? First, you need to know your THR range in BPM during exercise. Second, the midpoint in that range should be kept in mind specifically; you should be near this exercise target number when monitoring the heart rate as you work out. Third, for individuals beginning an aerobic workout program, it is recommended that the heart rate be monitored every 10 to 15 minutes during exercise. In order to do this and obtain meaningful heart rates, you must stop exercising. *As soon as you stop your aerobic activity and while standing, determine your heart rate by gently palpating the radial artery at the wrist.* Within 5 to 10 seconds of stopping your exercise, take a 10-second heart rate count. Multiply that number by six for BPM.

A longer delay in monitoring the heart rate following cessation of exercise decreases accuracy, and one may not assume that the BPM reading reflects the actual heart rate during exercise. Ideally, a heart rate correctly monitored will be on your target number or at least within your THR range. (There are biomedical, electronic devices on the market that will measure your actual exercising heart rate.)

During the aerobic workout, one attempts to keep the exercising heart rate in BPM in the THR range and fairly close to the target number. As an example, a 52-year-old runner with a resting heart rate of 42 BPM has a THR range from 124 to 140 BPM, with an exercise target number of 132 BPM. This means that the *10-second heart rate reading* when monitored during exercise should be 22 beats. A lower reading would indicate that the exercise intensity was below the THR range (e.g., 16 beats per 10-second count would be 96 BPM). This person would need to increase his or her running pace (intensity) slightly to elevate the exercising heart rate to at least 124 BPM. Conversely, if the 10-second heart rate reading during the run were counted at 25 beats (150 BPM), this individual should decrease the running pace. The intensity would be 10 BPM above his or her THR range.

It is important to stay within your THR range during aerobic work. You should find this range to be comfortable. Breathing should not be labored, and you should be able to talk with a companion while moving at a pace intense enough to produce your THR.

There is a dangerous myth about workout intensity perpetuated by a few masochistic cretins. It states, "No pain, no gain!" The exercise intensity guidelines noted above for your threshold heart rate *will not* produce pain. *Exercise intensity does not have to be painful to produce positive results.* The thought of perceived pain and continued discomfort turns people away from regular exercise because for normal people pain is not a motivator to exercise. From anatomical, physiological, psychological, and medical perspectives, extreme stress exercise that produces pain is contraindicated and counterproductive to human beings who wish to attain either performance or health-related fitness.

You can use any form of exercise as long as it is intense enough to keep you in your THR range. Most commonly these are jogging, running, swimming, cycling, and some court sports (singles tennis, handball, etc.). Can walking be an aerobic activity? Yes, it is for some people. If a brisk walk at a pace of 3 to 4 miles per hour moves you into your THR, you should not be running. Find an activity or activities you enjoy that will keep your exercising heart rate where it should be for the required duration of the workout. A vital key to this type of exercise is the enjoyment and satisfaction one has during daily workouts and in attaining short and long range goals! That is one "secret" to exercise continuity.

The other dimension of intensity of exercise noted above is your level of energy expenditure. This is measured in kilocalories. *The kilocalorie is described metabolically as the amount of heat required to raise the temperature of one liter of water one degree centigrade.* Commonly called "calorie," this unit is used by dieticians and exercise scientists for measuring energy intake (food) and energy expenditure (exercise/physical exertion). Everyone has heard about "calories" in one manner or another. Minimum and desired energy expenditure levels in kilocalories per week to maintain and develop health-related fitness were noted above for men (3,000 kcal/wk) and women (1,800 kcal/wk).

Table 8.2 Energy Expenditure Factors for Determining kcal/min

Horizontal Running	Factor
11 min 30 sec per mile	0.135
9 min per mile	0.193
8 min per mile	0.208
7 min per mile	0.228
6 min per mile	0.252
5 min 30 sec per mile	0.289
Swimming	
Backstroke	0.169
Breaststroke	0.162
Crawl stroke	0.156
Walking: 3–4 MPH	
Firm surface	0.080
Fields and hillsides	0.082
Grass	0.081
Cycling	
5.5 miles per hour	0.064
9.4 miles per hour	0.100
Racing	0.169

Note: This table should be used as follows: Convert your weight in pounds to kilograms by multiplying by 0.454. Multiply your weight in kilograms by the factor to determine your energy expenditure in kilocalories per minute. *Example*: A 147 pounder (66.74) kg utilizes 13.88 kcal/min while running at an 8-min-per-mile pace:

1. 147 pounds × 0.454 = 66.74 kg
2. 66.74 kg × 0.208 = 13.88 kcal/min

How can you monitor your kcal/week? Exercise physiologists have done metabolic measurements on humans involved in everything from target archery to sexual intercourse! So, energy expenditure values are available for most of the activities humans pursue. *The following is the procedure to determine energy expenditure for target archery practice:*

1. Change your body weight in pounds to kilograms by multiplying the pounds by *0.454.*
2. Multiplying your weight in kilograms by a factor of *0.065* will give you the kcal/min you use during target archery practice or tournament action.

Target archery for a 147 pounder (66.74 kg) for an hour would result in an energy expenditure of 260 kilocalories (4.34 kcal/min). If this person shot an hour per day for five days per week, the total weekly energy expenditure would be 1,300 kilocalories per week for target archery practice. He or she most likely would not reach THR intensity while shooting; so one can readily see that integration of aerobic activities with archery practice is needed to reach a desired energy expenditure level and a good cardiovascular endurance status. This is where supplemental running, cycling, swimming, or walking workouts can be utilized during the week in addition to target practice.

Table 8.2 provides energy expenditure factors to be used in the calculation of kcal/min for running, swimming, walking, and cycling.

If our 147-pound archer ran at an 8-minute-per-mile pace for 40 minutes per day at THR intensity four days per week, he or she would expend 2,220 kilocalories. Add three hours per week of target archery practice at 260 kilocalories per hour, and the total would be a very good level of energy expenditure intensity of 3,000 kcal/week. Such a regimen is desirable because it combines cardiovascular conditioning with shooting.

2. FREQUENCY: In order to produce positive adaptations in the blood chemistry (cholesterol, triglycerides, and glucose), the blood vascular transport system, and other parts of your cardiorespiratory anatomy, aerobic workouts at threshold heart rate intensity should be performed a minimum of four days per week. Ideally, workouts should be spaced about thirty-six hours apart. Some form of daily aerobic activity is recommended for individuals who have established good cardiorespiratory endurance with resting heart rates in the morning below 55 beats per minute.

3. DURATION: Thirty minutes of cardiovascular exercise at your threshold heart rate is considered to be the minimum time for a workout. Durations of 30 to 60 minutes per workout are adequate. If an individual is exercising six to seven days per week, it is a good idea to alternate such components as duration times and activities. For example, an hour bicycle ride on Monday could be followed by a 30-minute jog on Tuesday. *Activities chosen should be of interest and challenge the archer to attain his or her realistic short and long range goals.* Those are important considerations because long term continuity of exercise is a must in developing and maintaining performance-related fitness.

As indicated above, ski-archers and some bowhunters have a greater need to develop cardiovascular endurance to excellent levels than average target archers because of the physiologic demands of their sports. A year-round program of cardiovascular workouts is recommended. It is a mistake to "try to get in shape" in a few weeks or days prior to competing or going out on the hunt. If you stay "in shape," your workouts may be progressively more intense in terms of energy expenditure per workout for a few weeks before competing or going into the field.

Figure 8.5
Heel raise exercise—starting position.

Figure 8.6
Heel raise exercise—finish position. This exercise isolates and works the posterior calf or triceps surae muscle group.

Exercises for Stance Stability

All archers need above average strength in their *antigravity muscles* (fig. 8.2) to maintain a stable stance while shooting. A set of six exercises is recommended. Strength development should be the priority fitness factor for these antigravity muscle exercises. Therefore, the intensity, frequency, and duration guidelines outlined above for strength should be followed whenever possible while performing these exercises. Figures 8.5 through 8.13 serve as examples to demonstrate one method to exercise the antigravity muscle groups. There are several other excellent types of weight machines plus free weights and diverse exercise routines to work these muscle groups.

When resistance loads cannot be found to meet the intensity criterion for strength development, muscle endurance exercise intensity should be substituted. Some modest strength gain will be made while performing muscle endurance intensity exercise, and stance stability will be enhanced. Figures 8.5 through 8.13 show exercises (with the exception of fig. 8.8) that may be performed with or without machines to work the antigravity musculature.

Figure 8.7
The knee extension exercise for the anterior thigh, or quadriceps femoris muscle group.

Figure 8.8
The knee flexion exercise for the posterior thigh, or "hamstring," muscle group. These muscles flex the knee as shown and help extend the hip joints against resistance.

Figure 8.9
Double hip extension exercise—starting position.

Figure 8.10
Double hip extension exercise—finish position. Hip extension is caused by concentric contraction of the large buttocks muscle, the gluteus maximus.

Remember that there are times when neither free weights nor weight machines are necessary for muscle endurance and strength development exercise. The weight of the body working against and with gravity can be used for strength and muscle endurance gains.

Note: All exercises pictured and/or described in this chapter should be performed *slowly* against resistance and while moving with the gravitational field. Breathing should be as normal as possible, and the breath should not be held. That causes abnormal blood pressure shifts.

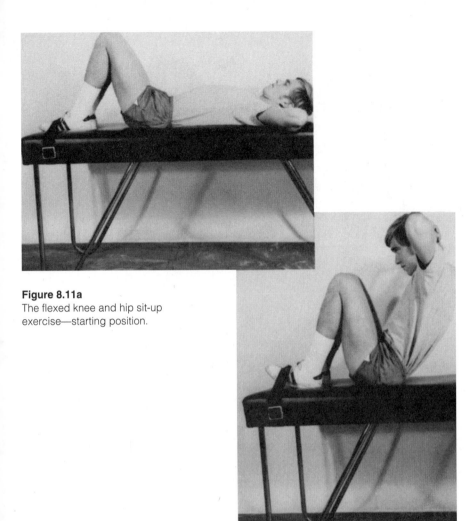

Figure 8.11a
The flexed knee and hip sit-up
exercise—starting position.

Figure 8.11b
The flexed knee and hip sit-up exercise—
finish position. This execise works the
abdominal musculature, "stomach muscles."

Figure 8.12
The back raise exercise—starting position.

Figure 8.13
The back raise exercise—finish position. Spinal extension is caused by the deep back muscle group, erector spinae.

Exercises for the Bow Arm

Steadiness of the bow arm is one of the most critical aspects of shooting. As you have learned, the major muscles most involved to produce this stability are located at the shoulder girdle, shoulder, and elbow joints. As a result, the archer needs considerable strength in the deltoid muscle of the shoulder as well as in the triceps and biceps brachii muscles that surround the elbow joint. Strength development guidelines need to be followed for the bow arm exercises.

Figures 8.14 and 8.15 are examples of exercises primarily designed to work the large deltoid muscle over the shoulder. This muscle must be strong enough to support the mass weight of the bow plus the literal weight of the arm against gravity. It

Trapezius

DELTOID

Triceps Brachii
Biceps Brachii
Serratus Anterior

Figure 8.14
A bow arm weight-training exercise using an Exer-Genie Exerciser pulley device. The arm is moved from the side into the shooting position (ABDUCTED) by the large shoulder muscle, the deltoid.

has to be strong enough to eliminate even minuscule arm motions during every shot in a target or field archery tournament and during a hunt. Being shaky during a shot "does not feed the bulldog" in archery!

Figure 8.14 illustrates a resistance exercise using a pulley device. The deltoid muscle is the muscle most involved as the arm is raised or abducted from the body in the same manner as moving the bow into the final shooting position. This exercise also works the important serratus anterior and trapezius muscles. As the arm is moved through its upward range of motion (abducted) against resistance, the scapula (shoulder blade) is upwardly rotated by lower fibers of the serratus anterior and upper and lower portions of the trapezius.

Figure 8.15 shows a traditional weight training exercise, the overhead press. This is also a good method to develop strength in the bow arm musculature. This exercise involves the large shoulder musculature, some back muscles, plus your triceps brachii muscle, which extends the elbow against resistance. Keeping the bow arm elbow fully extended at all times is critical while shooting. This requires considerable strength in the triceps brachii muscle.

Figure 8.15
The overhead press exercise is a good bow arm exercise. It strengthens the deltoid muscle at the shoulder and the triceps brachii muscle that extends the elbow against resistance.

Figure 8.16
The bench press exercise contributes strength to the bow arm unit by working the elbow extensor muscle, the triceps brachii, plus the deltoid and pectoralis major muscles of the chest.

Figure 8.17
The biceps brachii "curl exercise" adds anterior stabilizing strength to the extended elbow of the bow arm unit. The biceps brachii, as an elbow flexor, also adds strength to the drawing arm.

The bench press (shown in figure 8.16) is another weight training exercise designed to strengthen the triceps brachii on the posterior side of your elbow. Also, this exercise strengthens the deltoid as well as the large pectoralis major muscle on your chest. Work by the deltoid and triceps brachii during the bench press makes this a good exercise for the bow arm unit. As in the previous two exercises, crucial shoulder girdle musculature is also conditioned.

The elbow of the bow arm segment is held in the stable and extended position by all of the muscles surrounding the elbow joint. Therefore, the archer should strengthen not only the muscle on the back of the elbow, the triceps brachii, but also the biceps brachii on the front of the elbow. The "biceps curl" exercise as shown in figure 8.17 is designed to develop strength in the muscles that have an anterior or frontal spatial relationship to the elbow joint. The "biceps curl" exercise should be used on both elbows to enhance efficiency in the bow and drawing arms.

Exercises for the Drawing Arm

As noted previously, the main force for the drawing arm does not come from the arm muscles per se. The draw force is derived from strong shoulder and shoulder girdle muscles. Some of these are shown in figure 8.18. They include the *deltoid*,

Figure 8.18
A drawing arm exercise using a pulley device that isolates the critical muscles used to exert force to overcome the bow weight.

Figure 8.19
A drawing arm exercise using dumbbells for resistance. It is important to move the arms from the floor through the complete range-of-motion.

infraspinatus, teres minor, trapezius, and *rhomboid* muscles. (The latter are not seen in figure 8.18 because they lie beneath your trapezius muscle.) These are the "back muscles" that your archery instructor or coach wants you to concentrate on during target archery practice as you draw through your clicker. Since these muscles provide the force to overcome the bow weight during the draw, they must have above average strength to be functional. The stronger these muscles are, the easier it is for you to handle your bow weight during draws throughout a tournament. Also, with added strength in these muscles, the archer may be able ultimately to increase bow weight. That provides higher arrow velocities and flatter trajectories which can lead to better accuracy and higher scores.

Figure 8.18 shows a drawing arm resistance exercise performed with a pulley device. It is important for the archer to move the arms through the complete range-of-motion as indicated by the direction of the arrows. You should feel the shoulder blades move toward your spine (scapular adduction) as the arms are moved backward (horizontal abduction) as shown in figure 8.18.

Figure 8.20
Shoulder horizontal adduction exercise to complement the drawing arm exercise using a pulley device.

Figure 8.21
Shoulder horizontal adduction exercise using dumbbells to compliment the drawing arm exercise. It is important to move the arms through their complete range-of-motion from below the bench to touching the dumbbells above your head.

The same exercise is shown in figure 8.19 using free weights or dumbbells for resistance. The starting position is with the hands near the floor. It is very important to move the hands and arms as far as possible to the finish position shown in figure 8.19.

As a matter of scientific principle, *resistance exercises should be performed bilaterally, that is, muscle groups on opposite sides of the body should receive equal work to maintain strength, muscle endurance, and flexibility balance.* An exercise to work the chest and shoulder is depicted for use with a wall pulley and dumbbells in figures 8.20 and 8.21 respectively. The arms are brought forward (horizontally adducted) by the contracting muscles on the front of the shoulder and chest. This stretches "back muscles" involved while performing the exercise shown in figures 8.18 and 8.19. Strengthening front as well as back muscles will make the archer's draw easier to handle and prevent loss of shoulder range-of-motion (flexibility).

The Overload Draw Exercise

The archer should consider the bow a highly specific weight training device. The exercises previously described in this chapter can develop general strength and muscle endurance in muscle groups used by the archer. Workouts with free weights or weight machines have greater workloads available than found in most bow weights. Those heavier workloads are needed in the application of the SAID and Overload

Principles to attain your fitness objectives, particularly in strength. However, the archer can achieve a very specific muscle endurance overload by exercising with a bow weight in excess of the normal bow weight used in competition or while hunting. This type of exercise has the potential to develop strength and muscle endurance in muscle groups through the precise ranges of motion and at the specific joint angles utilized in drawing and holding the bow during a contest or hunt. Logan and McKinney have described this type of exercise in the literature as "Specifics."

As an added component of the conditioning process for archers, it is recommended that *overload draw exercises* be included within each set when conditioning for muscle endurance. (A used "exercise bow" a few pounds over the normal bow weight should be purchased and used exclusively for overload draw exercises. Your competitive tackle should not be used for this purpose.) A *minimum* of 20 draws should be made per exercise set to develop muscle endurance. That means the archer would complete a *minimum* of 60 overload draws during the three sets of a workout. (FITA Round shooters may want to complete 144 consecutive overload draws periodically just as a drill.)

The bow should be drawn to the anchor point as shown in figures 8.22, 8.23, and 8.24, and held statically long enough to simulate the release and follow-through phases. The bowstring must not be released. The string should be eased back to the starting position, and the next draw initiated within 15 to 20 seconds.

Overload drawing should be considered more than a weight training exercise. While overload drawing, the archer should *mentally practice shooting mechanics*. Each fundamental, body position, and joint angle should be thought through carefully. It is recommended that the position of a body part or segment be given specific attention during each set of overload draws, for example, the bow hand position at the pivot point during the first set, "back muscles" supplying the drawing force on the second set, bowstring to finger position on the third set, and so on.

Another approach to the "mental practice" aspect of overload drawing is to use information based on your shooting problems established during target practice and videotape analyses of your shooting fundamentals (see chapter 4). Use the overload draw time to mentally practice proper shooting technique. Mentally eliminate your major problem defined through videotape analyses and/or observations by your archery coach.

Ideally, the overload drawing workout should follow practice on a target range or field archery unit. The time spent should be an integration of the mental with the physical aspects of archery. Once the fundamentals have been learned, archery becomes more mental than physical.

Overload drawing is shown in figures 8.22, 8.23, and 8.24. It is recommended that most of these draws be smooth and continuous from the starting position to anchor. However, an occasional static hold at mid-position for 6 to 8 seconds—the position shown in figure 8.23—could facilitate some isometric strength gain. Also, the hold while at the anchor point, figure 8.24, can be for at least 6 to 8 seconds. The reader should refer to figures 8.4 and 8.18 while observing the changes in the superficial back and shoulder muscles of the archer in figures 8.22, 8.23, and 8.24. Several changes occur in the bow arm and drawing arm musculature. Some of these can be observed by comparing and contrasting the alterations in the external appearance of the back and shoulder muscles of the archer in figures 8.22 and 8.24.

Figure 8.22a
The overload draw exercise—starting
position. (Bow courtesy Black Widow
Custom Bows, Inc., 1201 Eaglecrest,
P.O. Box 2100, Nixa, MO 65714)

Figure 8.22b
The overload draw exercise—back
musculature—starting position.

Figure 8.23a
The overload draw exercise—
midposition.

Figure 8.23b
The overload draw exercise—back
musculature—midposition.

Figure 8.24a
The overload draw exercise—anchor position.

Figure 8.24b
The overload draw exercise—back musculature—anchor position.

Overload draws may be made periodically beyond the anchor point to work on flexibility in the shoulder-shoulder girdle segments. If more flexibility is desired, the draw should be slow and to the end of the range-of-motion of the draw arm *beyond the anchor point.* A static hold should be made at that point for 20 to 30 seconds. This procedure can be repeated ten to fifteen times during the workout, preferably when the archer's core temperature is slightly elevated. This flexibility exercise, for example, would be best following a running workout of about 30 minutes.

It was noted earlier in this chapter that total energy expenditure is important to consider in terms of kilocalories per week of exercise. If you perform the types of weight training exercises described herein for archers, table 8.3 can be used to help you determine your energy expenditure values for weight training.

Summary and Conditioning Recommendations

When the skill factor between competitors is equal, a target archer or field archer who has above average conditioning increases his or her probability of outscoring another archer who has only average or lower levels of muscle endurance, strength, and cardiovascular endurance. The serious bowhunter in good condition who must go after game in wilderness or rugged terrain will facilitate that task, assure his or her own survival, and increase the likelihood of making the kill and carrying out the meat for human consumption.

The following thirteen systematic activities are recommended as *one set* of exercises for archers. *Three sets should be performed to constitute a daily workout.* The guidelines for strength should be followed regarding intensity, frequency, and duration if that is the conditioning outcome desired by the archer. If muscle

Table 8.3   Energy Expenditure Factors for Determining kcal/min Values for Weight Training

Types of Equipment Used	Factor
Hydra-Fitness	0.132
Universal	0.116
Nautilus	0.092
Free weights	0.086

Note: This table should be used as follows: Convert your weight in pounds to kilograms by multiplying by 0.454. Multiply your weight in kilograms by the appropriate factor to determine your energy expenditure in kilocalories per minute. *Example*: A 166 pounder (75.36 kg) would use 6.48 kcal/min doing free weight exercise:

1. 166 pounds $\times$ 0.454 = 75.36 kg
2. 75.36 kg $\times$ 0.086 = 6.48 kcal/min

endurance is the priority, those conditioning guidelines for muscle endurance should be followed. Strength workouts could be pursued on alternate days, with muscle endurance weight loads providing a change of pace, if desired. (A variety of free weights, weight machines, pulley devices, and your own body moving against and with gravity may be used to perform these exercises.)

Stance

1. Heel raise (figs. 8.5 and 8.6)
2. Knee extension (fig. 8.7)
3. Knee flexion (fig. 8.8)
4. Hip extension (figs. 8.9 and 8.10)
5. Sit-up (fig. 8.11)
6. Back raise (figs. 8.12 and 8.13)

Bow Arm

7. Shoulder abduction (fig. 8.14)
8. Overhead press (fig. 8.15)
9. Bench press (fig. 8.16)
10. Biceps curl (fig. 8.17)—use for draw arm also

Draw Arm

11. Horizontal abduction (fig. 8.19)
12. Horizontal adduction (fig. 8.21)
13. Overload drawing (figs. 8.22 through 8.24)

When three sets of these exercises are completed at the intensity desired, it is recommended that the archer conclude the workout with a minimum of 30 minutes of cardiovascular endurance exercise (running, walking, cycling, swimming, etc.) at the threshold heart rate level of intensity most of the time.

Approximately 45 minutes are needed to complete the weight training exercises noted above. Let us assume that our 147-pound (66.74 kg) archer did this four times per week with free weights. That would be an energy expenditure of 1,032 kcal/week.

If he or she jogged at THR intensity at an 8-minute-per-mile pace for 30 minutes four times per week, 1,666 kilocalories would be expended. The total energy expenditure for these activities would be 2,698 kcal/week. Add to that four hours of archery practice per week for 1,040 kcals, and the grand total would be a very respectable 3,738 kcal/week of energy expenditure during supplemental exercise. RESULT: a better archer with a good level of health-related fitness!

Increasing the level of flexibility, strength, muscle endurance, and cardiovascular endurance produces important physiological and anatomical changes in the archer. It is of utmost importance that he or she continues target practice concurrent with these developmental modifications in the body. This procedure will ensure that changes in accuracy are also positive. If the archer conditions without shooting on a regular basis, it may take time to adjust the skill fundamentals to the anatomical and physiological changes. For the most positive results, the archer should condition using the recommended guidelines and practice shooting concurrently at least four days per week.

Review

1. Name the four important fitness parameters necessary to evaluate for each athlete. Of these, which has the lowest priority for archers?
2. When participating in an aerobic workout, how should you monitor your heart rate, at what intervals should you check it, and what is your THR and target level?
3. What are the chief differences in general conditioning among target archers, field archers, and bowhunters?
4. Compare and contrast the differences in the expected anatomic changes between strength development and conditioning for muscular endurance.
5. Why are rapid or ballistic movements contraindicated as exercises for increasing flexibility?
6. It takes 3,500 kilocalories of energy expenditure to rid one's self of one pound of stored, excess fat. How long would it take for you to get rid of one pound of your fat by using target archery practice as your only exercise?
7. Review the energy expenditure values. What activities can you use and for what duration to expend 2,000 to 3,500 kcal/week?
8. Discuss the specificity of training concept related to the overload draw exercise.
9. Write out a complete fitness program for yourself involving developmental activities for strength, muscle endurance, cardiovascular endurance, and skill. What are the frequencies for the activities? Have you adhered to the intensity criteria? What is the daily duration level for the activities chosen? What is the total energy expenditure per week in kilocalories?
10. Should you be guided in your exercise regimen by the often heard phrase "No pain, no gain?" Explain your response.
11. Substantiate the statement: "Overload drawing should be considered more than a weight training exercise."
12. Define and give an example of the SAID Principle.

Archery in Literature and Art

9

Since the bow and arrow have played such an important part in the survival of the human race for centuries, it is not surprising to find that authors of a wide variety of literature as well as artists throughout the world have included archers and archery feats in their creative and scholarly endeavors. The student of archery is encouraged to activate his or her intellectual curiosity and search for those literary and artistic works. It can be stimulating and fun!

The purpose of this chapter is to alert the student of archery to the strong presence of the subject of archery in literature and art produced throughout the ages. From an academic perspective, it is always interesting to look for relationships where one is not aware an association exists. *There are strong relationships between archery and the humanities.* (It should be noted that the scientific literature also contains an interesting body of knowledge about archery.) The exploration of those relationships can be fascinating for the individual who is intellectually curious because the topic encompasses many academic disciplines and virtually all societies and cultures throughout the history of the world.

A few references are listed in this chapter and in the bibliography for those readers who wish to begin looking at the literature and art of archery following this very brief introduction.

Literature

There is considerable mythology surrounding the constellation Sagittarius. Sagittarius is a large southern constellation that the Greeks called a centaur. The centaur is said to be shooting an arrow. The word *sagittarius* actually means "archer." Sagittarius is located south of Aquila and is partly in the Milky Way. It is east of Antares, one of the central stars in the constellation known as Scorpio. Sagittarius can be seen during the months of August and September in the United States. Figure 9.1 provides a schematic diagram of Sagittarius.

The various stars within Sagittarius form parts of the archer and his bow and arrow. Rukbat is the archer's knee; Arkab is the archer's tendon; Ascella is the archer's armpit or axillary region; Media is the midpoint of the bow; and Al Nasl is the arrow point. As the reader will note from figure 9.1, it took a vivid imagination to visualize an archer amidst that celestial configuration.

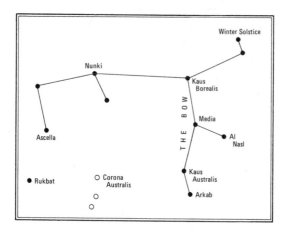

Figure 9.1
The Southern constellation known as Sagittarius, The Archer.

Greek mythological literature called the centaur of Sagittarius Chiron. Chiron was the famous son of Philyra and Saturn. The Roman poet Ovid reports that when Chiron was slain by Hercules with a poisoned arrow, Jupiter, the Father of the Gods, placed Chiron among the constellations. Ovid wrote: "Midst Golden Stars he stands refulgent now and thrusts the Scorpion with his bended bow." The reference is to the relationship between Al Nasl and Antares.

Apollo held many titles in mythological literature. One was The God of Archery. He was credited with numerous extraordinary feats with the bow and arrow. One of the most famous of these mythologic events is said to have taken place on Mount Parnassus. A great python was raiding families who lived in the area. The python smashed homes, ate human beings, and made a general nuisance of himself! Apollo decided to put a stop to that obstreperous behavior and took his bow and arrows in pursuit of the python. He ultimately found the python and invited him to fight. As is the case in most myths, good triumphed over evil. Apollo fought the python for four hours and finally used his great archery skill and killed the python with an accurately placed arrow.

Shortly following the battle with the python, Apollo encountered Eros, also known as Cupid. He insulted Eros by telling him that a boy should not play with a man's weapons. The reference, of course, was to the bow and arrows carried at all times by Eros. This verbal attack by Apollo enraged Eros. He decided to let Apollo know that he, Eros, was a highly skilled archer in his own right. He got even with Apollo by shooting him with a golden arrow of love. Shortly thereafter, Apollo fell in love with the beautiful Daphne, Goddess of Wild Things. Daphne was the daughter of Peneun, the River God. Eros promptly shot Daphne with a lead arrow of hate. That well-placed arrow made Daphne's feeling for Apollo one of utter disgust. Ultimately, she turned into a laurel tree to distance herself from her amorous pursuer. Apollo, in love with Daphne to the end,

Figure 9.2
The Education of Achilles by Chiron. (From E. G. Heath, *The Grey Goose Wing*)

showed his undying love by hanging his bow and quiver on her limbs. Eros not only took care of Apollo's attitude problem but taught him that archery is a sport for people of all ages and social status.

With his bow and arrows, Eros had many adventures in mythological literature. The term *eros* is rather interesting. It serves as the root word for the term "erotic" which coincides with one major purpose of the mythological existence of Eros. The term *eros* also gave rise to the word "arrow."

One of the greatest mythological archers was Hercules, or Herakles. Hercules is better known for his feats of strength, but he also achieved many remarkable accomplishments with the bow and arrow. It was with Hercules' bow that Philoctetes killed Paris during the Trojan War. Earlier, it will be remembered, Paris had shot Achilles with a poisoned arrow. That was a remarkable archery shot, because Paris shot Achilles in the heel, the only vulnerable portion of his body. Human anatomists continue to refer to the tendon from the *gastrocnemius* and *soleus* muscles (triceps surae) to the calcaneus bone as "the Achilles tendon." The concentric contraction force from these muscles via the Achilles tendon will plantar flex your ankle. This force, for example, moves you up on your toes in the standing position. This tendon and muscle group (fig. 8.2) are part of your antero-posterior antigravity muscles, which help to keep you upright in the shooting stance. An artist's portrayal of Achilles is shown in figure 9.2.

Figure 9.3
Odysseus, on returning from his many wanderings slays the suitors of Penelope, his wife. The use of a thumb release can be assumed due to the position of his bowstring hand—5th century B.C. (From E. G. Heath, *The Grey Goose Wing*)

In the *Iliad* and *Odyssey,* Homer, the eighth century B.C. Greek poet, wrote about numerous feats by archers. In the *Odyssey,* Homer describes ten years of adventures by Odysseus following the Trojan War. Figure 9.3 is an artist's depiction of the business he took care of when he finally arrived home and found his wife with some friendly and amorous folk from the neighborhood! A review of some contemporary homicides involving spouses indicates that the principal change in the scenario depicted in figure 9.3 is the weapon used to commit the crime. Human nature may not have changed much over the centuries.

Another minor constellation is known as Sagitta, or the Arrow. It is located in the Milky Way just north of a constellation known as the Eagle. In comparing and discussing Sagittarius and Sagitta, Aratos wrote, "There further shot another arrow but this with a bow. Towards it the Bird more northward flies." The references are to Sagittarius and the Eagle. Eratosthenes, a Greek mathematician and astronomer from Alexandria, considered Sagitta to be the shaft with which Apollo exterminated the Cyclops. Sagitta has also been referred to in mythological literature as one of Cupid's arrows.

As we move forward historically, other archers bordering on the mythological emerge in the literature, and additional information is derived from ballads. Robin Hood belongs in that category. There is no strong evidence that such a person actually lived. However, it is possible. As his legend grew, his feats with the bow and arrow became exaggerated. This is a common characteristic of mythology; that is, one is apt to find historically substantiated subject matter combined with feats and episodes purely mythological in nature.

There is an account in the literature of a legendary wand shoot between Robin Hood and an archer named Clifton. According to the tale, Clifton shot his arrow

Figure 9.4
An eighteenth-century engraving of Robin Hood by Thomas Bewick. (From E. G. Heath, *The Grey Goose Wing*)

first and hit the two-inch wand at 100 yards (91.44 meters in England). Before Clifton's arrow stopped vibrating, Robin Hood released an arrow from his longbow and completely split the shaft of Clifton's vibrating arrow. The mathematical probability of that occurring, even with the finest Olympic or compound bows with matching graphite arrows, is infinitesimal.

The best contemporary trick-shot archers usually make their shots at distances of 10 to 20 yards. Some movie stunt men do not rely on skill alone for those close-up shots you have seen of arrows penetrating a human body and blood gushing forth profusely! To accomplish that dramatic effect, the arrow is mounted on a very thin wire and guided directly to its mark. The arrow penetrates a large pad with a bag filled with red fluid strategically placed under the stunt man's clothing. Such procedures by contemporary professional archers make the story of Robin Hood's wand shot appear even more fantastic. But, as you will recall, virtually every Robin Hood movie ever made features some unbelievable shots. That is why they call it "show business."

Wand shooting is referred to periodically in English literature. A formal Wand Round for competitive purposes evolved as a result. The Wand Round consists of shooting thirty-six arrows at a piece of balsa wood two inches in width projecting six feet upward from the ground. The scoring is simple, but achieving a score is extremely difficult! Any arrow embedded in the wand counts as a hit. Also, a witnessed rebound from the wand counts as a hit. The challenge of wand shooting lies in the distances involved. Men shoot at the two-inch wand from 100 yards, intermediate boys from 80 yards, and women as well as intermediate girls shoot at the wand from 60 yards. This is an extremely difficult task. The reader may want to try to duplicate the alleged feat of Robin Hood. To fully appreciate the difficulty, use a longbow with wooden arrows!

There is a grave in England supposedly occupied by Robin Hood. A portion of the epitaph reads, ". . . No archer was like him so good; his wildness named him Robin Hood." (His real name was supposed to be Robert, Earl of Huntington.) It is rather interesting to note that "hood" is a vernacular term now used to describe someone who lives a tumultuous life outside the law.

Robin Hood stories have fascinated people for years. As a result, the character and his associates have been portrayed by numerous artists. An eighteenth century engraving is shown in figure 9.4.

Johann Friedrich von Schiller, the late eighteenth-century dramatist, wrote a famous drama about the legendary archer, Wilhelm Tell. (Gioacchino Rossini wrote the opera *William Tell,* about the exploits of the same archer.) The tale centers around a Swiss crossbowman who defied a new regime he did not like. As punishment, he was forced to demonstrate his skill by shooting through an apple sitting on his son's head. A shot like Tell's in real life would have been remarkable because the father had to shoot at his son in a stressful situation with a crossbow unlike those in use today. According to the legend, Tell came prepared in the event that he missed the shot and killed his son. He carried a second bolt that day for his crossbow, and he intended to fire it at the individual who ordered that he shoot at his son.

The student of archery and literature may want to attempt to duplicate some of the legendary archery feats found within the literature. This is recommended while using tackle close to the type used during the event described in the old tales. This helps to check on the validity of the literary account of the shot. In the case of the Wilhelm Tell tale, however, it would be wise to place the apple on a balloon or some other inanimate object rather than on the head of a loved one.

Shooting at another human can be "shaky business," and it is not recommended even for academic validation! Some bowhunters even experience "the shakes" when they have game animals in their sights. And, there is the bowhunting phenomenon known as "buck fever" where the individual "freezes" when the game animal comes into shooting range. This means that the archer can not release the arrow.

James Fenimore Cooper wrote many portrayals of the American Indian. There are factual events in Cooper's books regarding how the Indian constructed and used bows and arrows. Cooper researched his material very carefully. He also lived and wrote at a time when many Indians were still pursuing their desired life-style and had not been completely relegated to life on reservations. Some of Cooper's books are *The Pioneers, The Last of the Mohicans, The Pathfinder, The Deerslayer,* and *The Prairie.*

Henry Wadsworth Longfellow's famous poem *Song of Hiawatha* is a good example of factual material being combined with feats bordering on the mythological. Longfellow, however, gave an accurate account of how some Indians made bows and arrows. Iagoo made a bow for Hiawatha from ash. The arrows were made of oak. Flint was used for the point, and the bowstring was of dried deerskin. These kinds of materials were used by Indians to make archery tackle in various places throughout the United States and Canada. (See chapter 6.)

According to Longfellow, Hiawatha was so fast that he could shoot an arrow on a horizontal trajectory and outrun the arrow. That is fast, even with the relatively inefficient tackle of a nineteenth-century American Indian! If any archery student or person reading this book can duplicate this feat, he or she should report to the Olympic Track Coach.

Longfellow also mentioned that Hiawatha could shoot ten arrows vertically so fast that the last arrow would be flying skyward before the first arrow had fallen. This would be extremely difficult if not impossible with the tackle described in the poem. However, this can be accomplished with contemporary tackle and an abundance of open space.

It is recommended that the archery student look for archery references and accomplishments in literature and analyze their feasibility. The reader is referred to the following books as a starting point:

1. Aeschylus. *Agamemnon.*
2. Arnold, Elliot. *Blood Brother.*
3. Clemens, Samuel (Mark Twain). *A Connecticut Yankee in King Arthur's Court.*
4. Defoe, Daniel. *The Adventures of Robinson Crusoe.*
5. Gillespy, Frances. *Laymon's Brut: A Comparative Study in Narrative Art.*
6. Homer. *Iliad* and *Odyssey.*
7. Lucian. *Dialogues of the Gods.*
8. Millar, George. *A Cross Bowman's Story.*
9. Morley, Christopher. *The Arrow.*
10. Ovid. *The Metamorphoses.*
11. Shakespeare. *Macbeth.*
12. ———. *Pericles.*
13. Stevenson, Robert Louis. *The Black Arrow.*
14. Swift, Jonathan. *Gulliver's Travels.*
15. Thucydides. *The History of the Peloponnesian War.*

There are several good references in the Bibliography concerning the study of archery as it relates to the humanities.

Art

There are thousands of works of art involving archery in public museums, art museums, and private collections throughout the world. Some of these, like the Bayeux Tapestry, are very famous. But, others remain obscure. In cave drawings, among the earliest art forms, bowhunters are depicted in pursuit of game. Bows have appeared in Mesopotamian seals, on Egyptian tomb paintings, and on Assyrian monumental reliefs. These date back thousands of years. Artists in the Far East and Near East commonly used archers and archery as a theme in their paintings. American Indians also drew bowhunters in pursuit of game on stone in the locales where they lived several hundred years ago.

The student interested in art is invited to search for sculptures, carvings, drawings, and other art forms involving archery throughout history. Archery tackle from throughout the world and covering the history of mankind is one aesthetic aspect of archery that should never be overlooked as an art form. A classic example of this type of art can be seen in the Grayson Archery Collection housed at the Museum of Anthropology at the University of Missouri in Columbia. This extensive collection of archery artifacts was donated by Dr. Charles E. Grayson. His interests in archery tackle over the years lie in the areas of history, function, and form. His excellent collection reflects those concerns. This collection of archery tackle is historically and artistically significant.

Several examples of artists' depictions of archers or the use of archery have been used as a succinct introduction to archery in art throughout this book. The reader should scrutinize those that appear in chapters 1, 2, 4, and this chapter. They show various artists' concepts of archers in action, archery feats, tackle, and events. It is useful to critically analyze each of these for the following: (1) artistic quality and merit, (2) tackle design for the era, as compared with contemporary tackle, (3) aesthetic impact, and (4) the artist's concept of shooting mechanics. The trained artist, of course, would look for much more in these works of art.

Richard Pardons Robin Hood—A.D. 1184 (Briggs: Beale)

Sennacherib (Assyria). (Courtesy of H. Armstrong Roberts. Printed by permission.)

Cupid with bow—Chas. Lemiore (Louvre). (Courtesy of H. Armstrong Roberts. Printed by permission.)

Diana—Goddess of Wild Things.

Battle of Marathon (Briggs: Beale)

Roman war elephant.

Buffalo hunt with wolfskin mask—George Catlin #13.

Review

1. Who was the God of Archery in mythological literature and how did he happen to be shot with a golden arrow of love?
2. Which constellation supposedly depicts a centaur shooting a bow and arrow? When can this constellation be observed in the United States?
3. Cite examples of literature, music, and art in which archery or archers are prominent.
4. Traditional liberal arts and study of the humanities involve such areas as literature, philosophy, and art. Reflect on your studies in these areas and determine how authors and artists integrated archery into their themes.
5. What characters in mythological literature were directly involved with archery in some form?
6. What is a wand shoot?
7. Describe the plot of the famous drama and opera, *William Tell*. What kind of bow was used to shoot the legendary archer's arrow?
8. When you visit museums and art galleries, make note of the quantity and quality of paintings, sculptures, and drawings where archery is depicted in one of its forms.
9. From what term is the word "arrow" derived?
10. What was the feat supposedly performed by Hiawatha that could be accomplished today but was extremely unlikely to have been achieved using Hiawatha's bow?

The Language of Archery

10

Archery, like any other sport or specialized area, has a distinctive vocabulary. There are some words or terms below that have other meanings when used in different contexts, but they have a precise definition to the archer. This is necessary so archers can communicate with one another succinctly and precisely.

The following list of terms are commonly used in the archery sports:

Addressing the Target
The archer's stance straddling the shooting line prior to shooting the arrow.

Aim
The placement of a sight pin on the center of the target; if a sight is not used, placement of the tip of the arrow on a specific point while shooting at a target over a given distance.

AMO
Archery Manufacturer's Organization.

Anchor Point
The placement of the archer's bowstring hand on the chin or face with the bow at full draw.

Archer's Paradox
The aerodynamically stabilizing condition of the arrow after it deflects around the bow handle at release.

Arm Guard
A leather protective device for the radioulnar (forearm) and wrist joint areas of the bow arm.

Arrow Plate
The piece to which the arrow rest is attached.

Arrow Rest
A device mounted just above the arrow shelf on the bow to maintain arrow position from nocking until the arrow has cleared the bow at release.

Arrow Shelf
The lowermost area of the sight window on the bow.

Arrowsmith
An individual who specializes in making arrows and arrowheads.

BAA
The Bowfishing Association of America; established in 1990.

Back
The side of the bow limb away from the archer when the bow is in the draw position.

Barb

The part of the point on a fishing arrow point used to hold the fish; one of the hairlike branches growing from the shaft of a feather.

Bare Bow

A method of shooting that does not include using a bowsight.

Belly

A synonym for the face of the bow or the side of the bow nearest the string.

Blunt

A flattened arrow point usually made of rubber or metal designed to kill small game by impact force.

Bolt

The projectile shot from a crossbow.

Bow Arm

The arm that the archer prefers to use for holding the bow during shooting.

Bow Bracer

A device designed to ensure safety for the archer during the process of bracing or stringing the bow.

Bow Hand

The hand that the archer prefers to use for holding or supporting the bow during shooting.

Bowman

An archer.

Bowsight

An adjustable device attached to the bow that facilitates the aiming process for the archer.

Bow Square

A device used to measure string and nocking heights accurately.

Bowstrap

A leather strap that enables the archer to maintain contact with the bow without actually gripping the handle.

Bow Tip Protector

A cap that fits over the tip of the lower limb of the bow to protect it from damage produced by contact with the ground or floor.

Bow Window

The center shot or sight window area of the bow handle immediately above the grip, which aids the archer during the aiming process.

Bowyer

An individual who specializes in making bows.

Brace Height

The bow manufacturer's recommended distance from the pivot point of the bow to the bow string. Replaces the older term *fistmele*.

Bracing
The process of stringing the bow in preparation for shooting; placing the bowstring loops into position in the notches of the bow.

Break-over
The reduction of bow weight pressure felt by the archer when drawing a compound bow and holding it at full draw.

Broadhead
A multiple-edged and razor-sharp arrow point utilized in bowhunting, flight shooting, and field archery.

Brush Button
A silencer device, usually rubber, placed toward each end of the bowstring to reduce string noise following release during bowhunting.

Bull's Eye
The center of the target or that part of the target face with the highest scoring value.

Butt
The term used for target backing when the target face is mounted on a straw or hay bale.

Butt Hook
A curved metal, plastic, or wood hook attached to the butt end of a crossbow stock as an aid in steady aiming.

Cam Wheels
Noncircular wheels mounted at the tips of the limbs on compound bows.

Cant
Tilting the bow left (counterclockwise) or right (clockwise) by lateral or medial rotation of the shoulder joint of the bow arm.

Cast
The velocity that the bow can impart to the arrow, and the horizontal distance the arrow can traverse.

Centerline
The relationship of the bowstring to the bow limbs which, when viewed from the face side, should divide the limbs evenly.

Center Shot Bow
A bow designed to allow the arrow rest to be placed in the center of the upper limb instead of at the extreme lateral side of the bow.

Channel Groove
A grooved section down the length of a crossbow barrel, which allows the cock feather to move along the barrel when shot.

Clearance
The ability of the arrow and fletching to pass by the bow and arrow rest without contact. Tuning adjustments to the arrow nocks, arrow rest, and cushion plunger will improve clearance.

Clicker

A small metal device mounted on the sight window in front of the arrow rest that indicates full draw has been attained by snapping off of the arrow point with an audible click.

Clout

An NAA round shot over relatively long distances at a 15-meter (diameter) target drawn on the surface of the ground.

Collapse

An undesired spinal rotation by the archer prior to arrow release, causing the bow arm to move backward while the drawing arm moves forward.

Composite Bow

A bow manufactured by utilizing two or more types of materials such as wood and fiberglass.

Compound Bow

A bow invented by H. W. Allen in 1966 designed with an eccentric pulley system to maximize pull weight poundage at mid-draw and to minimize stacking at full draw.

Creeping

An undesired forward motion of the bowstring from the anchor point immediately prior to release.

Crest

The colored identification bands on the arrow immediately below the fletching.

Crossbow

A tool for shooting bolts. It consists of a short bow mounted crosswise near the end of a wood, metal, or plastic stock.

Cushion Pressure Point

A plastic or leather device that will absorb some of the shock of the arrow as it passes after release.

Dead Release

Extension of the interphalangeal joints of the fingers gripping the bowstring due to the kinetic energy of the bowstring instead of muscular force.

Draw

The process of moving the bowstring with nocked arrow from brace height to the archer's anchor point on the face.

Draw Weight

See "Weight."

Drift

The lateral displacement of an arrow from its normal trajectory due to crosswind velocity.

End

A set number of arrows shot before going to the target to score and retrieve them; the number may be three, five, or six in target archery.

Eye

The loop at the end of the bowstring that fits into the notch of the bow during bracing.

Face
The side of the bow limb closest to the archer when the bow is in the draw position—replaces the term *belly*.

Field Captain
The person in charge of an archery tournament.

Field Point
A point used in field archery that can be as heavy as a broadhead.

Finger Sling
A small piece of leather with loops at each end designed to fit around the archer's thumb and index or middle finger during shooting. It helps prevent the bow from falling to the ground after release.

Finger Tab
A leather device worn to prevent blistering on the anterior surface of the three drawing fingers.

Fishtailing
The condition when the arrow appears to be moving from side to side during its flight toward the target. Tuning adjustments involving the cushion plunger, bow weight, and bowstrings may help to minimize fishtailing.

FITA
Fédération Internationale de Tir à L'Arc—The organization responsible for conducting world championship contests in archery.

Fletcher
An arrow maker.

Fletching
The stabilizing feathers or plastic vanes attached to an arrow between the nock and crest.

Flight Shooting
An archery event in which the shooting objective is to attain the greatest distance possible for the arrow or bolt.

Flinching
An undesired and sudden motion of the bow arm (usually horizontal abduction of the bow shoulder or elbow flexion) at release.

Flu-Flu
An arrow with large or spiraled fletching designed to increase the drag coefficient in order to diminish flight distance.

Follow-through
The act of holding the release position until the arrow has struck the target.

Foot Markers
Devices used to mark the placement of the feet during the stance once the target is addressed by the archer on the shooting line.

Freestyle
A method of shooting where the archer uses a bowsight to aim.

Freeze
The inability to release the arrow while at full draw.

Gap Shooting

An aiming technique whereby the archer estimates the distance (gap) between a selected point and the target. Release is made when the gap no longer exists.

Goat's Foot

A cocking-assist device used with crossbows to lever the string back to its cocked position.

Gold

The center of the target used in target archery.

Grip

The center portion of the bow where the hand exerts pressure during the draw. (*Grip* is often used interchangeably with the term *handle*.)

Grouping

The arrangement of the end of arrows on the target face after they have been shot.

Handle

The middle portion of the bow.

Handle Riser

The area just below and above the bow grip.

Hanging Arrow

An arrow that does not penetrate the target mat but dangles across the target face.

Hen Feathers

The two feathers on either side of the index feather. Traditionally, these feathers are not as flamboyant as the index feather.

Hit

An arrow that embeds itself within one of the scoring areas on the target face.

Holding

The act of maintaining the bow and arrow in a stable position at full draw prior to release.

Index Feather

The feather at a right angle to the slit in the nock of the arrow and usually different in color from the remaining feathers. This term replaces the older term, *cock feather*.

Jig

A device used for making and repairing fletching and bowstrings.

Keeper

A piece of material used to hold the bowstring to the nock when the bow is not braced.

Kiss Button

A contact point on the bowstring for the archer's lips to touch to ensure consistency and accuracy of the anchor point.

Lady Paramount

The woman in charge of an archery tournament.

Laminated Bow

A bow constructed of several layers of different materials glued together.

Limbs
The energy-storing parts of the bow located above and below the riser.

Longbow
A bow with no built-in curvatures to increase leverage.

Loop
The ends of the bowstring made to attach securely into the bow notches when braced.

Loose
The act of releasing or shooting the arrow.

Mass Weight
The actual or physical weight of the bow in pounds.

Mat
The firmly constructed area of the target upon which the target face is mounted; also written as *matt*.

Minnowing
A high intensity side to side movement of the arrow in its flight toward the target; movements are more rapid and smaller than seen when arrows fishtail in flight. Minnowing is due to inadequate clearance and by fletching striking the arrow rest after release.

NAA
National Archery Association of the United States.

NFAA
National Field Archery Association of the United States.

Nock
The plastic device on the end of the arrow opposite the point, made with a groove for holding the arrow to the bowstring when placed in position for shooting.

Nocking
The technique of placing the arrow on the bowstring in preparation for shooting.

Nock-locator
The stops on the serving of the bowstring that mark the exact nocking point for the arrow.

Nose
The solid metal portion at the front of the crossbow that retains the prod.

Oblique Stance
A foot position whereby the toe of the foot nearest the target is placed on a line to the target and then rotated laterally 45 degrees. The heel of the foot farthest from the target is placed in line with the center of the target.

Olympic Bow
The recurve bow equipped for target archery competition as required by FITA and NAA rules and regulations.

Open Stance
A foot position whereby the line to the target is from the instep of the foot farthest from the target while the leg nearest the target has been extended at the hip to form at least a toe-heel relationship with the foot on-line to the target.

Overbowed

The act of drawing a bow that has a weight out of proportion to the archer's strength.

Overdraw

Drawing the arrow beyond the face of the bow or drawing the bow to its point of maximum stress on the limbs; or, a device placed on a hunting bow that allows the arrow to be drawn safely past the face of the bow, thereby increasing bow weight and arrow velocity.

Overstrung

The use of a bowstring too short for the bow, a condition that results in an excessive brace height and inefficiency in shooting.

PAA

Professional Archer's Association.

Palm Rest

A device that extends below the midportion for a crossbow stock and is placed in the shooter's nontrigger hand.

Pass Through

Used in target archery scoring to designate an arrow that has gone completely through the target matt or butt.

Peeking

Undesired motion of the archer's head (neck or cervical flexion) at the time of release in an attempt to follow the arrow trajectory into the target.

Perfect End

A situation when all arrows shot are grouped tightly into the highest scoring area on the target face.

Petticoat

The outermost perimeter of the target face outside the scoring area. Arrows that land in this area are not scored as hits.

Pile

A synonym for arrow point.

Pinch

The undesired act of squeezing the arrow nock too tightly during the draw, causing the arrow to move off the arrow rest.

Pivot Point

The part of the bow grip farthest from the string when the bow is braced.

Plucking

Undesired lateral motion of the string hand and arm away from the bowstring at the time of release.

Point-blank range

The distance at which the archer may utilize the center of the target as an aiming point.

Point-of-Aim

An antiquated technique of aiming whereby the archer uses a mark unattached to the bow and usually placed on the ground as an alignment point.

Porpoising
A condition where the arrow moves up and down during its flight toward the target. An incorrect nocking point location is the cause of porpoising.

Pressure Point
The place on the arrow plate against which the arrow lies and exerts pressure when the arrow is released; it can be cushioned or spring loaded.

Prism Sight
A sophisticated aiming device utilizing refraction principles to gain a clear view of the target.

Prod
The bow section of the crossbow.

Pull
The process of disengaging embedded arrows from the target.

Pushing
The undesired process of moving the bow forward and parallel to the earth at the time of release.

Quiver
Any device designed to hold arrows for the archer during the process of shooting.

Range
(1) A specified distance to be shot during a round; (2) an outdoor or indoor shooting area designated for target archery.

Rebound
An arrow that does not penetrate the target face or mat but bounces off a scoring area on the target.

Recurve Bow
A bow manufactured so the ends of the limbs deflect toward the back of the bow to increase leverage when the bow is braced. The recurve is also known as the Olympic Bow.

Reflexed Bow
A bow with straight limbs where the backs form an obtuse angle at the conjunction of the handle riser and grip.

Release
The act of putting the arrow into flight due to a release of pressure on the bowstring by either the fingers (target archery) or a release device (bowhunting).

Round
The term used to designate the number of arrows to be shot from precise distances at specified target faces or targets.

Roving
An archery game of shooting at natural targets in woods and fields.

Scatter
Arrows distributed unevenly over a large portion of the target face and/or ground.

Scoring Area
The concentric circles on the target face worth prescribed point values.

Self Bow

A bow consisting of one complete piece of wood or raw material. Primarily yew and elm woods were used to construct bows of this type.

Serving

The protective thread wrapped around the bowstring where the arrow is nocked.

Shaft

The body of the arrow upon which the nock, fletching, and point are mounted, and the crest is painted.

Shooting Glove

A three-fingered protective device utilized by some archers for the bowstring-gripping fingers; used in lieu of a finger tab.

Shooting Line

The line straddled by archers during shooting that indicates a specific distance from the target in target archery.

Sight Bar

The piece of the bowsight to which the sight block is attached.

Sighter Arrows

The practice arrows shot to enable the target archer to adjust to range and environmental conditions prior to tournament competition; six sighter arrows are usually allowed before a round in target archery.

Sight Pin

The part of the bowsight placed on the center of the intended target during aiming.

Sight Window

The area of the bow cut away to allow the arrow rest to be mounted in the center of the bow.

Skirt

The outer cloth on a target face that holds the face on the mat; sometimes called the *petticoat.*

Snake

Embedding of an arrow under grass and horizontal to the ground, making the arrow extremely difficult to locate.

Spine

The measured deflection in inches of an arrow shaft when it is depressed by a two-pound weight at its center.

Stabilizer

A weighted device added to the handle-riser areas of the bow and designed to reduce torque and absorb shock upon release.

Stacking

A disproportionate increase in bow weight during the last few inches of the draw.

Stirrup

A cocking device that allows the shooter to hold the crossbow in a stationary position while using both hands to cock the bowstring.

String Fingers
The fingers used to hold the nocked arrow in place on the bowstring during the draw.

String Height
See "Brace Height."

String Notch
The grooves at the end of the bow limbs designed to hold the bowstring when the bow is braced.

String Peep
An oval insert into the strands of the bowstring at eye level, used as a rear-mounted aiming device by the archer.

Tackle
All equipment used by an archer.

Target Captain
The individual at each target designated to determine and call the score of each arrow and pull each arrow from the target.

Target Face
The scoring area of a target.

Target Mat
The protective backing of the target that the arrows penetrate.

Tassel
A piece of cloth material used to clean arrows.

Timber
A verbal warning given in field archery that an arrow is being released or is about to land where it should not be landing.

Tip
The ends of the bow limbs.

Torque
An undesirable twisting of the bow and/or bowstring during any part of the shooting process.

Toxophilite
An individual involved in archery either as a performer and/or serious student of the sport.

Trajectory
The parabolic flight pattern of an arrow following release.

Tree Stand
A portable platform that can be anchored in a tree. It is used as a place to observe and shoot game animals by bowhunters.

T-Square
A device used by archers to measure brace height and locate the nocking point on the bowstring.

Tuning
An adjustment of the arrow rest, pressure point, string height, and nocking height to improve arrow flight; includes determination of correct spine.

Underbowed

The act of drawing a bow with a weight too light to enable the archer to accomplish the shooting objective.

Understrung

A bow with a bowstring too long which results in an improper brace height and reduced efficiency.

Unit

A fourteen-target course in field archery, including all official shots; the field archery shooting range.

Vane

A term used most commonly when fletching is made of plastic or rubber instead of feathers.

Waiting Line

A line located five meters behind the shooting line in target archery behind which the archers must remain while waiting to shoot.

Wand

A historic type of target; a piece of balsa wood two inches in width embedded in the ground and projecting six feet upward.

Weight

The bow manufacturer's determined number of pounds required to draw each bow's string a given distance.

Windage

The left-right adjustment of the bowsight or the pin on the bowsight; or, wind direction and velocity on the shooting range or unit.

Wrist Sling

A device that fits around the bow and the archer's wrist designed to prevent the bow from falling to the ground as the arrow is released.

Yarn Tassel

A tuft of yarn used by archers to clean arrows.

Yaw

Unstable or erratic motion of the arrow during its trajectory toward the target.

Official Wildlife Agencies in the United States and Canada

Information regarding current bowhunting and/or bowfishing rules, regulations, seasons, and license fees may be obtained by contacting the specific wildlife agency in the American state or Canadian province where you plan to hunt and/or fish. It is recommended that this be done several months in advance of your trip. Their addresses and phone numbers are listed below for the reader's convenience:

United States

Alabama Department of Conservation
    and Natural Resources
64 North Union Street
Montgomery, AL 36130
(205) 261–3468

Alaska Department of Fish and Game
Box 3–2000
Juneau, AK 99802
(907) 465–4190

Arizona Game and Fish Department
2222 West Greenway Road
Phoenix, AZ 85023
(602) 942–3000

Arkansas Game and Fish Commission
#2 Natural Resources Drive
Little Rock, AR 72205
(501) 223–6300

California Department of Fish and
    Game
1416 Ninth Street
Sacramento, CA 95814
(916) 324–8347

Colorado Division of Wildlife
Department of Natural Resources
6060 Broadway
Denver, CO 80216
(303) 297–1192

Connecticut Department of
    Environmental Protection
Franklin Wildlife Management Area
RR1, Box 241
North Franklin, CT 06254
(203) 642–7239

Delaware Division of Fish and Wildlife
P.O. Box 1401
Dover, DE 19903
(302) 736–5297

District of Columbia Metropolitan
    Police
300 Indiana Avenue NW
Washington, DC 20001

Florida Game and Freshwater Fish
    Commission
620 South Meridan Street
Tallahassee, FL 32399–1600
(904) 488–4676

Georgia Department of Natural
    Resources
Floyd Towers East, SE
205 Butler St., Suite 1362
Atlanta, GA 30334
(404) 656–3523

Hawaii Division of Forestry and
    Wildlife
1151 Punchbowl Street
Honolulu, HI 96813
(808) 548–2861

Idaho Department of Fish and Game
P.O. Box 25
600 South Walnut
Boise, ID 83707
(208) 334–3746

Illinois Division of Fish and Wildlife
Resources
P.O. Box 286
Monmouth, IL 61462
(309) 374–2492

Indiana Division of Fish and Wildlife
607 State Office Building
Indianapolis, IN 46204
(317) 232–4080

Iowa Department of Natural
Resources
Wallace State Office Building
Des Moines, IA 50319
(515) 281–6154

Kansas Department of Wildlife and
Parks
Box 54A, RR2
Pratt, KS 67124
(316) 672–5911

Kentucky Department of Fish and
Wildlife
#1 Game Farm Road
Frankfort, KY 40601
(502) 564–4406

Louisiana Department of Wildlife and
Fisheries
P.O. Box 4004
Monroe, LA 71211
(318) 343–4044

Maine Department of Inland Fisheries
and Wildlife
284 State Street
Augusta, ME 04333
(207) 289–2871

Maryland Forest, Park and Wildlife
Service
P.O. Box 68
Wye Mills, MD 21679
(301) 827–8612

Massachusetts Division of Fisheries
and Wildlife
100 Cambridge Street
Boston, MA 02202
(617) 727–3151

Michigan Department of Natural
Resources
P.O. Box 30028
Lansing, MI 48909
(517) 373–1263

Minnesota Department of Natural
Resources
Box 7,500 Lafayette Road
St. Paul, MN 55146
(612) 296–3344

Mississippi Department of Wildlife
Conservation
P.O. Box 451
Jackson, MS 39205
(601) 961–5300

Missouri Department of Conservation
P.O. Box 180
Jefferson City, MO 65102
(314) 751–4115

Montana Department of Fish,
Wildlife, and Parks
1420 East 6th Avenue
Helena, MT 59620
(406) 444–2535

Nebraska Game and Parks
Commission
P.O. Box 30370
Lincoln, NE 68503
(402) 464–0641

Nevada Department of Wildlife
P.O. Box 10678
Reno, NV 89520
(702) 789–0500

New Hampshire Fish and Game
Department
34 Bridge Street
Concord, NH 03301
(603) 271–2462

New Jersey Division of Fish, Game
and Wildlife
CN 400
Trenton, NJ 08625
(609) 292–2965

New Mexico Department of Game
and Fish
State Capitol
Santa Fe, NM 87503
(505) 827–7885

New York Department of
Environmental Conservation
Wildlife Resources Center
Delmar, NY 12054
(518) 439–0098

North Carolina Wildlife Resources
Commission
512 North Salisbury Street
Raleigh, NC 27611
(919) 733–7291

North Dakota Game and Fish
Department
100 North Bismarck Expressway
Bismarck, ND 58501
(701) 221–6300

Ohio Division of Wildlife
Fountain Square
Columbus, OH 43224
(614) 265–6305

Oklahoma Department of Wildlife
Conservation
1801 North Lincoln
P.O. Box 53465
Oklahoma City, OK 73152
(405) 521–2739

Oregon Department of Fish and
Wildlife
P.O. Box 59
Portland, OR 97207
(503) 229–5403

Pennsylvania Game Commission
P.O. Box 1567
Harrisburg, PA 17105–1567
(717) 787–5529

Rhode Island Department of
Environmental Management
Division of Fish and Wildlife
Government Center
Wakefield, RI 02879
(401) 789–0281

South Carolina Wildlife and Marine
Resources Department
P.O. Box 167
Columbia, SC 29202
(803) 734–3888

South Dakota Department of Game, Fish,
and Parks
445 East Capitol
Pierre, SD 57501
(605) 773–3485

Tennessee Wildlife Resources Agency
P.O. Box 40747
Nashville, TN 37204
(615) 360–0500

Texas Parks and Wildlife Department
4200 Smith School Road
Austin, TX 78744
(512) 389–4800

Utah Division of Wildlife Resources
1596 W. N. Temple
Salt Lake City, UT 84116
(801) 533–9333

Vermont Fish and Wildlife Department
103 S. Main St.
Waterbury, VT 05676
(802) 244–7331

Virginia Commission of Game and
Inland Fisheries
P.O. Box 11104
Richmond, VA 23230–1104
(804) 367–1000

Washington Department of Game
600 North Capitol Way
Olympia, WA 95804
(206) 753–5700

West Virginia Department of Natural
Resources
1800 Washington Street
Charleston, WV 25305
(304) 348–2771

Wisconsin Department of Natural
Resources
P.O. Box 7921
Madison, WI 53707
(608) 266–2621

Wyoming Game and Fish Department
5400 Bishop Boulevard
Cheyenne, WY 82002
(307) 777–7735

Canada

Alberta Forestry, Lands and Wildlife
Fish and Wildlife Division
Main Floor, Information Center
Bramalea Bldg.
9920 108 Street
Edmonton, AB T5K 2G6
(403) 427–3590

British Columbia Wildlife Branch
780 Blanshard
Victoria, BC V8V 1X5
(604) 387–9737

Manitoba Department of Natural
Resources
1495 Saint James Street
Winnipeg, MB R3H OW9
(204) 945–6784

New Brunswick Fish and Wildlife
Branch
P.O. Box 6000
Fredericton, NB E3B 5H1
(506) 453–2440

Newfoundland Department of
Development and Tourism
P.O. Box 2006, Suite 502
Herald Tower
Corner Brook, NF A2H 6J8
(709) 637–2280

Northwest Territory Renewable
Resources
Government of NWT
Box 2668
Yellowknife, NWT X1A 2P9
(403) 873–7181

Nova Scotia Wildlife Division
Box 516
Kentville, NS B4N 3X3
(902) 678–8921

Ontario Wildlife Branch
Room 4640, 99 Wellesley W.
Toronto, ON M7A 1W3
(416) 965–4252

Quebec Department of Recreation,
Hunting and Fishing
P.O. Box 22000
150 East Saint Cyrille
Quebec City, PQ J1K 7X2
(418) 643–2464

Saskatchewan Department of Parks
and Renewable Resources
Wildlife Branch
3211 Albert Street
Regina, SK S4S 5W6
(306) 787–9071

Yukon Department of Renewable
Resources
Box 2703
Whitehorse, YK Y1A 2C6
(403) 667–5237

Archery Organizations

Archery organizations around the world that function to meet the needs and interests of individuals for the archery sports are listed below. The reader is encouraged to contact any of the organizations either by mail or phone in which he or she has an interest. Information and details regarding the purposes, functions, and programs offered by the organization will be mailed or given to you over the phone.

American Archery Council
604 Forest Avenue
Park Rapids, MN 54670
(218) 732–7747

Archers Who Care
16144 E. Palisades Blvd.
Fountain Hills, AZ 85268
(602) 837–3119

Archery Hall of Fame
1555 S. 150W., Dept. USA
Angola, IN 46703
(219) 665–1604

Archery Manufacturer's Organization
2622 C-4 N.W. 43rd Street
Gainesville, FL 32606
(904) 377–8262

Archery Range and Retailers
Organization
4609 Femrite Drive
Madison, WI 53716
(608) 221–2697

Archery Shooter's Association
Old Valdosta Road
P.O. Box 5078
Nashville, GA 31639
(912) 686–7402

Association of Professional Archers
4702 Big Springs Road
Dept. USA
Greenback, TN 37742
(717) 896–8123

Boone and Crockett Club
Old Milwaukee Depot
250 Station Drive
Missoula, MT
(406) 542–1888

Bowfishing Association of America
619 Elm Court
Monticello, AR 71655
(501) 367–2554

Bowhunters Who Care
P.O. Box 269, Dept. USA
Columbus, NE 68602
(402) 564–7177

Crossbow Archery Development
Association
Frost Street
Wolverhampton WV4 6UD
England

Fédération Internationale de Tir à
l'Arc (FITA)
Via Cerva 30
20122 Milano, Italy

Fred Bear Sports Club
4600 S.W. 41st Boulevard
Gainesville, FL 32601
(904) 376–2327

International Armburst Union
(International Crossbow Shooting
Association)
Schosslirain 9
CH-6006 Luzern
Switzerland

International Bowhunting
Organization of the USA
P.O. Box 398
3409 E. Liberty Ave.
Vermilion, OH 44089
(216) 967–2137

International Field Archery
Association
31 Dengate Circle
London, Ontario, Canada N5W IV7
(519) 453–1103

NAA Flight Shooting Committee
2782 McClelland Street
Salt Lake City, UT 84106
(801) 467–3084

National Archery Association
One Olympic Plaza
1750 East Boulder Street
Colorado Springs, CO 80909–5778
(303) 578–4576
E-mail address:
102036.3634@compuserve.com

National Archery Association
Permanent Resident Athlete Program
1750 Wueste Road
Chula Vista, CA 91915
(619) 482–6156

National Bowhunter Education
Foundation
P.O. Box 2007
Fond du Lac, WI 54936
(414) 923–5238

National Field Archery Association
31407 Outer Interstate 10
Redlands, CA 92373
(909) 794–2133

National Handicapped Sports and
Recreation Association
Capitol Hill Station
P.O. Box 18664
Denver, CO 80218
(303) 733–9349

National Wheelchair Athletic
Association
3617 Betty Drive
Suite S
Colorado Springs, CO 80907
(719) 597–8330

National Wheelchair Athletic
Association
Archery Section
Courage Center
3915 Golden Valley Road
Golden Valley, MN 55422
(612) 588–0811

NFAA Bowfisher Program
31407 Outer Interstate 10
Redlands, CA 92373
(909) 794–2133

Pope and Young Club (Big Game
Records)
Post Office Box 548
Chatfield, MN 55923
(507) 867–4144

Professional Archer's Association
P.O. Box 291
Lincoln, CA 95648
(916) 645–1985

The Association of Professional
Archers
4702 Big Springs Rd., Dept. USA
Greenback, TN 37742
(717) 896–8123

The British Long Bow Society
65 Chiltern Close
North Common, Warmley, Bristol
BS155UL
England, United Kingdom

The National Crossbow Hunter's
Association
8740 West 86th Avenue
Arvada, CO 80005

The National Crossbowmen of the
United States
203 Washington Grove Lane
Washington Grove, MD 20880
(301) 926–0492

The North American Bowhunting
Club
739 W. Littleton Blvd.
Littleton, CO 80120
(303) 797–9618

The Society for Creative
Anachronisms (Crossbow)
Office of the Registry
P.O. Box 360743
Milpitas, CA 95035–0743

United States Armburst Association
(Crossbow)
P.O. Box 261
Cape May Court House, NJ 08210

U.S. Match–Crossbow Shooting
Association
P.O. Box 261, Winding Way
Cape May Court House, NJ 08210

U.S. National Senior Sports Classic
(Archery)
11516 Natural Bridge
Bridgeton, MO 63044
(314) 731–1600

World Bowhunting Association
604 Forest Avenue
Park Rapids, MN 56470
(218) 732–7747

Selected Bibliography

American Bowhunter. Rt. 1, Box 41E, Pilager, MN 56473.

Archery. 31407 Outer I-10, Redlands, CA 92373.

Archery Business. Suite 101, 319 Barry Ave. S., Wayzata, MN 55391.

ASCHAM, ROGER. *Toxophilus.* London: A. Murray and Son, 1545.

AUSTIN, NORMAN. *Archery at the Dark of the Moon.* Berkeley: University of California Press, 1975.

BAIER, PATRICIA, and others. *The National Archery Association's Instructor's Manual.* Colorado Springs: National Archery Association of the United States, 1982.

BARRETT, JEAN A. *Archery.* S.O.: Scott, Foresman and Company, 1980.

BEAR, FRED. *The Archer's Bible.* Garden City, NY: Doubleday and Company, 1980.

———. *World of Archery.* Garden City, NY: Doubleday and Company, 1979.

BERGMAN, C. A.; McEWEN, E.; AND MILLER, R. "Experimental Archery: Projectile Velocities and Comparison of Bow Performances." *Antiquity* 62 (December 1988): 658–70.

Bow and Arrow Magazine. P.O. Box HH, Capistrano Beach, CA 92624.

Bowfishing Digest. 727 Holiday Lane, Claremore, OK 74117.

Bowfishing Magazine. P.O. Box 2005, Wausau, WI 54402–2005.

Bowfish Sports. P.O. Box 102, Grand Haven, MI 49417.

Bowhunter. 3808 South Calhoun Street, Fort Wayne, IN 46807.

Bowhunting World Magazine. 601 Lakeshore Parkway, Suite 600, Minnetonka, MN 55305–5215.

BROWN, KEN. *The Ken Brown Guide to Bowfishing.* Hugo, OK: Ken Brown Publications, 1980.

BURKE, EDMUND H. *Archery Handbook.* New York: Arco, 1965.

———. *The History of Archery.* New York: William Morrow, 1957.

BUTLER, DAVID F. *The New Archery.* New York: A. S. Barnes, 1968.

CAMPBELL, DONALD W. *Archery.* Englewood Cliffs, NJ: Prentice-Hall, 1971.

———. ed. *Archery Instruction Manual (Fourth Edition).* Dubuque, IA: Kendall/Hunt Publishing Company, 1993.

CLARK, J. G. D. "Neolithic Bows from Somerset, England, and the Prehistory of Archery in North-West Europe." *Proceedings of the Prehistoric Society* 29 (December 1963): 50–98.

COMBS, ROGER, ed. *Crossbows.* Northbrook, IL: DBI Books, 1987.

Crossbow Shooting International Magazine. 9 Manor Street, Tettenhall, Wolverhampton, WV6 8RA England.

DRISCOLL, MARGARET L., ed. *Selected Archery Articles.* Washington, DC: American Association for Health, Physical Education, and Recreation, 1971.

ELMER, ROBERT P. *American Archery.* Ronks, PA: National Archery Association of the United States, 1917.

ELMER, ROBERT P. *Archery.* Philadelphia: PA, 1926.

ELMER, ROBERT P., and FARIS, NABIH A. *Arab Archery.* Princeton, NJ: Princeton University Press, 1945.

FOLEY, VERNARD; PALMER, GEORGE; and SOEDEL, WERNER. "The Crossbow." *Scientific American* 252 (January 1985): 104–10.

FORD, HORACE A. *Archery: Its Theory and Practice.* London: J. Buchanan, 1856.

FREY, GILBERT. "A History of Crossbow Target Archery in the United States." *The U.S. Archer* 9 (November–December 1990): 306–7.

GANNON, ROBERT. *The Complete Book of Archery.* New York: Coward-McCann, 1964.

GILLELAN, G. HOWARD. *The Complete Book of the Bow and Arrow.* Harrisburg, PA: The Stackpole Co., 1977.

The Glade: International Magazine for Archers.
62 Hook Rise North, Tolworth, Surrey KT6
7JY, England.

GROGAN, HIRAM J. *Modern Bow Hunting.*
Harrisburg, PA: The Stackpole Co., 1958.

HAUGEN, ARNOLD O., and METCALF, HARLAN.
Field Archery and Bowhunting. New York:
Ronald Press, 1963.

HEATH, E. G., ed. *Anecdotes of Archery.*
London: The Tabard Press, 1970.

HEATH, E. G. *The Grey Goose Wing.* Reading,
Berkshire, England: Osprey, 1971.

———. *A History of Target Archery.* South
Brunswick: A. S. Barnes, 1974.

HENDERSON, AL. *On Target for Understanding
Target Archery.* Mequon, WI: Target
Communications, 1983.

HERRIGEL, EUGEN. *Zen in the Art of Archery.*
New York: Pantheon, 1953.

HERTER, GEORGE L., and HOFMEISTER, RUSSELL.
*Professional & Amateur Archery
Tournament and Hunting Instructions and
Encyclopedia.* Waseca, MN: Herter's, 1963.

HICKMAN, C. N.; NAGLER, F.; and KLOPSTEG,
PAUL E. *Archery: The Technical Side.*
Redlands, CA: National Field Archery
Assoc. of the U.S., 1947.

HILL, HOWARD. *Hunting the Hard Way.* Chicago:
Follet, 1953.

HONDA, SHIG; LAMMERS, MARJORY E.; and
NEWSON, RALPH W. *Archery.* Boston: Allyn
& Bacon, 1975.

KELLY, GENE. "Memorial Lands: A Bowmaker's
Legacy." *Missouri Conservationist* 48
(December 1987): 28–29.

KLANN, MARGARET L. *Target Archery.* Reading:
PA: Addison-Wesley, 1970.

KLOPSTEG, P. E. "Physics of Bows and Arrows."
American Journal of Physics 11 (August
1943): 175–92.

———. *Turkish Archery and the Composite
Bow.* 3rd ed. Manchester: Simon Archery
Foundation, 1987.

LIEBERMAN, STEPHEN B., ed. *FITA Constitution
and Rules.* Milan: FITA, 1992.

LOGAN, GENE A., and MCKINNEY, WAYNE C.
Anatomic Kinesiology. Dubuque, IA: Wm.
C. Brown, 1982.

LONGMAN, C. J., and WALROND, H. *Archery.* New
York: Frederick Ungar, 1894.

LOVE, ALBERT J. *Field Archery Technique.*
Corpus Christi, TX: Dotson, 1956.

MARKHAM, GERVASE. *The Art of Archerie.*
London: Arms and Armour Press, 1968.

MCEWEN, EDWARD; MILLER, ROBERT; and
BERGMAN, CHRISTOPHER A. "Early Bow
Design and Construction." *Scientific
American* 264 (June 1991): 76–82.

MCKINNEY, WAYNE C. "Effect of Varying
Energy Expenditures During Supplemental
Exercise On Cardiovascular Fitness and
Cardiac Risk: Longitudinal Research in
Progress, 1986–Date."

North American Bowhunter Magazine. P.O. Box
5487, Tucson, AZ 85703.

NORTHRIP, JOHN W.; LOGAN, GENE, A.; and
MCKINNEY, WAYNE C. *Analysis of Sport
Motion: Anatomic and Biomechanic
Perspectives.* Dubuque, IA: Wm. C. Brown,
1983.

POPE, SAXTON. *Yahi Archery.* Berkeley:
University of S.O. Press, 1918.

———. *The Adventurous Bowman.* New York:
G. P. Putnam's Sons, 1926.

———. *Hunting with Bow and Arrow.* New
York: G. P. Putnam's Sons, 1947.

The Professional Bowhunter Magazine. P.O.
Box 5275, Charlotte, NC 28225.

PSZCZOLA, LORRAINE. *Archery.* Philadelphia:
W. B. Saunders, 1983.

RHODE, ROBERT J. *Archery Champions.*
Norristown, PA: The Archer's Publishing
Co., 1961.

SCHAAR, JOHN. *Modern Archery Ballistics.*
Tempe, AZ: Grand Slam Archery, 1986.

SCHUMM, MARYANNE M. *Clarence N. Hickman:
The Father of Scientific Archery.* Minisink
Hills, PA: Maples Press, 1983.

SHORE, PAUL T. "Ramboat, Part I, The Ultimate
Bowfishing Machine." *Bowfishing* 1
(Fall/Winter 1986): 8–12.

———. "Ramboat, Part II, The Ultimate
Bowfishing Machine." *Bowfishing* 1
(Winter/Spring 1987): 4–6.

SHULTZ, JOHN H. "The World of Archery Comes
to Missouri." *Missouri Conservationist* 55
(April 1994): 24–27.

STERLING, SARA. *Robin Hood and His Merry
Men.* Philadelphia: George W. Jacobs, 1921.

The U.S. Archer. 7315 North San Anna Drive,
Tucson, AZ 85704.

THOMPSON, MAURICE. *The Witchery of Archery.*
New York: Charles Scribner's Sons, 1878.

THOMPSON, MAURICE, and THOMPSON, WILL H.
How to Train in Archery. New York: E. I.
Horsman, 1879.

WALKER, DOROTHY. *Instructor Manual for Basic
Archery.* Jefferson City, MO: Missouri
Department of Conservation, 1981.

Index